IMAGES
of America

Maltese in Detroit

On The Cover: This photograph was taken during the 1950 wedding of Chuck and Mary Brincat at St. Paul's Maltese Church in Corktown. (Courtesy of Mary and Chuck Brincat.)

IMAGES
of America

MALTESE IN DETROIT

Diane Gale Andreassi with a Foreword by
Larry Zahra, U.O.M., Hon. Consul General of Malta

ARCADIA
PUBLISHING

ISBN 978-0-7385-8337-2

Published by Arcadia Publishing
Charleston, South Carolina

Printed in the United States of America

Library of Congress Control Number: 2010937730

For all general information, please contact Arcadia Publishing:
Telephone 843-853-2070
Fax 843-853-0044
E-mail sales@arcadiapublishing.com
For customer service and orders:
Toll-Free 1-888-313-2665

Visit us on the Internet at www.arcadiapublishing.com

This book wouldn't have been written without the encouragement, ideas, technical support, and sacrifices from my husband, Domenic, who happily accompanied me on many photograph-seeking missions and helped in too many ways to name. My son, Dan, nudged me forward with a "you can do it" attitude during frustrating times, especially when it was necessary to upgrade equipment. Recently he also showed me by example how to overcome even the most difficult obstacles and to do it with quiet determination. My daughter, Lia, offered ideas, accompanied me while I gathered photographs, and took many pictures used in the book. She was my saving grace during computer glitches, and she was the rock I turned to when I needed reassurance.

Contents

Acknowledgments		6
Foreword		7
Introduction		8
1.	Early Immigration to Detroit	9
2.	You Are What You Eat	43
3.	The Backbone of Maltese Communities	47
4.	Maltese Become Entrepreneurs	61
5.	Maltese Get a Kick Out of Soccer	65
6.	The Maltese's Place in the History of Corktown	71
7.	Clubs Serve the Community at Large	103
8.	Maltese Today	121

ACKNOWLEDGMENTS

It would not have been possible to write *Maltese in Detroit* without the help of all those immigrants and Maltese descendents who so fervently wanted to share a piece of their family's history. A hearty thank you goes out to all those people who offered pictures, stories, documents, and most of all an interest in the project.

I am most grateful to my parents, James and Rita Gale, for teaching us about family loyalty and devotion to the Roman Catholic faith and for instilling strong values that seem to be typical in Maltese families. My sisters, Linda Morasso and Rose D'Amato, helped beyond measure, introducing me to Maltese people in the community, tracking down photographs, and providing endless support now and throughout my life. My brothers, James Gale and Charles Gale, gave their time and energy, especially during my other family commitments, which lightened my load and maintained my sanity.

Tess Vella was a networking gem, who opened doors to so many generous and hospitable Maltese people, such as Chuck and Mary Brincat, who spent hours showing their photographs. Without Vella's help, the book would not have happened. She readily dropped what she was doing to provide insight and ideas for the book.

I want to thank Paul Borg, president of the Maltese American Community Club in Dearborn and consulate of Malta to the State of Michigan, for his work in collecting photographs and providing information. His insights and suggestions were priceless.

Lena (Cassar) Cunningham seemed to call and send photographs at opportune times during the gathering process. Her persistence and interest are greatly appreciated and became a motivator during the early months.

Maltese consul Larry Zahra showed tremendous commitment to obtaining photographs, background information, and other details that helped in so many ways. Thank you, too, for writing the foreword.

Terise Attard Okasinski shared old pictures, documents, and introduced me to many Maltese people living in Corktown. She also provided a wonderful tour through the neighborhood that opened my eyes to many beautiful Maltese landmarks.

Joe Formosa, vice president of the Maltese American Community Club in Dearborn, was most helpful digging out old photographs from a storage room at the club and patiently tracked down identities of the people in the pictures.

All the information in this book was done with consideration and diligence toward accuracy; however, it was based on peoples' recollections, and sometimes that can lead to errors. Other extended help came from Joe Muscat, Tony Mifsud, John Caruana, Charlie Schembri, and Norma Jean Philip.

Foreword

Delivering my address to the Convention of Maltese Associations of Maltese Abroad, I quoted the following well-known words that were written by Emma Lazarus in 1883: "Give me your tired, your poor, / Your huddled masses yearning to breath free, / The wretched refuse of your teeming shores. / Send these, the homeless, tempest-tossed, to me."

All of these words apply to Maltese immigrants. The island has the distinguished recognition of being the first country to be bestowed with an American consulate, which occurred during the wars with the French and the English. Also during these wars, Malta became a safe port for American ships. The famous pirate, La Fete, who fought on the side of the Americans, recruited many sailors from Malta. These sailors were rewarded for their deeds after the wars and given land in New Orleans and Virginia, making them the first Maltese immigrants in these areas. Others followed after World War I and World War II. However, those who came after World War II had to have a sponsor put up a bond of $10,000 on their behalf. These bonds were put in place to help prevent these new immigrants from being financially dependent on the government.

I have lived in the United States for over 58 years, and one thing I can say about the Maltese immigrant is that he is a conscientious, hard-working individual who tries to give his newly found home as much as—or more than— he gets. In my journeys across the United States, I have always been inspired by the comments of the employers of Maltese immigrants and their descendants. At Ford Motor Company, for instance, I became acquainted with one of the vice presidents, and he said, "Maltese have a place at Ford any time. They are well-liked, hard-working, and very industrious people."

I believe this book should be in the homes of all Maltese Americans, so that their children, grandchildren, and great-grandchildren can be proud of their Maltese heritage.

—Larry Zahra, Officer of the Order of Merit
Hon. Consul General of Malta

INTRODUCTION

Maltese were among the many people around the world who heard about the job opportunities in the automobile industry that Detroit offered. The first immigrants had a wanderlust and adventuresome drive that took them to new shores. While the streets were not paved in gold, for most immigrants their new land provided a better way of life.

Maltese immigrated in droves to Detroit after World War I. They grew in number from between 6,000 to 7,000, according to a December 12, 1920, *Detroit Free Press* article. They left the archipelago of six islands of which Malta, Gozo, and Comino are inhabited. Located in the center of the Mediterranean, Malta is 58 miles from Sicily and 180 miles from Libya. The Maltese islands are soaked in history with temples dating from 5,000 BC. The Phoenicians colonized the islands around 800 BC, and the Romans made Malta part of their empire in 218 BC. Malta was under Arab rule in the 9th and 10th centuries, which strengthened the Semitic roots of the Maltese language.

In 1530, the king of Spain and the Holy Roman emperor, Charles V, gave Malta to the Knights of the Sovereign Military Hospitaller Order of St. John of Jerusalem. They survived a three-month siege by the Turks in 1565 and governed until 1798, when Malta fell to Napoleon. In 1800, the Maltese expelled the French with the assistance of the British Royal Navy, and in 1814 Malta became a British colony. It became independent in September of 1964.

Malta was an important naval base, as it is strategically placed between Europe and North Africa. During World War II, the country was subjected to a long blockade and a five-month bombing raid by the Axis powers. Malta was devastated but did not surrender. The bombing raid during the war made Malta the most bombed country on the face of the planet. It had more bombs dropped on its people in two months than London had in two years. The George Cross was awarded to the island of Malta in April 1942 from King George VI to honor the Maltese people for their bravery during World War II.

Maltese immigrants were proud of this honor—and their homeland—but they came to Detroit in an effort to improve their lives and the lives of generations that would follow.

One

Early Immigration to Detroit

Maltese who came to the United States were pioneers willing to leave their families and homes to try a new life in a new land. From the tiny island nation, Maltese immigrants took with them the importance of values, loyalty to family and friends, and that Catholic faith, which they passed down to their children. Today these are the hallmarks of Maltese families in Detroit and its surrounding areas.

After World War I, many people in the country of Malta were out of work. The Maltese naval dockyard provided work for 15,000 men during the war, and by 1919 it was decided that only 5,000 workers were needed to work at the dockyard. Other military branches were letting workers go, and unemployment reached over 20,000 people.

According to *The Great Exodus 1918–1939*, written by Fr. Lawrence Attard, some 10,000 Maltese left their homeland to find work abroad, mostly in American cities, between 1919 and 1920. However, official census figures are thought to be low, considering some people entered the country illegally as stowaways or by crossing the Canadian border undetected. Those people, of course, would not have been included in the count.

Unemployment, poverty, and political frustration were some of the main factors that prompted people to leave their island homes. Detroit was building cars, and people around the world learned of jobs that were available. Detroit became the largest Maltese colony outside the islands.

When some of the immigrants arrived, they found that life was not as easy as they might have believed. The Americanization Committee of Detroit established a Maltese Information Bureau that provided a newsletter to help the Maltese assimilate in their new country.

The immigrants' devotion to the Roman Catholic Church drew them to others of the same faith. According to Fr. Lawrence Attard, some women who attended Holy Trinity Catholic Church even started sponsoring social events in order to bring Maltese immigrants closer to American Catholics.

Some Maltese immigrants changed their family names in an attempt to sound American. Some of the family names that assimilated included Farrugia, which modified to Farr; Camilleri, which transformed to Miller; Mizzi, which converted to Mitchell; and Galea, which changed to Gale.

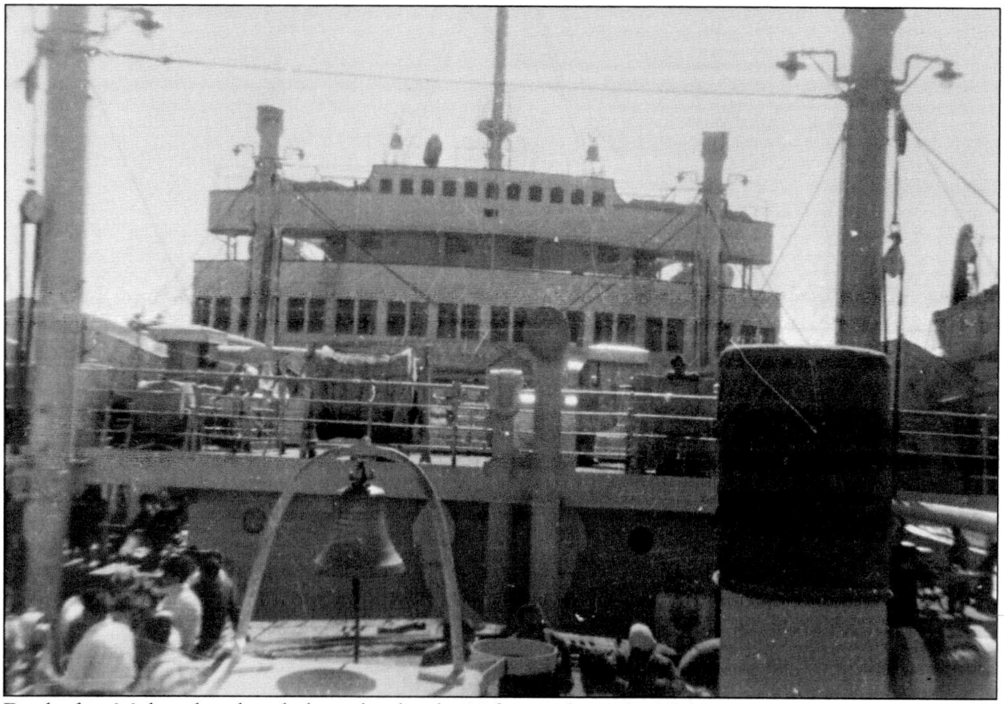

Docked in Malta, this ship, believed to be the *Vulcania*, brought Maltese immigrants to Canada—some of whom readily made the short trip to Detroit. It was important to first establish a connection with other Maltese immigrants in Detroit and then find work, which would help pave the way for their permanent settlement in the Motor City. (Courtesy of Tony Pons.)

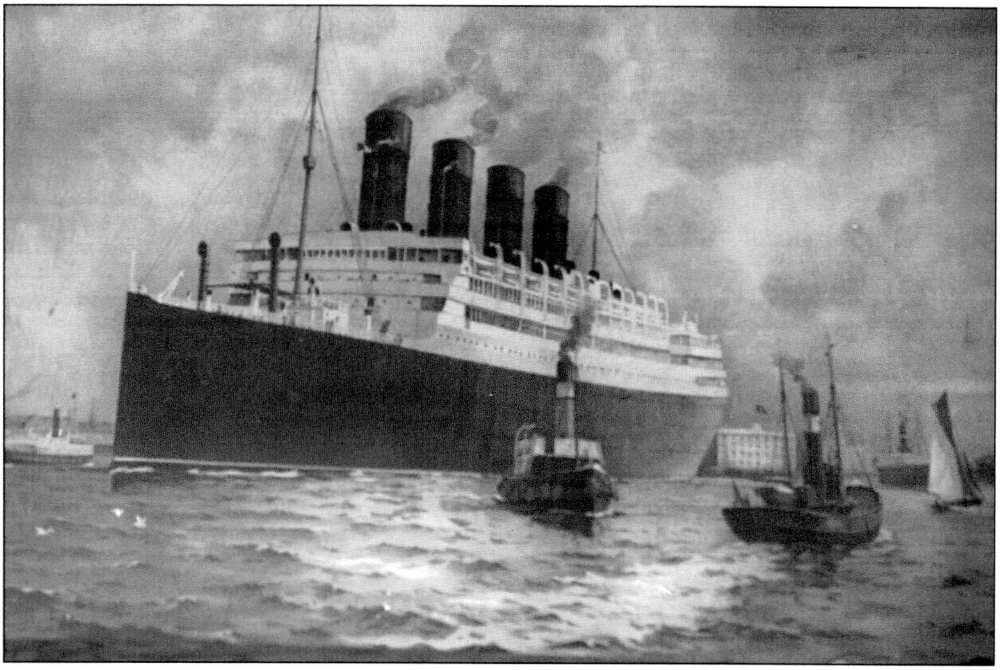

One of the first ships, the *Conardo*, is leaving Malta and destined for the United States. The date of the image is unknown. (Courtesy of Paul Borg.)

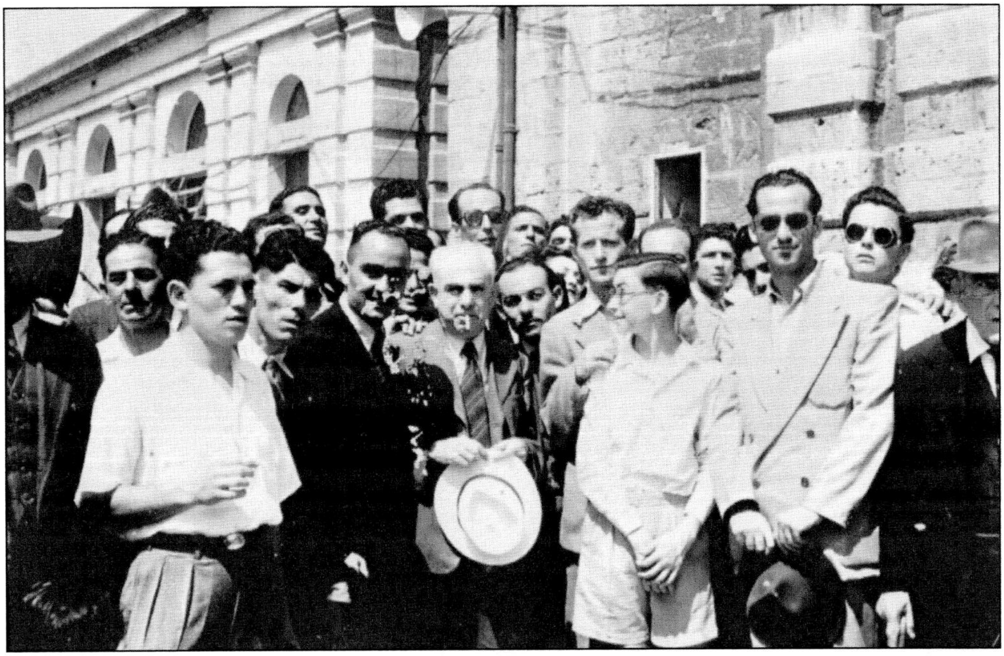

A group of immigrants set out for North America, going either to Canada or Detroit, around 1947. (Courtesy of Tony Pons.)

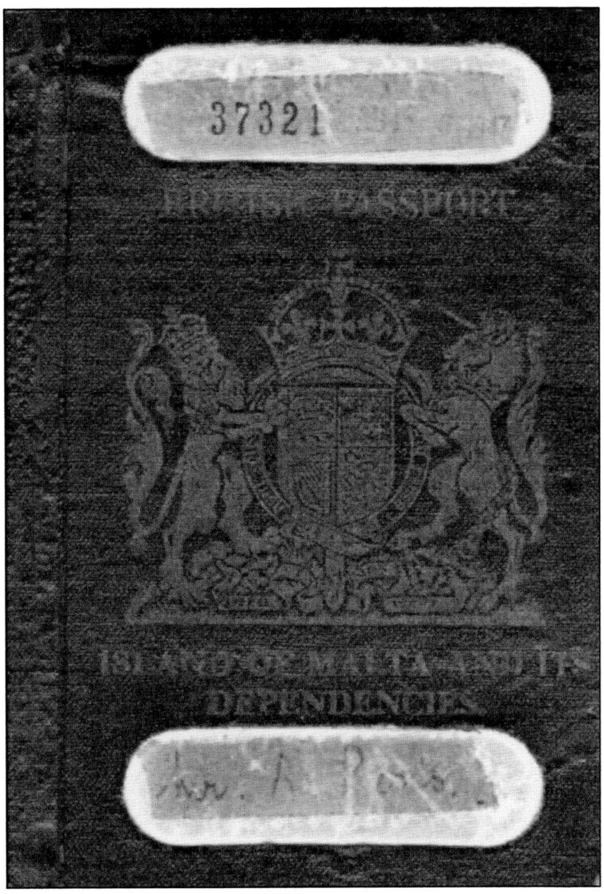

Tony Pons used this passport when he left Malta in June 1948. He sailed to Canada on the *Vulcania*. It was a nine-day journey. The ship brought 380 people, making it one of the biggest groups of Maltese going to the United States and Canada. After meeting his future wife, Cathie White, Pons moved to Detroit in 1952. (Courtesy of Tony Pons.)

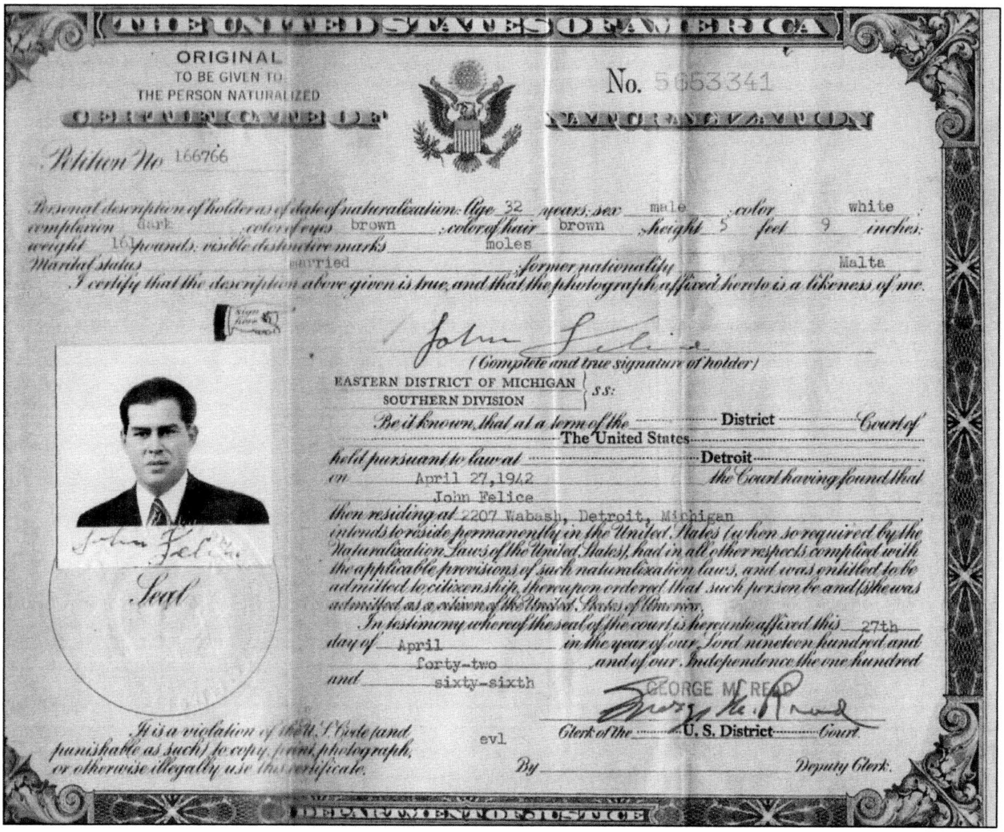

THE UNITED STATES OF AMERICA

ORIGINAL
TO BE GIVEN TO
THE PERSON NATURALIZED

No. 5653341

CERTIFICATE OF NATURALIZATION

Petition No. 166766

Personal description of holder as of date of naturalization: Age 32 years; sex male; color white; complexion dark; color of eyes brown; color of hair brown; height 5 feet 9 inches; weight 161 pounds; visible distinctive marks moles
Marital status married; former nationality Malta
I certify that the description above given is true, and that the photograph affixed hereto is a likeness of me.

John Felice
(Complete and true signature of holder)

EASTERN DISTRICT OF MICHIGAN
SOUTHERN DIVISION } ss:

Be it known, that at a term of the District Court of The United States held pursuant to law at Detroit on April 27, 1942 the Court having found that John Felice then residing at 2207 Wabash, Detroit, Michigan intends to reside permanently in the United States (when so required by the Naturalization Laws of the United States), had in all other respects complied with the applicable provisions of such naturalization laws, and was entitled to be admitted to citizenship, thereupon ordered that such person be and (s)he was admitted as a citizen of the United States of America.

In testimony whereof the seal of the court is hereunto affixed this 27th day of April in the year of our Lord nineteen hundred and forty-two and of our Independence the one hundred and sixty-sixth

Seal

GEORGE M. READ
Clerk of the U.S. District Court.

evl

By Deputy Clerk.

It is a violation of the U.S. Code (and punishable as such) to copy, print, photograph, or otherwise illegally use this certificate.

DEPARTMENT OF JUSTICE

Shown above and below are the naturalization certificates for John and Elsie Felice. Issued from the U.S. government, this paperwork is proof of having obtained U.S. citizenship. (Both courtesy of Norma Jean Philip.)

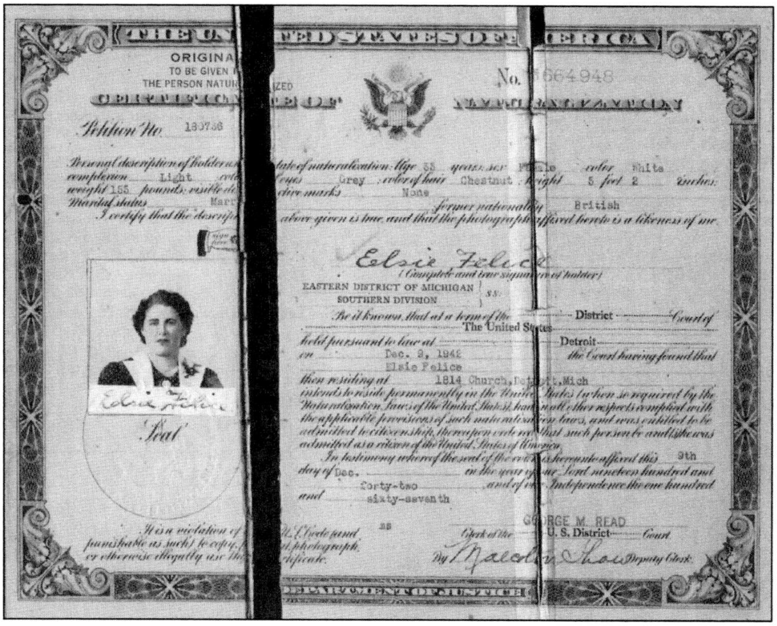

THE UNITED STATES OF AMERICA

ORIGINAL
TO BE GIVEN TO
THE PERSON NATURALIZED

No. 5664948

CERTIFICATE OF NATURALIZATION

Petition No. 183736

Personal description of holder as of date of naturalization: Age 33 years; sex female; color White; complexion Light; color of eyes Grey; color of hair Chestnut; height 5 feet 2 inches; weight 155 pounds; visible distinctive marks None
Marital status Married; former nationality British
I certify that the description above given is true, and that the photograph affixed hereto is a likeness of me.

Elsie Felice
(Complete and true signature of holder)

EASTERN DISTRICT OF MICHIGAN
SOUTHERN DIVISION } ss:

Be it known, that at a term of the District Court of The United States held pursuant to law at Detroit on Dec. 9, 1942 the Court having found that Elsie Felice then residing at 1814 Church, Detroit, Mich intends to reside permanently in the United States (when so required by the Naturalization Laws of the United States), had in all other respects complied with the applicable provisions of such naturalization laws, and was entitled to be admitted to citizenship, thereupon ordered that such person be and (s)he was admitted as a citizen of the United States of America.

In testimony whereof the seal of the court is hereunto affixed this 9th day of Dec. in the year of our Lord nineteen hundred and forty-two and of our Independence the one hundred and sixty-seventh

Seal

GEORGE M. READ
Clerk of the U.S. District Court.

By Malcolm Shaw Deputy Clerk.

It is a violation of the U.S. Code (and punishable as such) to copy, print, photograph, or otherwise illegally use this certificate.

DEPARTMENT OF JUSTICE

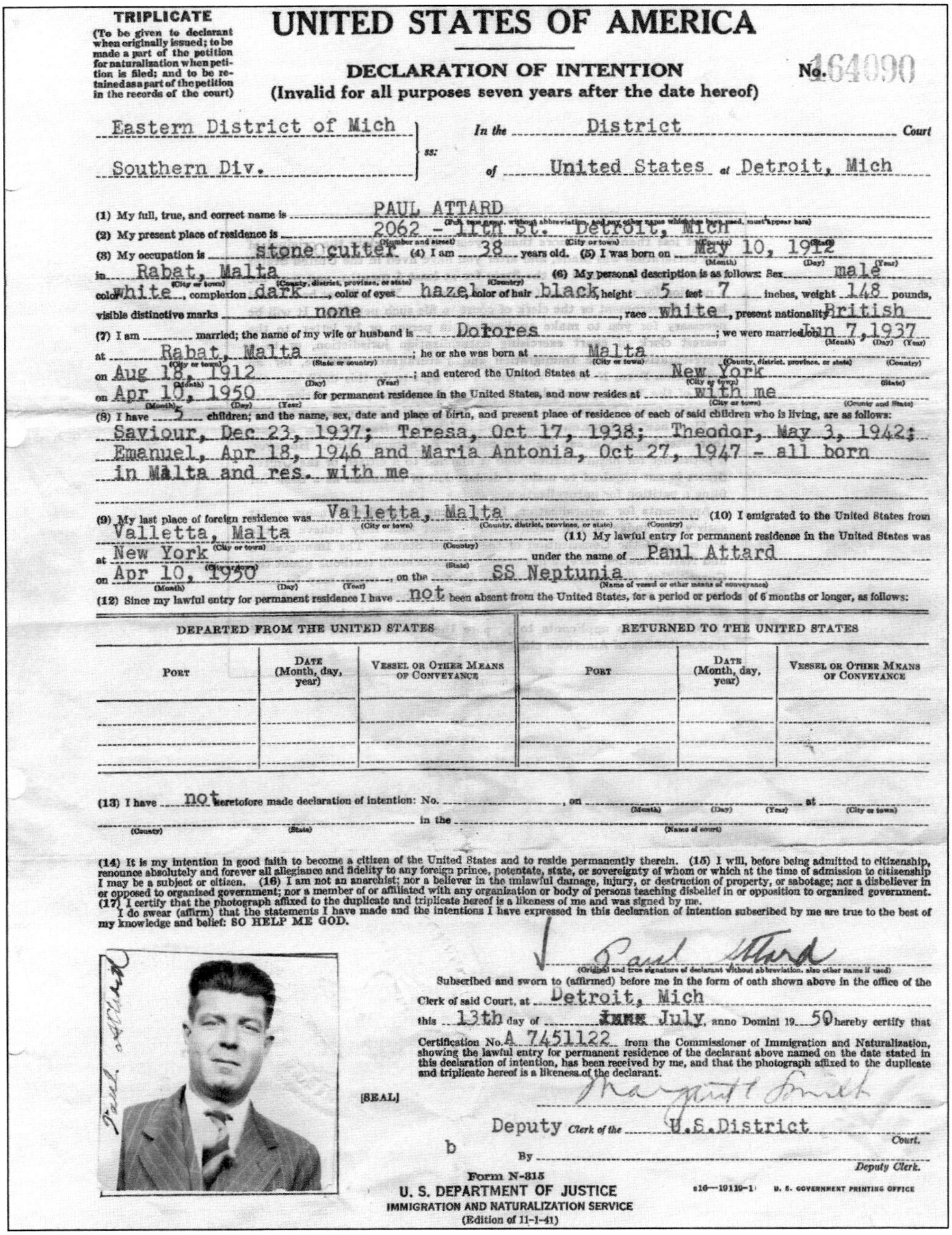

TRIPLICATE
(To be given to declarant when originally issued; to be made a part of the petition for naturalization when petition is filed; and to be retained as a part of the petition in the records of the court)

UNITED STATES OF AMERICA

DECLARATION OF INTENTION

No. 164090

(Invalid for all purposes seven years after the date hereof)

Eastern District of Mich, Southern Div. ss: In the District Court of United States at Detroit, Mich

(1) My full, true, and correct name is PAUL ATTARD (Full, true name, without abbreviation, and any other name which has been used, must appear here)

(2) My present place of residence is 2062 - 11th St. Detroit, Mich (Number and street) (City or town) (State)

(3) My occupation is stone cutter (4) I am 38 years old. (5) I was born on May 10, 1912 (Month) (Day) (Year) in Rabat, Malta (City or town) (County, district, province, or state) (Country) (6) My personal description is as follows: Sex male color white, complexion dark, color of eyes hazel, color of hair black, height 5 feet 7 inches, weight 148 pounds, visible distinctive marks none, race white, present nationality British

(7) I am married; the name of my wife or husband is Dolores; we were married Jun 7, 1937 (Month) (Day) (Year) at Rabat, Malta (City or town) (State or country); he or she was born at Malta (City or town) (County, district, province, or state) (Country) on Aug 18, 1912 (Month) (Day) (Year); and entered the United States at New York (City or town) (State) on Apr 10, 1950 (Month) (Day) (Year) for permanent residence in the United States, and now resides at with me (City or town) (County and State)

(8) I have 5 children; and the name, sex, date and place of birth, and present place of residence of each of said children who is living, are as follows: Saviour, Dec 23, 1937; Teresa, Oct 17, 1938; Theodor, May 3, 1942; Emanuel, Apr 18, 1946 and Maria Antonia, Oct 27, 1947 - all born in Malta and res. with me

(9) My last place of foreign residence was Valletta, Malta (City or town) (County, district, province, or state) (Country) (10) I emigrated to the United States from Valletta, Malta (City or town) (Country) (11) My lawful entry for permanent residence in the United States was at New York (City or town) (State) under the name of Paul Attard on Apr 10, 1950 (Month) (Day) (Year), on the SS Neptunia (Name of vessel or other means of conveyance)

(12) Since my lawful entry for permanent residence I have not been absent from the United States, for a period or periods of 6 months or longer, as follows:

DEPARTED FROM THE UNITED STATES			RETURNED TO THE UNITED STATES		
Port	Date (Month, day, year)	Vessel or Other Means of Conveyance	Port	Date (Month, day, year)	Vessel or Other Means of Conveyance

(13) I have not heretofore made declaration of intention: No. ______, on ______ (Month) (Day) (Year) at ______ (City or town) ______ (County) (State) in the ______ (Name of court)

(14) It is my intention in good faith to become a citizen of the United States and to reside permanently therein. (15) I will, before being admitted to citizenship, renounce absolutely and forever all allegiance and fidelity to any foreign prince, potentate, state, or sovereignty of whom or which at the time of admission to citizenship I may be a subject or citizen. (16) I am not an anarchist; nor a believer in the unlawful damage, injury, or destruction of property, or sabotage; nor a disbeliever in or opposed to organized government; nor a member of or affiliated with any organization or body of persons teaching disbelief in or opposition to organized government. (17) I certify that the photograph affixed to the duplicate and triplicate hereof is a likeness of me and was signed by me.
I do swear (affirm) that the statements I have made and the intentions I have expressed in this declaration of intention subscribed by me are true to the best of my knowledge and belief: SO HELP ME GOD.

Paul Attard
(Original and true signature of declarant without abbreviation, also other name if used)

Subscribed and sworn to (affirmed) before me in the form of oath shown above in the office of the Clerk of said Court, at Detroit, Mich this 13th day of July, anno Domini 1950. I hereby certify that Certification No. A 7451122 from the Commissioner of Immigration and Naturalization, showing the lawful entry for permanent residence of the declarant above named on the date stated in this declaration of intention, has been received by me, and that the photograph affixed to the duplicate and triplicate hereof is a likeness of the declarant.

[SEAL]

Margaret Smith
Deputy Clerk of the U.S. District Court.
By ______ Deputy Clerk.

Form N-315
U. S. DEPARTMENT OF JUSTICE
IMMIGRATION AND NATURALIZATION SERVICE
(Edition of 11-1-41)
16—19110-1 U. S. GOVERNMENT PRINTING OFFICE

Here is Paul Attard's Declaration of Intention. The back of the document states, "Not less than two nor more than seven years after the date the original of his declaration was made, and after you have lived in the United States for at least five years and in the State for at least six months, you may petition for naturalization (or second papers)." (Courtesy of Terise Attard Okasinski.)

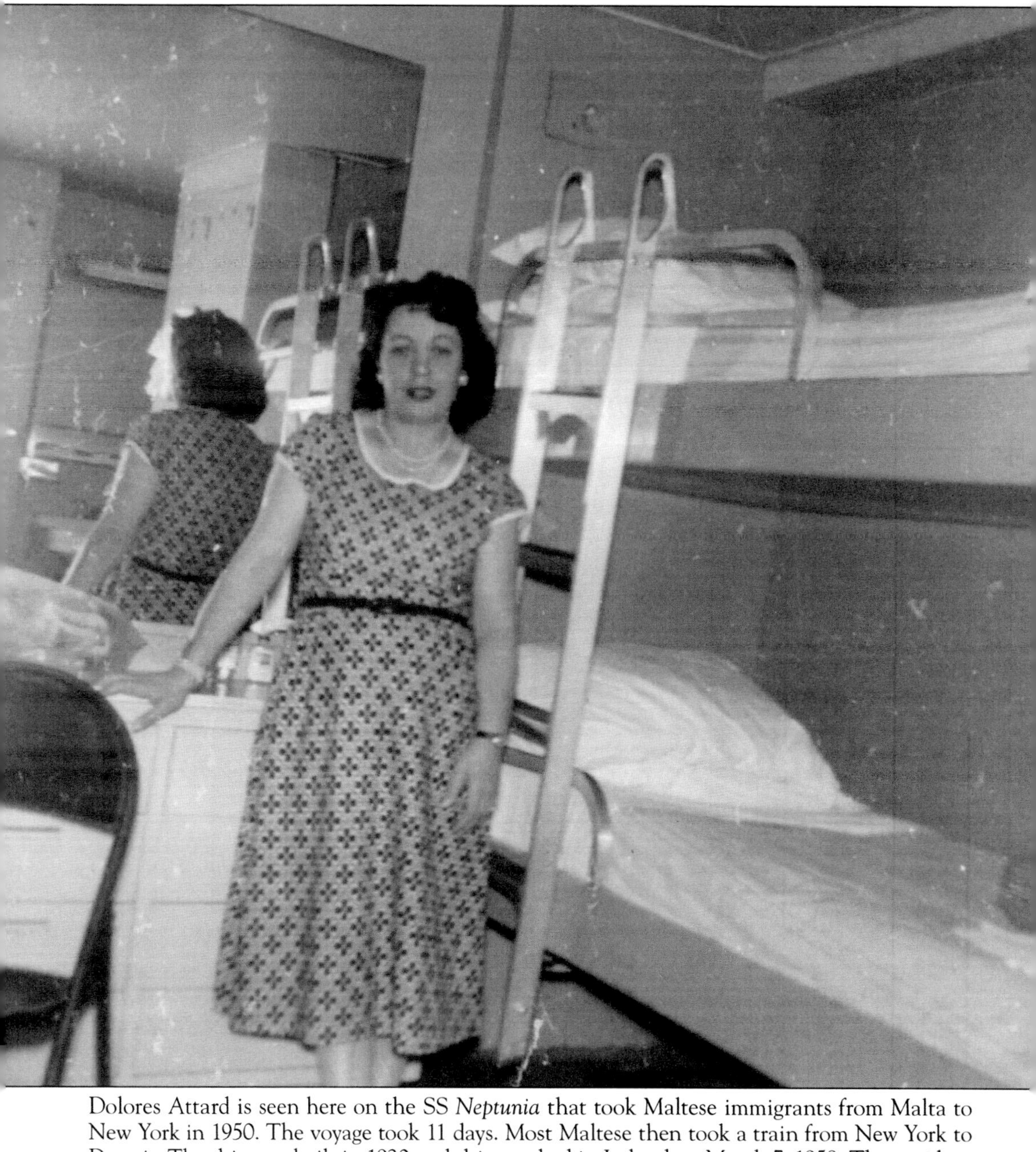

Dolores Attard is seen here on the SS *Neptunia* that took Maltese immigrants from Malta to New York in 1950. The voyage took 11 days. Most Maltese then took a train from New York to Detroit. The ship was built in 1920 and shipwrecked in Ireland on March 7, 1958. The accident was a total loss of the vessel, but no one died. (Courtesy of Terise Attard Okasinski.)

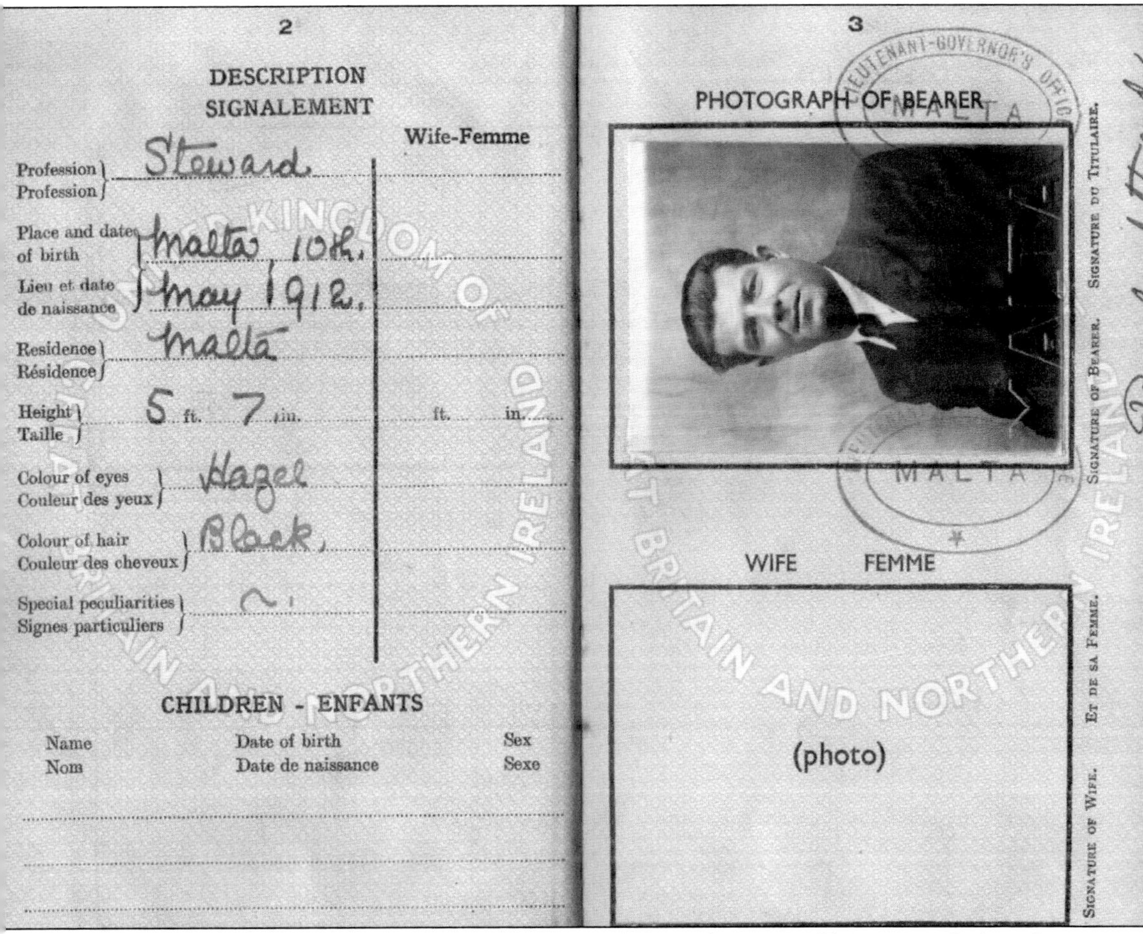

Here is Paul Attard's passport. Attard was in the British Navy during World War II, and when the war was over unemployment in Malta was high. Wanderlust seemed to be in his blood, because before the Navy he was in the Merchant Marines. He had brothers who had moved to the United States and decided to do the same, bringing his wife, Dolores, and five children. (Courtesy of Terise Attard Okasinski.)

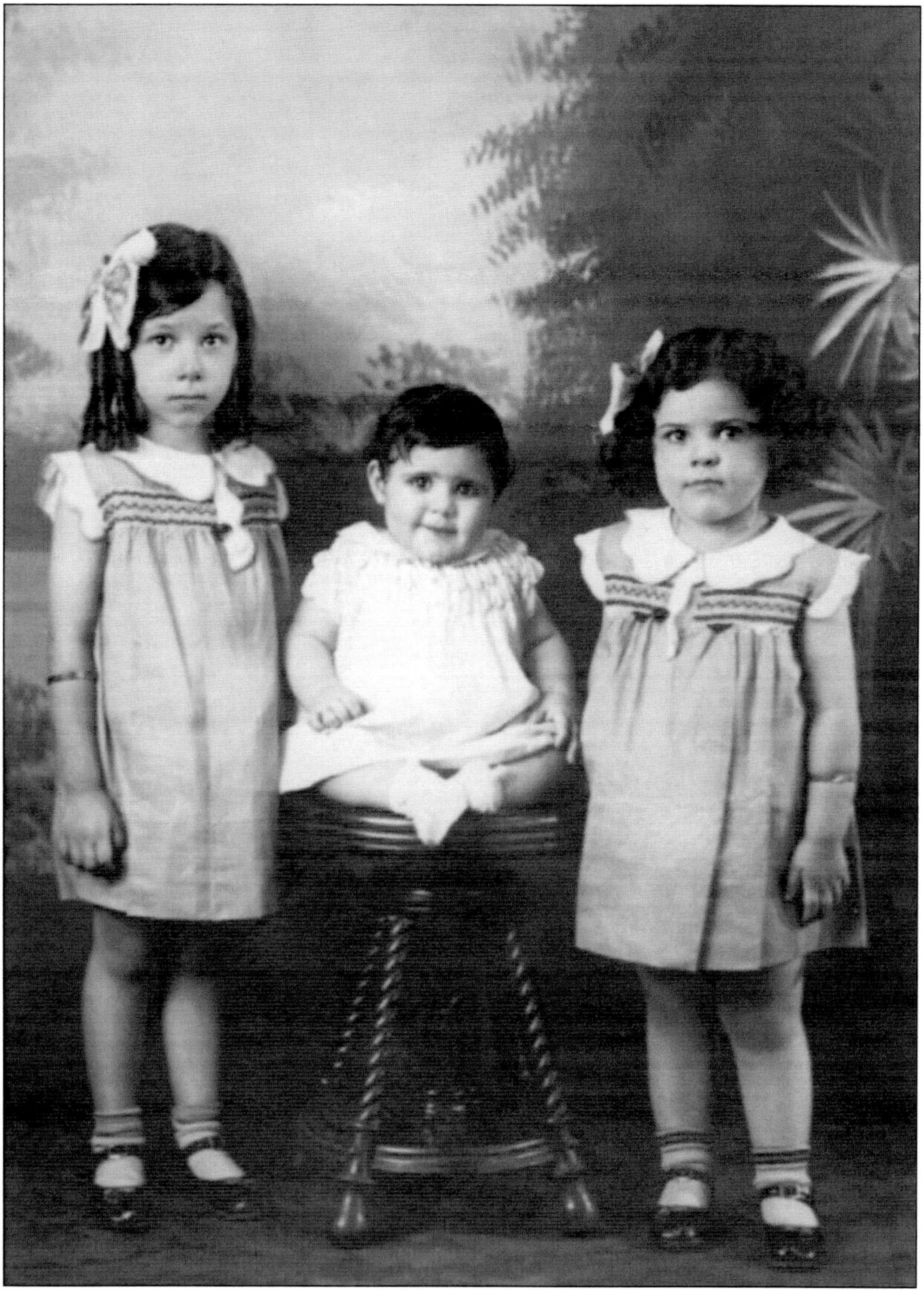

Pictured from left to right are Carmella, Jenny (seated), and Stella Bonnici in 1934 or 1935. The girls grew up in Corktown, and Jenny later worked for the Corktown Development Corporation. (Courtesy of Stella Grima.)

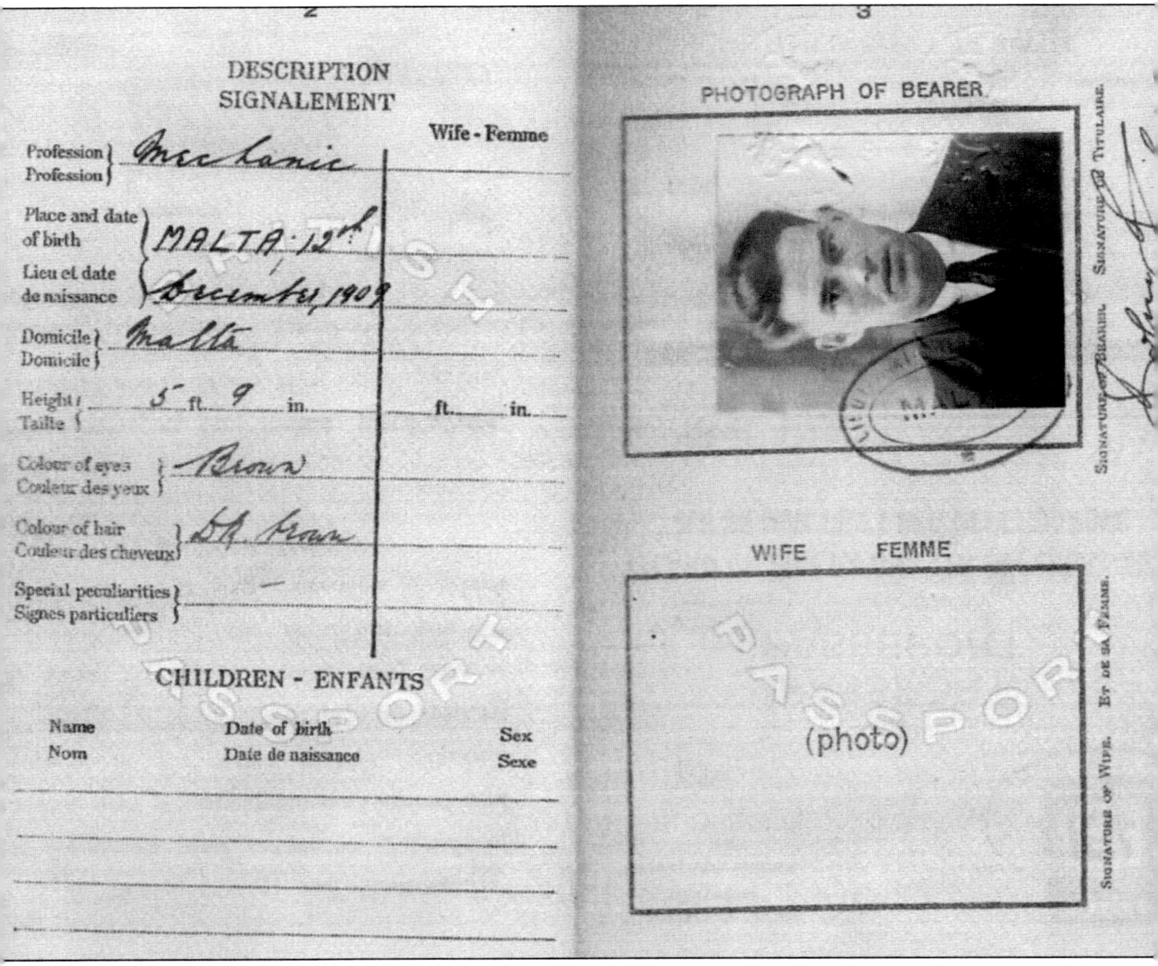

John Felice's passport was issued in October 1936. Malta was a British colony at that time and only gained its independence in 1964. (Courtesy of Norma Jean Philip.)

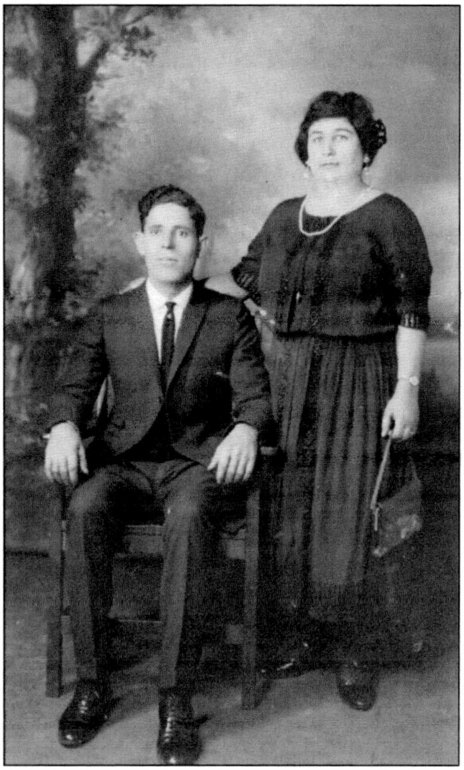

Agnes and Grazio DeBono were married in 1918 in Malta. They came to Detroit around 1921 and raised six boys and six girls. Three children were born in Malta, and nine were born in Detroit. (Courtesy of DeeDee DeBono.)

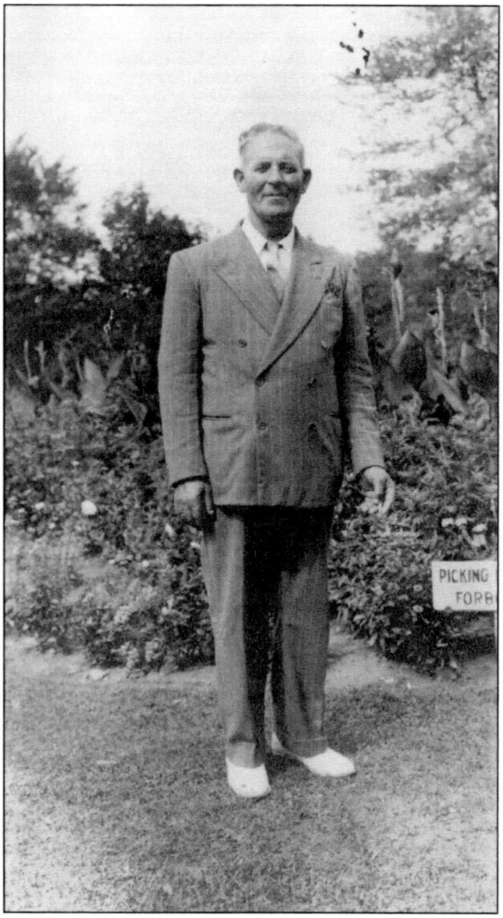

Grazio DeBono was about 25 years old when he came to Detroit. He worked in the foundry at Ford Motor Company for 30 years. (Courtesy of DeeDee DeBono.)

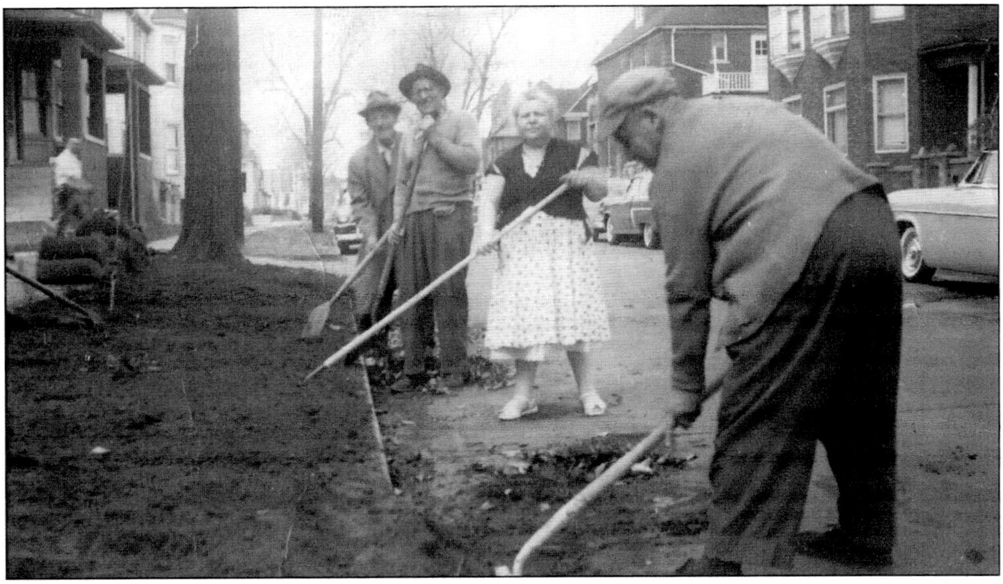

In this photograph, Joe and Velina Portelli, with the help of the DeBono, put in sod at a home in Corktown around 1957.

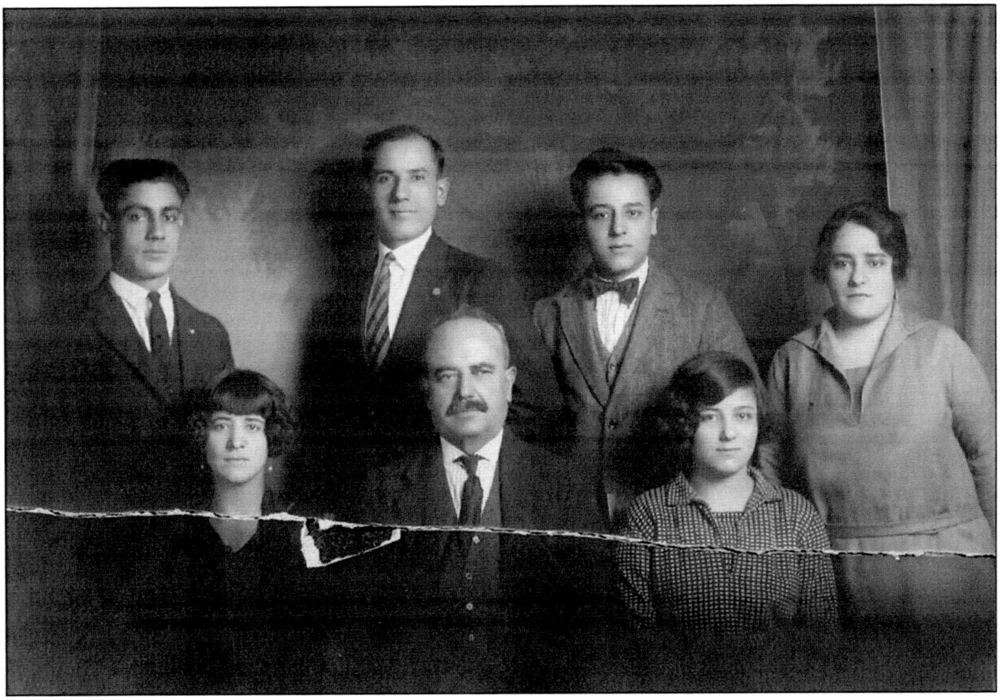

Amabile and Maria (Cacciottolo) Borg had 18 children, of which 12 lived past infancy. Upon arrival to the United States, Amabile Borg (seated, center) and some of his older children had their portrait taken. Other family members came to the United States later. Some of the names of the children pictured include Paul Borg, Emmanuel Borg, Carmena (Borg), and Delores Borg DeBono (seated, right). (Author's collection.)

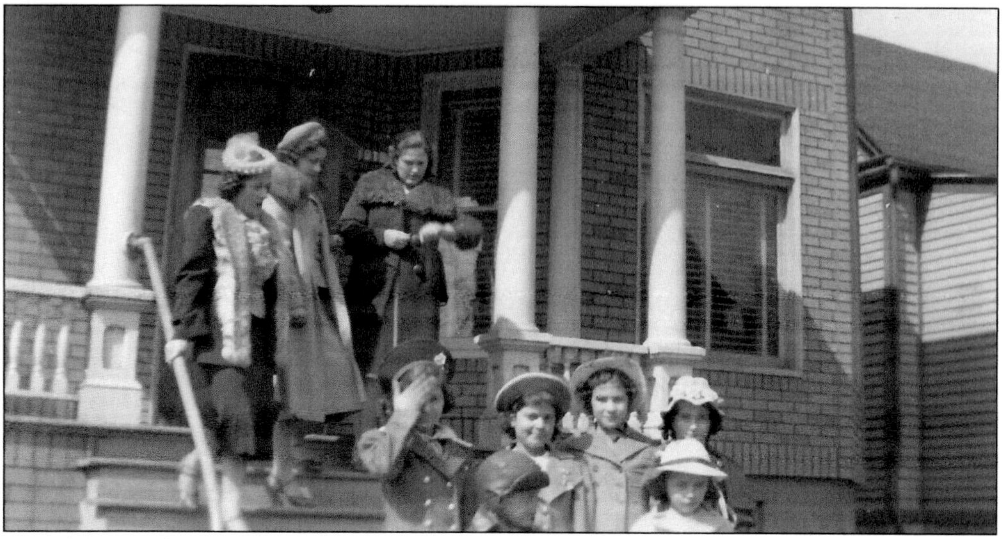

From left to right, sisters Rita and Judy Borg and their friend Vivian Smith pose in their best clothes in front of the Borg home in Corktown on Easter Sunday around 1940. Many Maltese-born women who came to Detroit were proficient seamstresses. Maltese women in Corktown dressed immaculately, often with fur around their coat collars, big brimmed hats, heeled shoes, and matching gloves to complete their outfits. (Courtesy Tess Vella.)

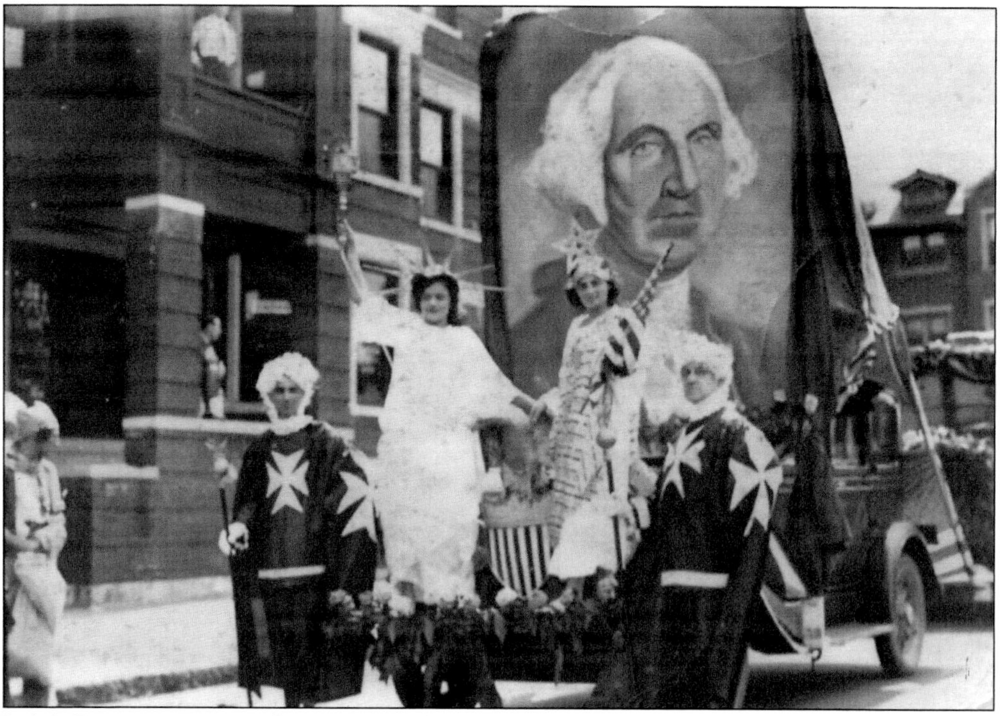

Judith Borg is portraying the Statue of Liberty on a Maltese float in a Corktown parade around 1935. The theme of the float was perfect for a group of people who did their utmost to assimilate to their new country. Honoring the Statue of Liberty was a perfect way to recognize their new home, while references to Malta on the float were a reflection of their Maltese heritage. (Courtesy Rose D'Amato.)

Rita and James Gale were married at St. Paul's Maltese Church in 1941. They had four of their five children—James, Charles, Linda, and Rose— while living in Detroit's Corktown area. They later moved to the west side of Detroit, which was where they had their last child, Diane. (Author's collection.)

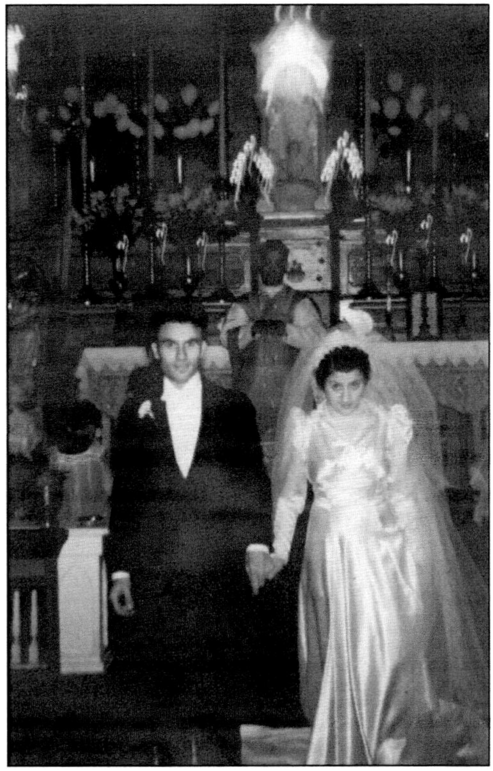

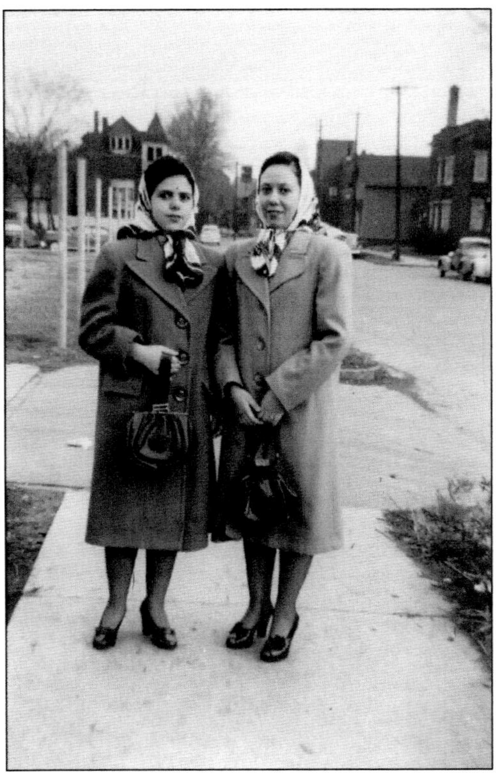

Sisters Stella and Carmela Bonnici are pictured here on Eleventh Street. They graduated from Holy Trinity Elementary School and St. Vincent de Paul High School. Carmella and Stella worked at Detroit Edison at different times. (Courtesy of Stella Grima.)

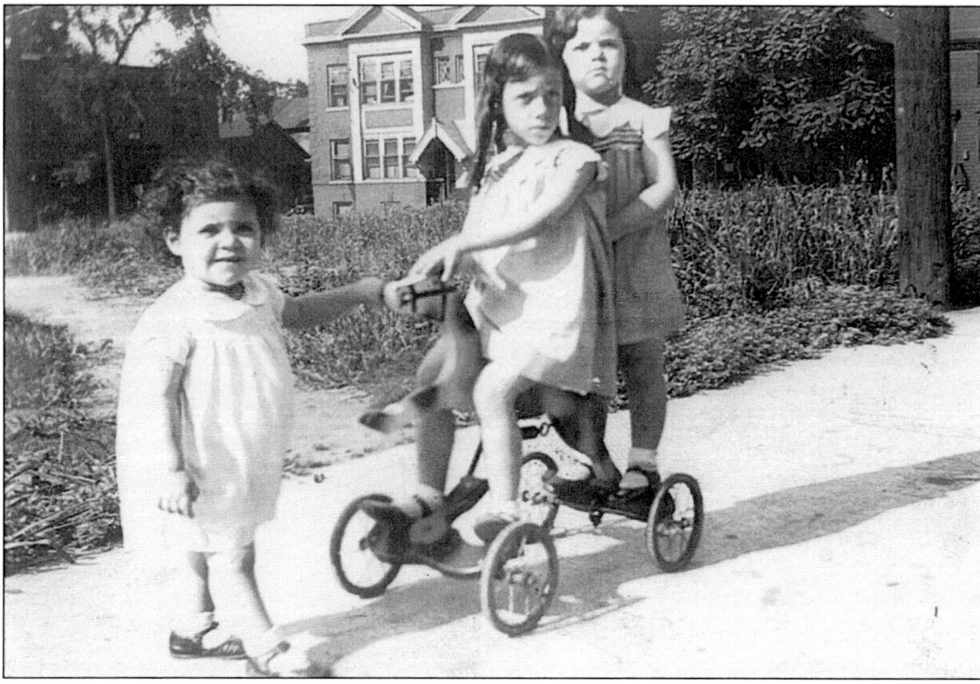

Jenny, Carmella, and Stella Bonnici pause for a picture on a sidewalk around 1935 in Corktown. (Courtesy of Stella Grima.)

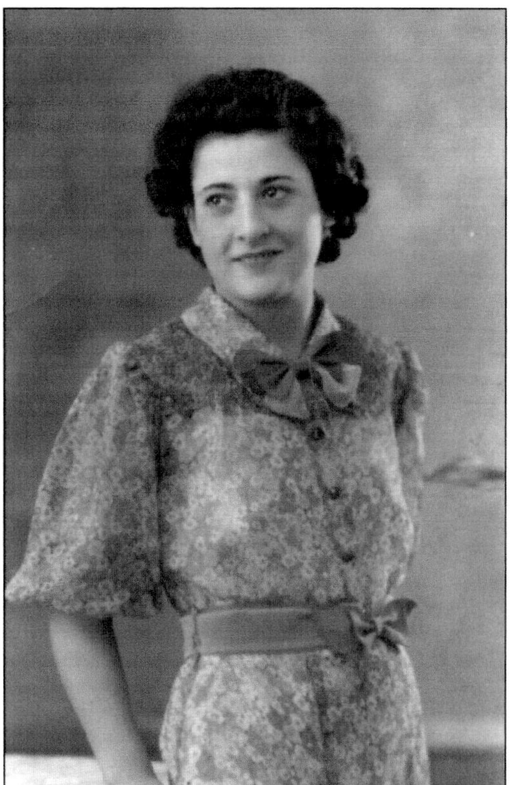

Rita Borg's brother Emmanuel Borg owned Borg Studios in Corktown. She and other members of the family were often used as models while he tried various photographic techniques. He spent countless hours in the library researching and studying photography and was known for his attention to detail. (Author's collection.)

Nina Borg and John B. Haley (Hili) were married in 1925 by Fr. Michael Borg, who was the pastor representing the Maltese people in Corktown. Nina and John met in Detroit and had two children, Tess, who was born in 1932, and Paul, who died at birth in 1933.

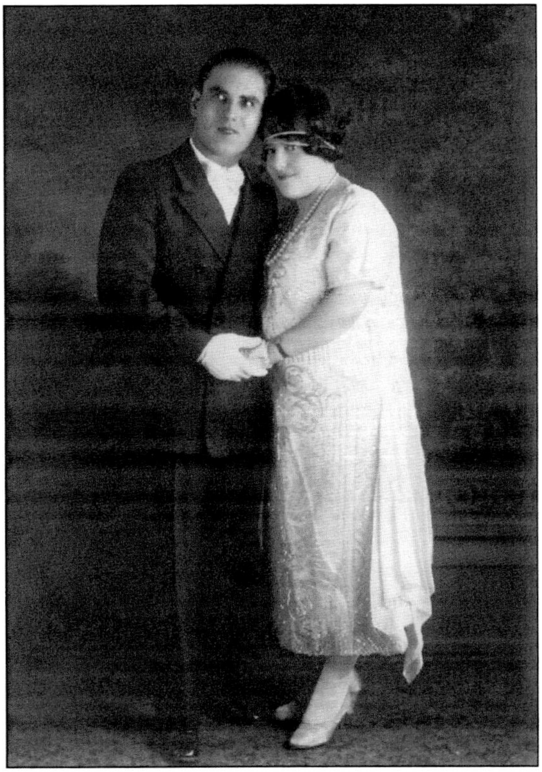

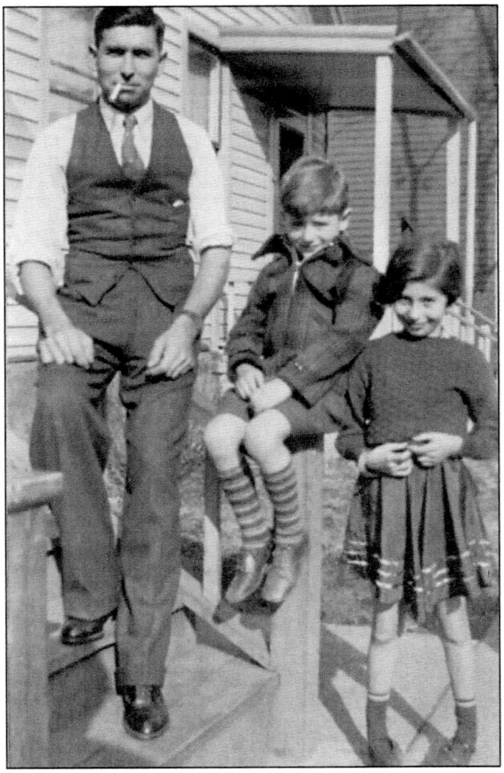

John Fenech is with his children Robert and Frances Fenech. John was born in Veletta, which is the capitol of Malta. He left behind his sweetheart, Helen Venturi, and sent for her to join him in Detroit in 1930. They were married shortly after she arrived. Even death could not keep them separated for too long—they died within three days of each other. Helen passed away on December 25, 1968, after suffering from the Hong Kong flu that developed into spinal meningitis, and John died from cancer on December 28, 1968. (Courtesy Tess Vella.)

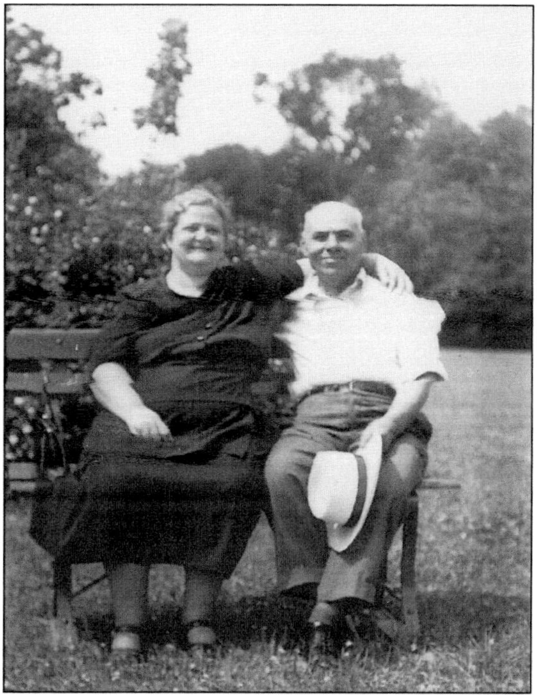

Maria and Raphael Bonnici pose at Patton Park in Detroit around 1950. They were married in Malta in 1929 before coming to Detroit and raising five children. (Courtesy of Stella Grima.)

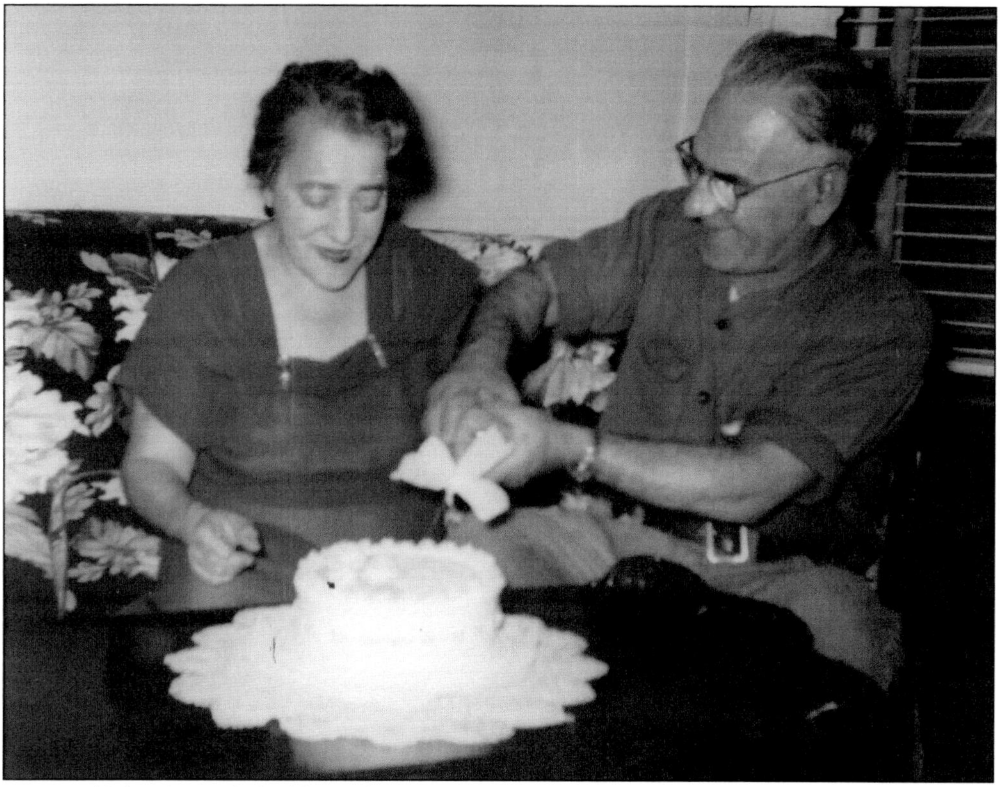

Nina and John B. Healy (Hili) cut their 40th anniversary cake in their home on Leverette Street in Corktown. (Courtesy Tess Vella.)

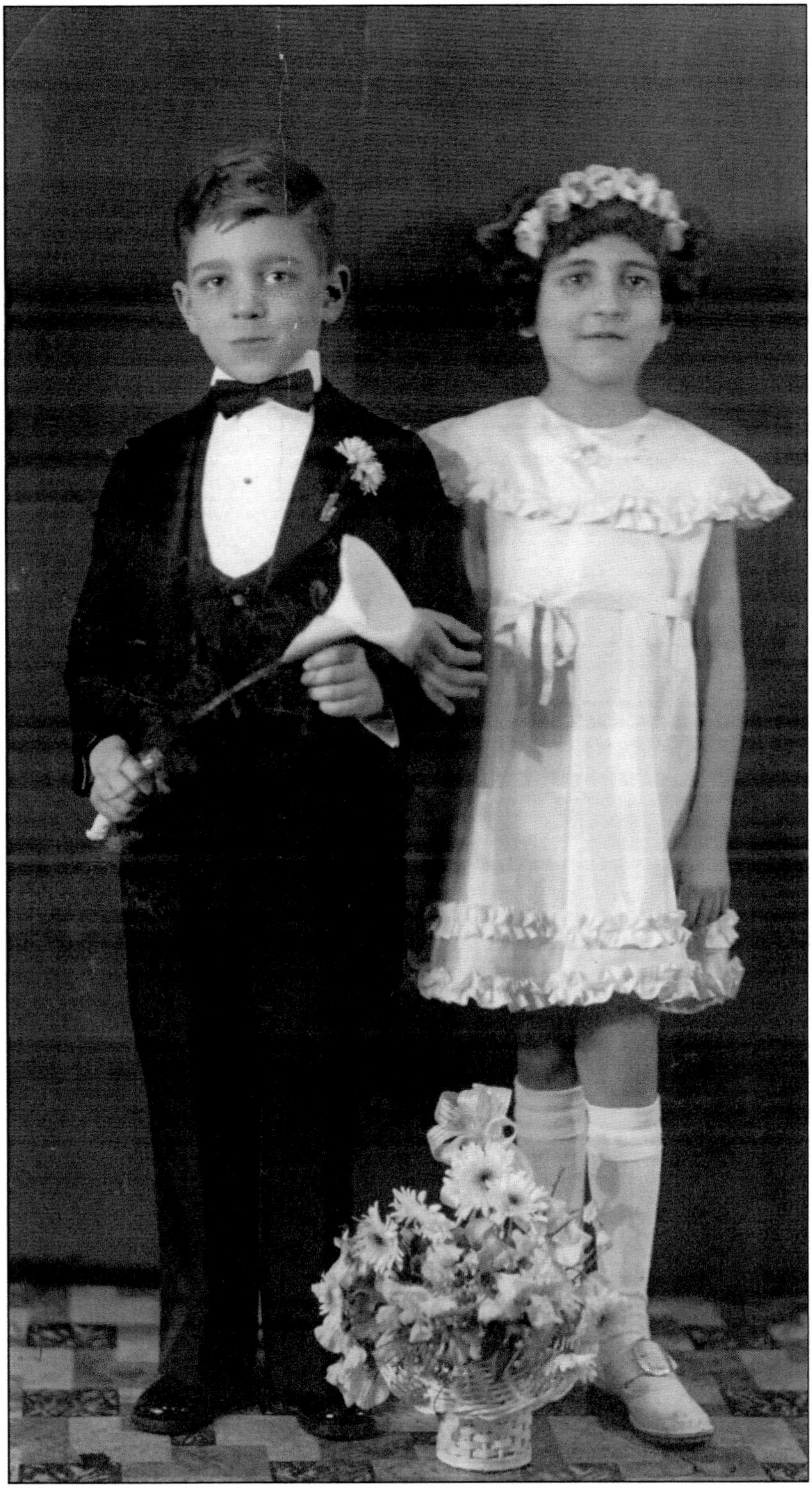

Joseph Vella and Angie DeBono helped with a wedding in St. Paul's Maltese Church. Both were seven years old at the time this photograph was taken. (Courtesy of DeeDee DeBono.)

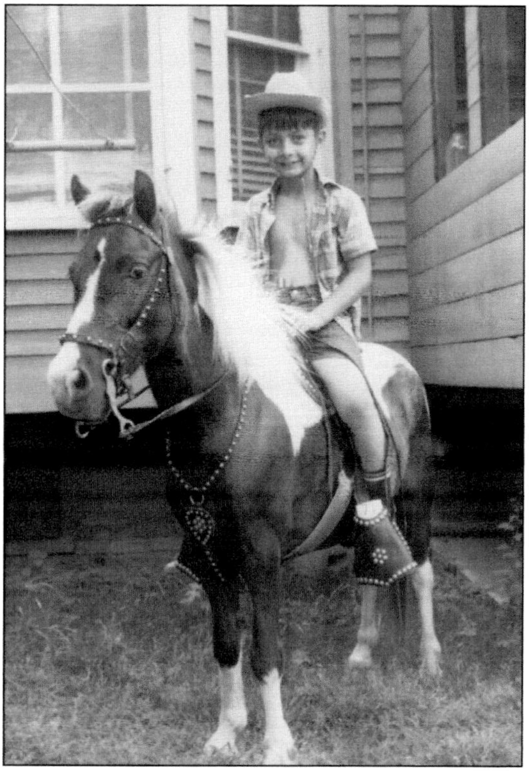

Six-year-old Paul Attard took a pony ride outside his home in Corktown. He grew up to become a Detroit fireman. He worked for the City of Detroit in personnel for a number of years, but a career as a fireman was something he always wanted. He never applied, because his mother worried about his safety. After his mother's death, the 29-year-old applied for his dream job and was accepted. (Courtesy of Terise Attard Okasinski.)

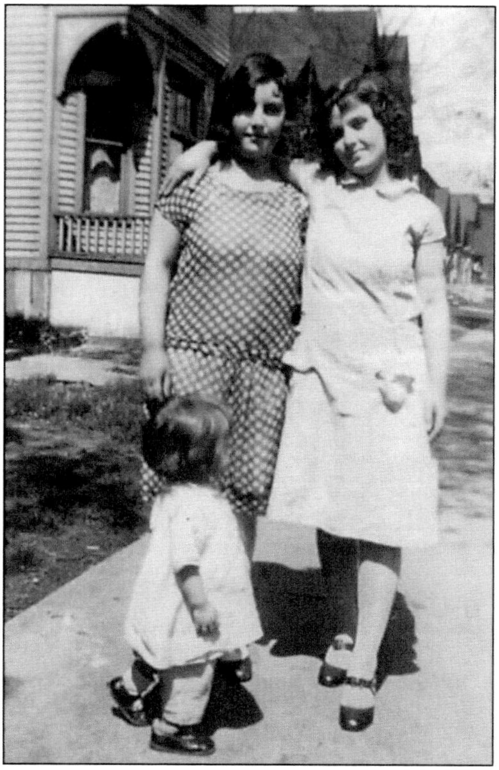

This photograph of Mary Cassar (left), Josephine Cassar (right), and Mary's daughter Esther was taken around 1930 on LaBrosse Street in Detroit. (Courtesy of Christina Setlock.)

Here is Lawrence Cassar with Mary, Jean, and Esther Cassar around 1929. Lawrence, who was born in Gozo, Malta, arrived on Ellis Island in 1920. Mary, who was born in Mosta, Malta, arrived in Detroit when she was nine. Lawrence rented a room in Corktown from Mary's parents. She was 15 years old when they married. (Courtesy of Christina Setlock.)

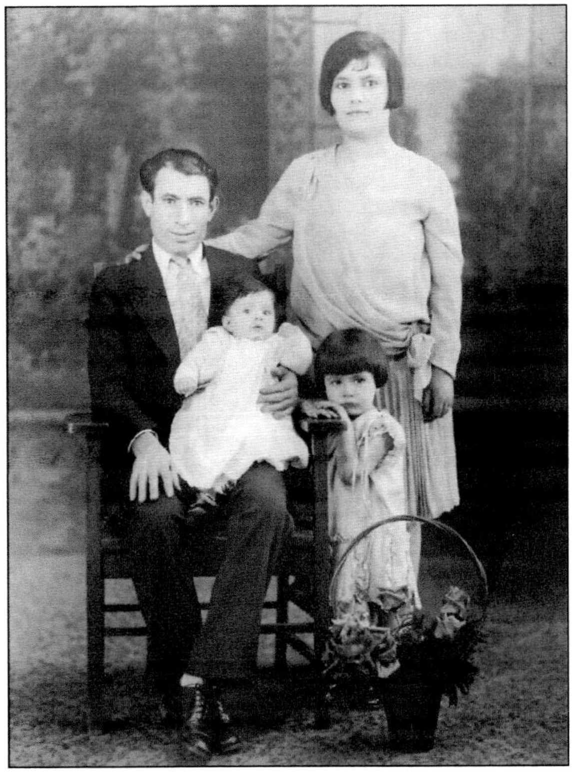

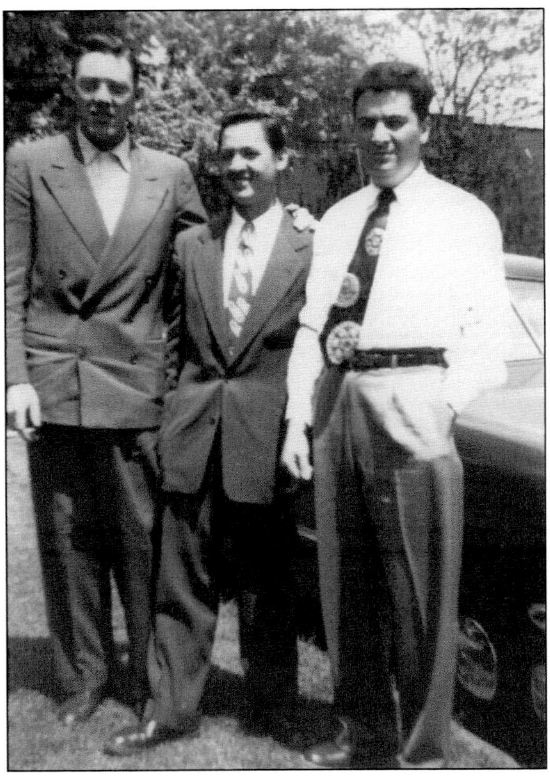

From left to right, David Campbell, Charlie Mifsud, and Frank Mifsud are pictured in 1951 in Detroit. Frank came to the United States in 1950. He married, Evelyn Campbell, and they raised five children. (Courtesy of Rose Mifsud.)

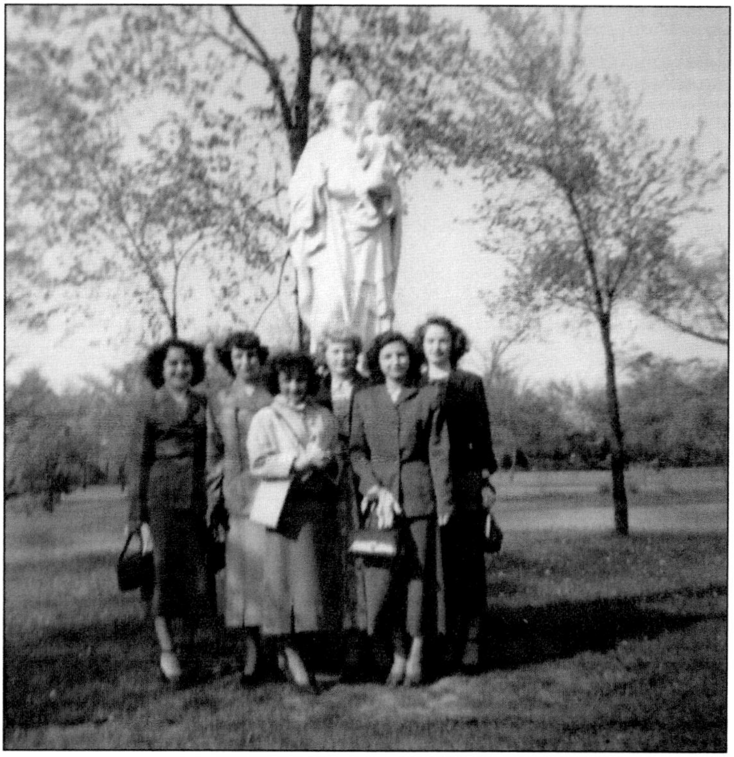

Here is a group of girls from St. Vincent High School that visited a convent in Monroe about 1946. They are, from left to right, Virginia Sanchez, Helen Brincat, Tess Haley, Rose Adams, Louise Tabone, and Florence Leeds.

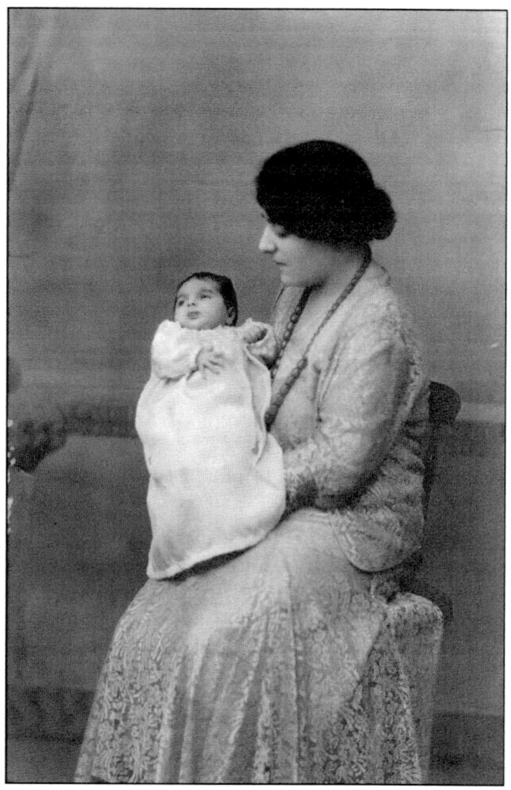

Nina Haley holds her baby, Tess, shortly after her birth in 1932. Tess was born and raised in Corktown and married John Vella, who also grew up in Corktown. They had eight children and eventually moved to Livonia.

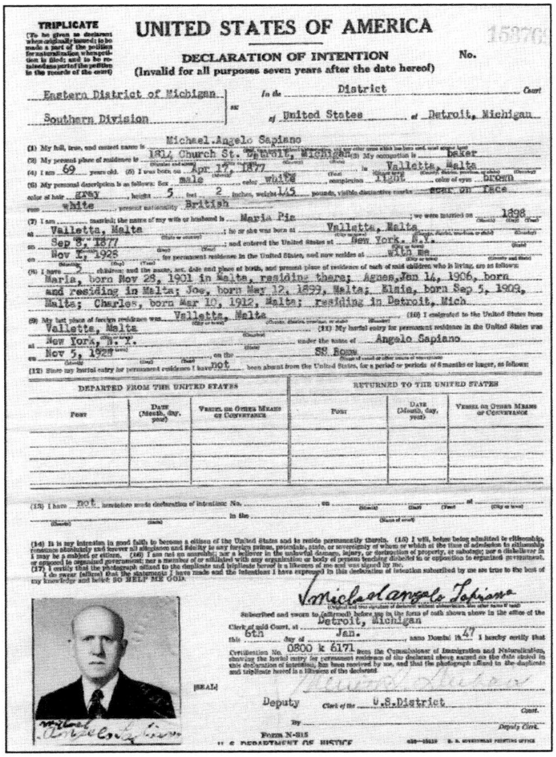

TRIPLICATE

UNITED STATES OF AMERICA

DECLARATION OF INTENTION

(Invalid for all purposes seven years after the date hereof)

No.

Eastern District of Michigan — Southern Division — In the District Court of United States at Detroit, Michigan

(1) My full, true, and correct name is Michael Angelo Sapiano
(2) My present place of residence is 1814 Church St. Detroit, Michigan (3) My occupation is baker
(4) I am 69 years old. (5) I was born on Apr 17, 1877 in Valletta, Malta
(6) My personal description is as follows: Sex male, color white, complexion light, color of eyes brown, color of hair grey, height 5 feet 2 inches, weight 145 pounds, visible distinctive marks scar on face, race white, present nationality British
(7) I am married; the name of my wife or husband is Maria Pia; we were married on 1898 at Valletta, Malta; he or she was born at Valletta, Malta on Sep 8, 1877 and entered the United States at New York, N.Y. on Nov 5, 1928 for permanent residence in the United States, and now resides at with me.
(8) I have 5 children; and the name, sex, date and place of birth, and present place of residence of each of said children who is living, are as follows: Maria, born Nov 28, 1901 in Malta, residing there; Agnes, Jan 14, 1906, born and residing in Malta; Joe, born May 12, 1899, Malta; Elsie, born Sep 5, 1909, Malta; Charles, born Mar 10, 1912, Malta; residing in Detroit, Mich.
(9) My last place of foreign residence was Valletta, Malta (10) I emigrated to the United States from Valletta, Malta (11) My lawful entry for permanent residence in the United States was at New York, N.Y. under the name of Angelo Sapiano on Nov 5, 1928 on the SS Roma
(12) Since my lawful entry for permanent residence I have not been absent from the United States, for a period or periods of 6 months or longer, as follows:

DEPARTED FROM THE UNITED STATES			RETURNED TO THE UNITED STATES		
Port	Date (Month, day, year)	Vessel or Other Means of Conveyance	Port	Date (Month, day, year)	Vessel or Other Means of Conveyance

(13) I have not heretofore made declaration of intention: No. ... on ... at ... in the ...

(14) It is my intention in good faith to become a citizen of the United States and to reside permanently therein. ... SO HELP ME GOD.

Michael Angelo Sapiano

Subscribed and sworn to (affirmed) before me in the form of oath shown above in the office of the Clerk of said Court, at Detroit, Michigan this 6th day of Jan. anno Domini 1947. I hereby certify that Certification No. 0800 k 6171 from the Commissioner of Immigration and Naturalization, showing the lawful entry for permanent residence of the declarant above named on the date stated in this declaration of intention, has been received by me, and that the photograph affixed to the duplicate and triplicate hereof is a likeness of the declarant.

[SEAL]

Deputy Clerk of the U.S. District Court.

Form N-315

Here are the passports for Michael Angelo Sapiano and Ersilia Sapiano. Ersilia, a concert pianist, was married to Giovanni Felice, a tenor. They professionally performed together in the Detroit area. Giovanni worked at Ford Motor Company when he came to the United States. Michael Angelo owned a bakery in Malta and worked for the Michigan Italian Bakery Company after moving to Detroit. (Both courtesy of Norma Jean Philip.)

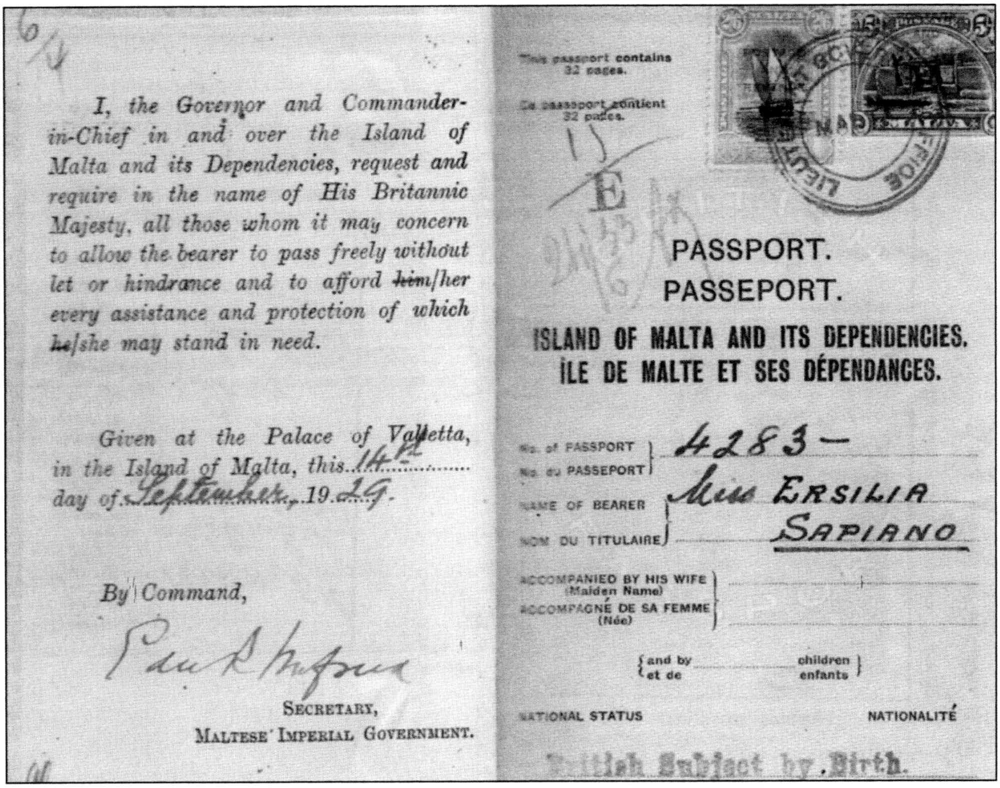

I, the Governor and Commander-in-Chief in and over the Island of Malta and its Dependencies, request and require in the name of His Britannic Majesty, all those whom it may concern to allow the bearer to pass freely without let or hindrance and to afford ~~him~~/her every assistance and protection of which ~~he~~/she may stand in need.

Given at the Palace of Valletta, in the Island of Malta, this 14th day of September, 1929.

By Command,

SECRETARY,
MALTESE IMPERIAL GOVERNMENT.

This passport contains 32 pages.
Ce passeport contient 32 pages.

PASSPORT.
PASSEPORT.
ISLAND OF MALTA AND ITS DEPENDENCIES.
ÎLE DE MALTE ET SES DÉPENDANCES.

No. of PASSPORT / No. du PASSEPORT: 4283 —
NAME OF BEARER / NOM DU TITULAIRE: Miss ERSILIA SAPIANO
ACCOMPANIED BY HIS WIFE (Maiden Name) / ACCOMPAGNÉ DE SA FEMME (Née)
and by / et de ... children / enfants
NATIONAL STATUS / NATIONALITÉ: British Subject by Birth.

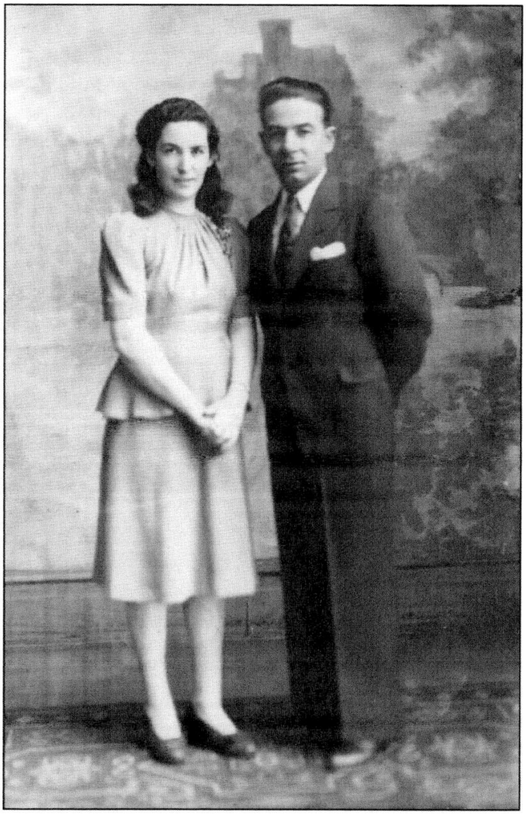

Here are Colleen Micallef and Charles Attard. Colleen was born in Malta and raised in Toronto. She married Charles in 1939, and they moved to Detroit. (Courtesy of Theresa [Attard] Srock.)

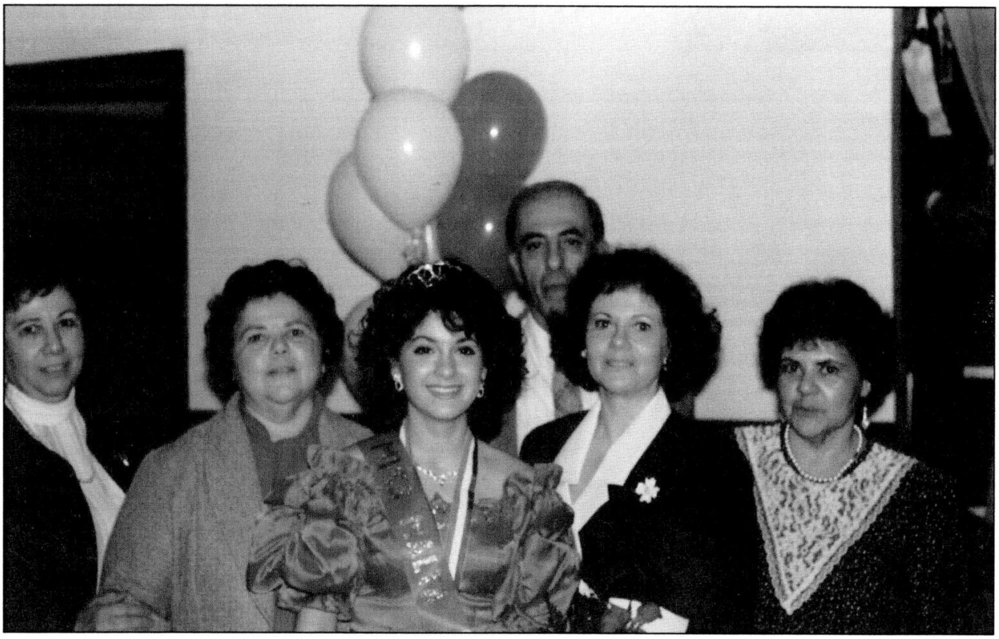

From left to right (front) are Carmella Bonnici, Stella Grima, Miss Malta 1989–1990 Stephanie Acho, and her mom Rita Acho; (back) John Grima and Jennie Bonnici. Carmella, Stella, and Jennie are Stephanie's aunts; John is her uncle. (Courtesy of Stella Grima.)

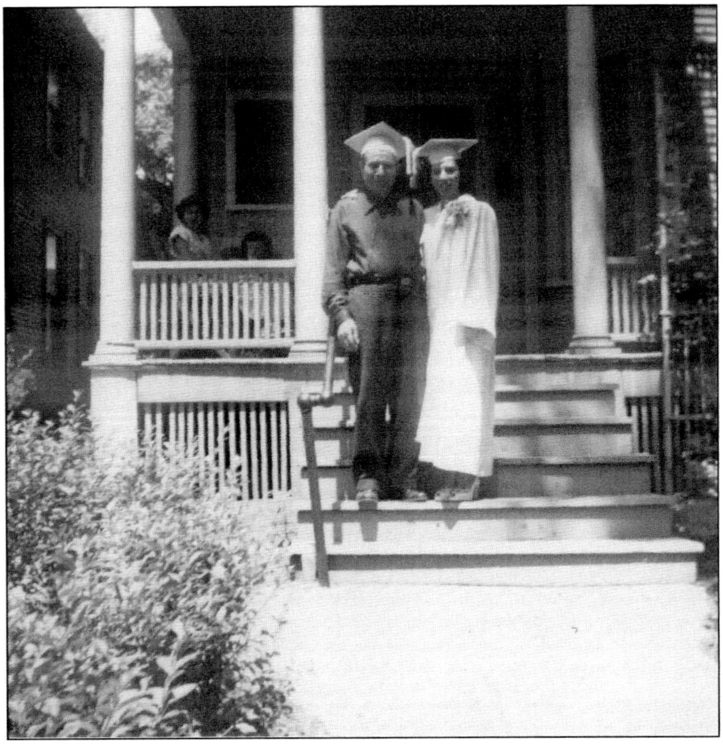

Pictured here in 1950, Lawrence Cassar stands on the porch of his home in Corktown with his youngest daughter, Lena. She graduated from St. Vincent de Paul High School and went on to marry and have three children. (Courtesy of Lena Cunningham.)

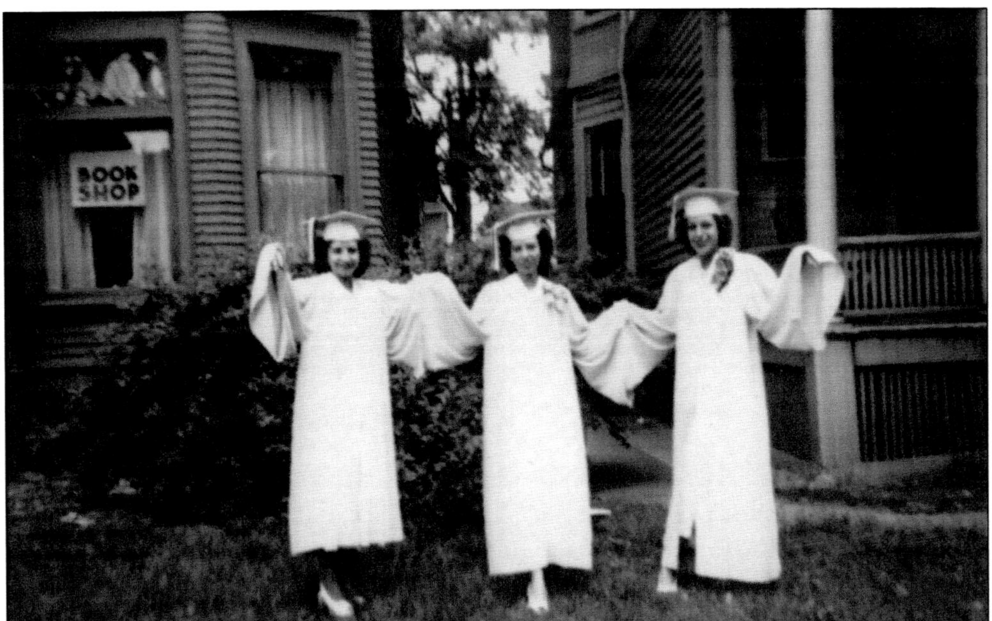

From left to right, Louise Tabone, Lena Cassar, and Helen Brincat were neighbors on Leverette Street in Corktown. This picture was taken in 1950. As neighbors, they grew up together and remained friends for more than 60 years. Their friendship remained strong even as they left the city and moved to various Detroit suburbs. (Courtesy of Lena Cunningham.)

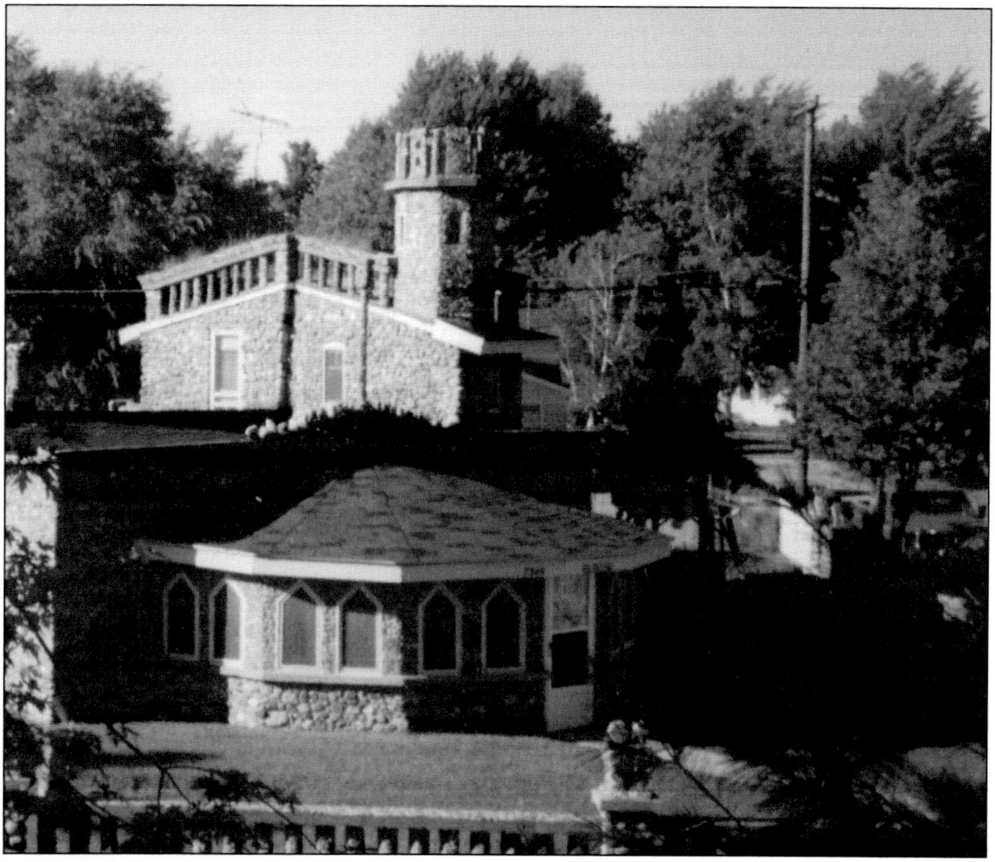

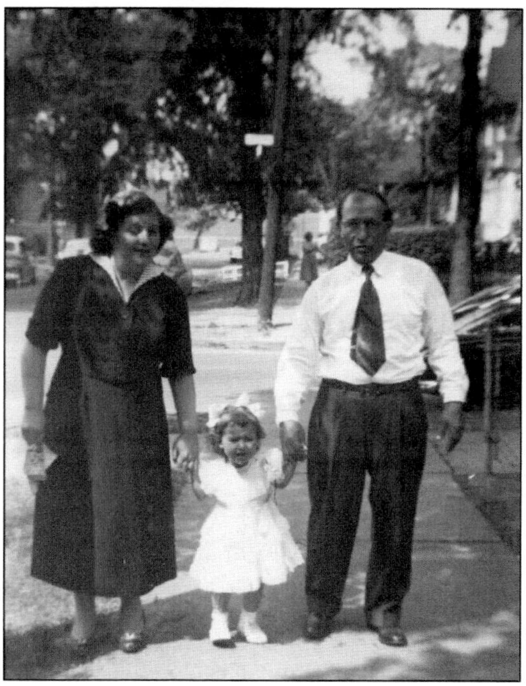

A Maltese family owned this stone house in Lexington, Michigan, which was a popular area for Maltese to buy summer homes. Others moved there to live year-round.

Ann Marie Tabone Sheehan poses with Hannah and John Tabone. As of 2010, Ann Marie still remains at the family homestead on Leverette Street. (Courtesy of Lena Cunningham.)

Tess Haley takes a break from a photograph session at a grotto of the Blessed Mother in Orchard Lake on the day of her graduation. (Courtesy Tess Vella.)

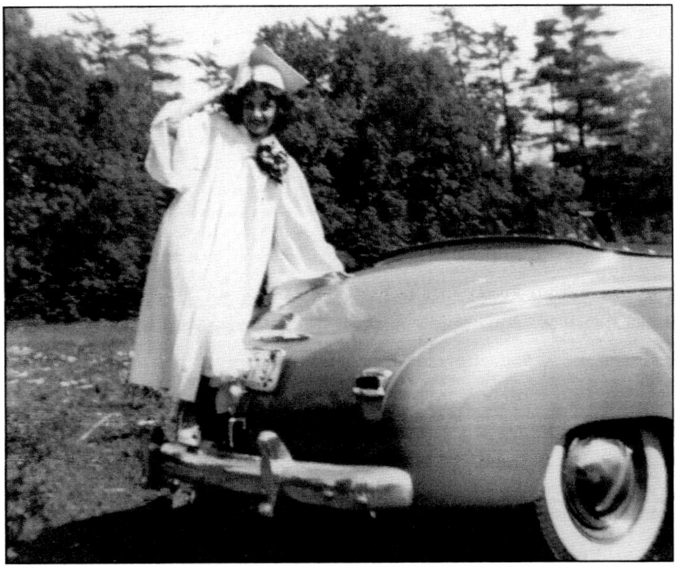

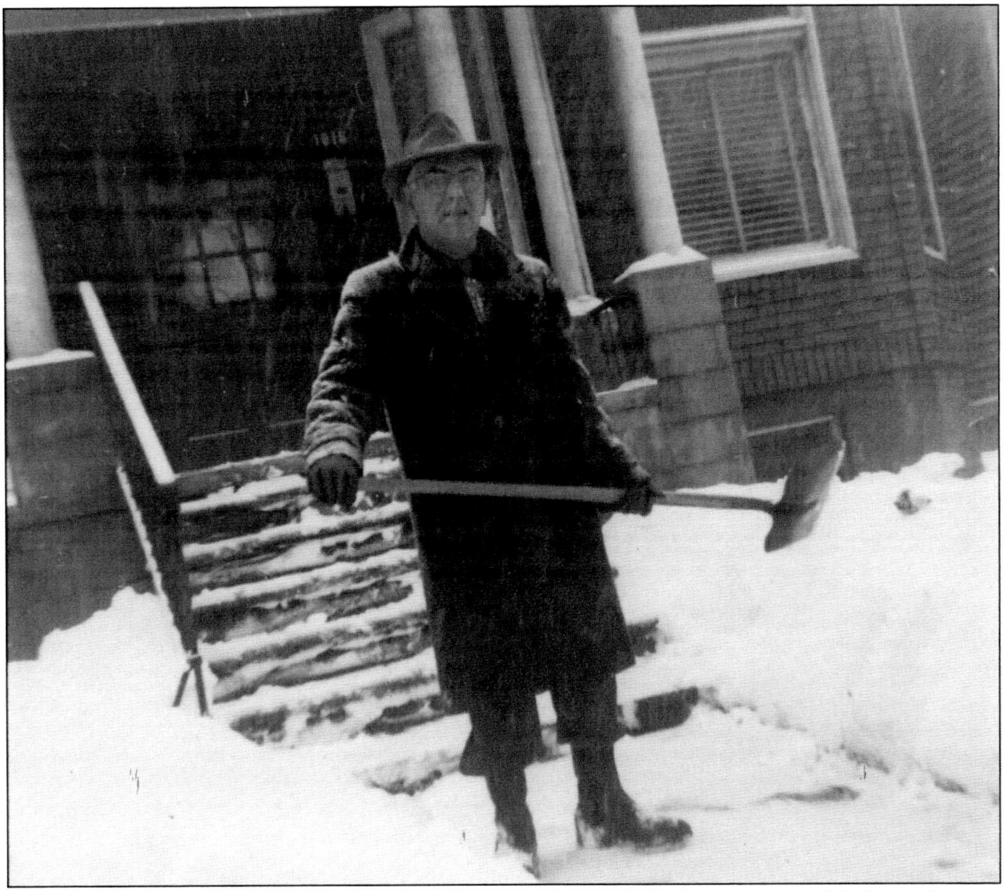

John B. Haley (Hili) shovels snow at 1816 Leverette Street in Corktown around 1950. Haley was known for his strength, and legend has it that he could raise the back of a car single-handedly. (Courtesy Tess Vella.)

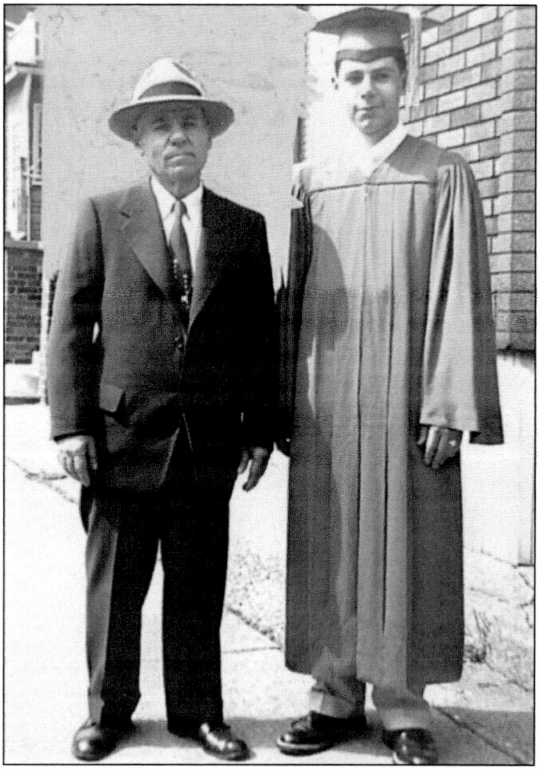

Ralph Bonnici and his son Leon pose for the camera after Leon's graduation from St. Vincent de Paul High School in 1954. Ralph and his wife, Maria, came from Malta in 1929. Their five children were born in Corktown, and Ralph worked for Dodge Motors. Leon worked for Michigan Consolidated Gas Company, served in U.S. Army, and married Kathleen. They, too, had five children. (Courtesy of Stella Grima.)

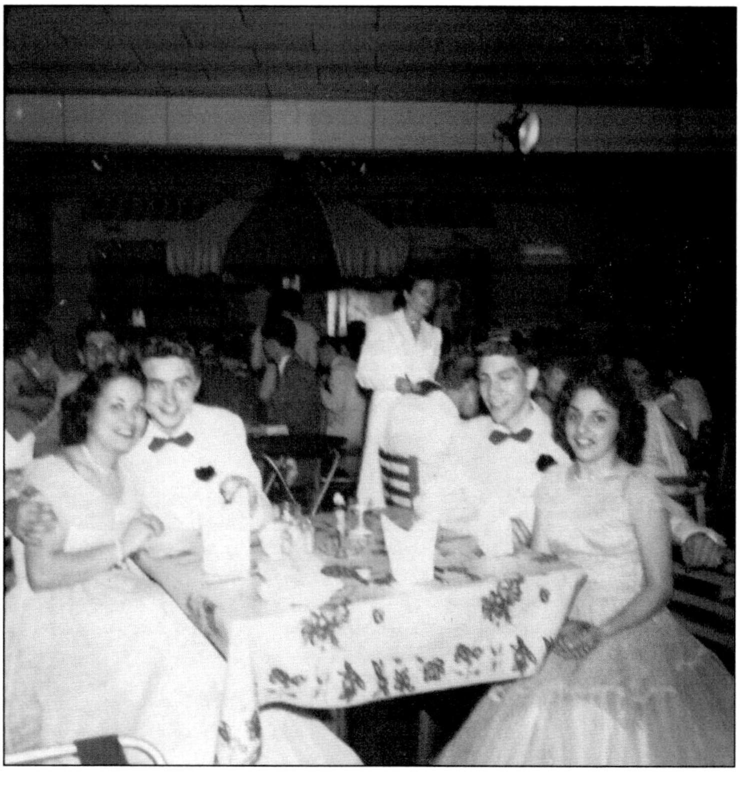

After prom in 1950, graduates from St. Vincent de Paul High School went to a restaurant. Shown here are Agnes Ellul and Leonard Kotarski with John Vella and Tess Haley. (Courtesy Tess Vella.)

Seen here from left to right are (front row) Maria Bonnici and Rita Bonnici; (back row) Jenny, Leon, and Carmela Bonnici. This picture was taken at the Bonnicis' cousin's house in Detroit. (Courtesy of Stella Grima.)

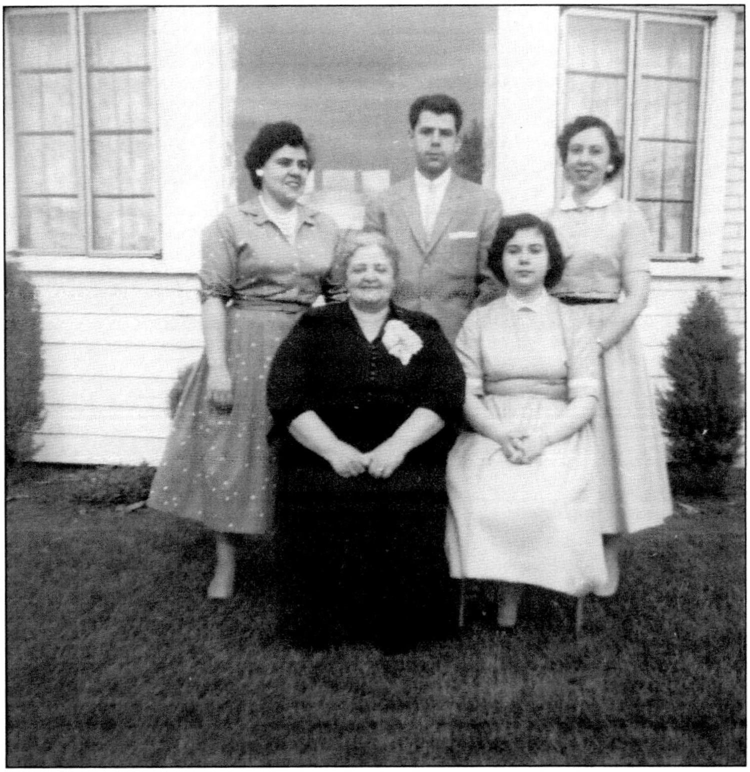

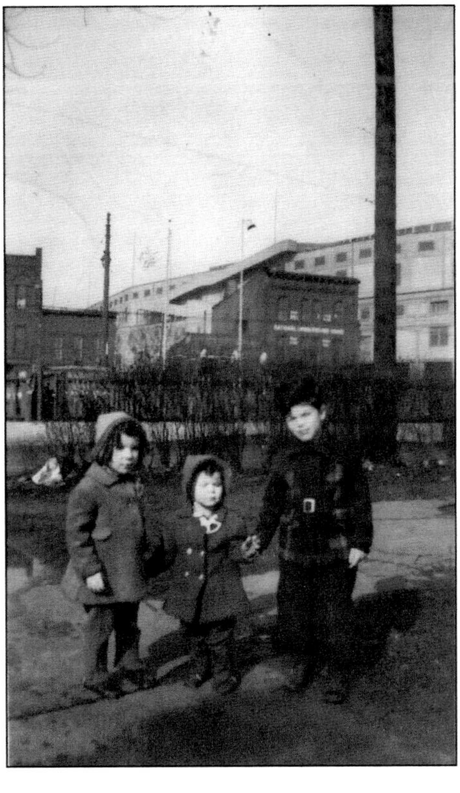

Theresa, Fred, and Carmen Attard lived on Eleventh Street and Michigan Avenue from 1940 to 1952. The three children were born to Charlie and Colleen Attard of Corktown and were longtime residents who graduated from St. Vincent de Paul Elementary School and High School. (Courtesy of Theresa [Attard] Srock.)

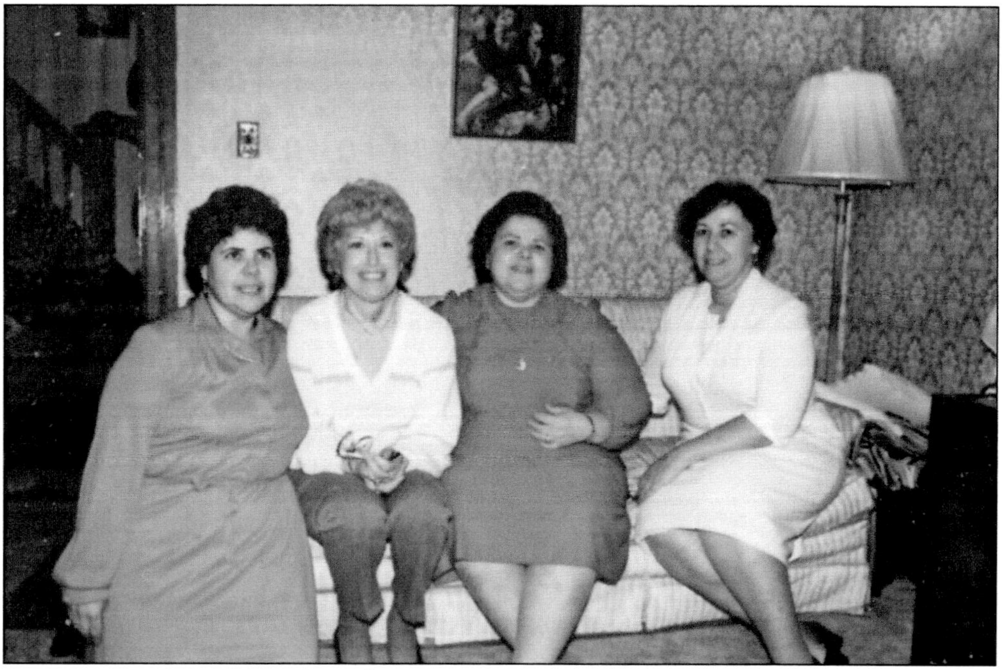

Jenny Bonnici, Frances Fenech, Stella Bonnici, and Carmella Bonnici are pictured at the Bonnici home on Eleventh Street around 1979. Frances lived around the corner on Leverette Street. The girls were best friends before elementary school and remain good friends in 2010. (Courtesy of Frances Fenech.)

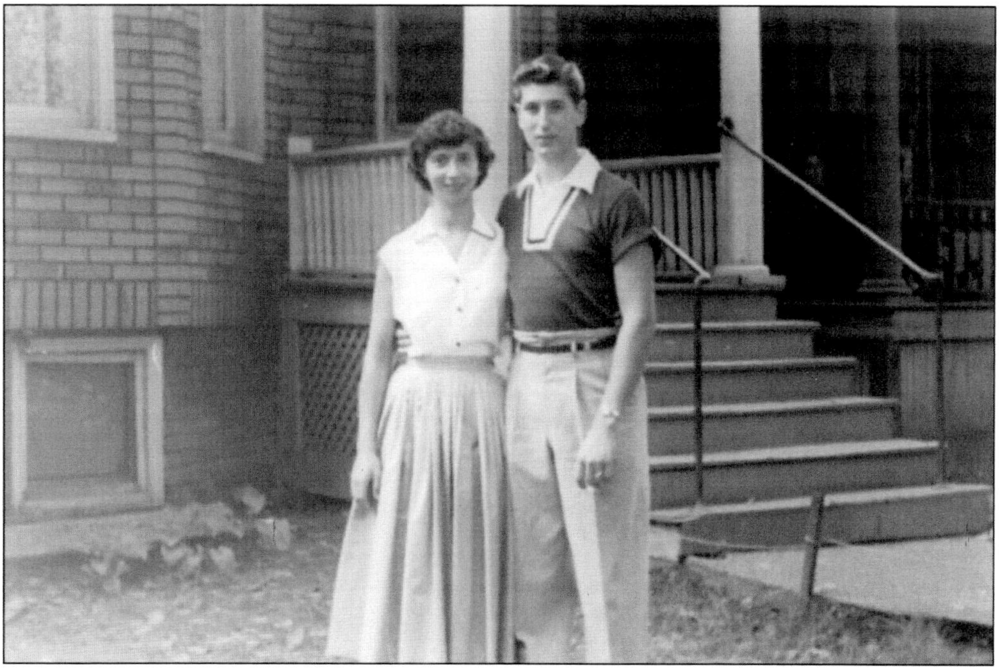

Josephine Sammut and Robert Fenech were neighbors on Leverette Street growing up, and they later married each other. (Courtesy of Frances Fenech.)

Ninette Capace (left) and Helen Fenech are shown at the Fenech home on Leverette Street. Ninette lived next door to Helen, and the ladies were cousins. (Courtesy of Frances Fenech.)

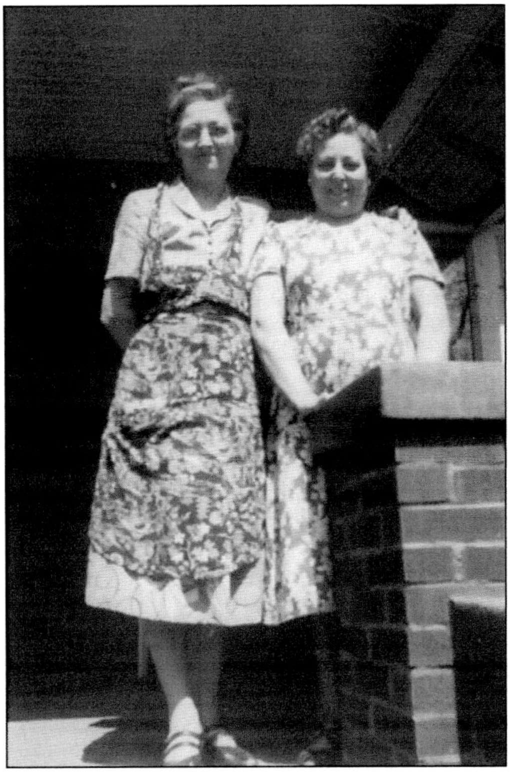

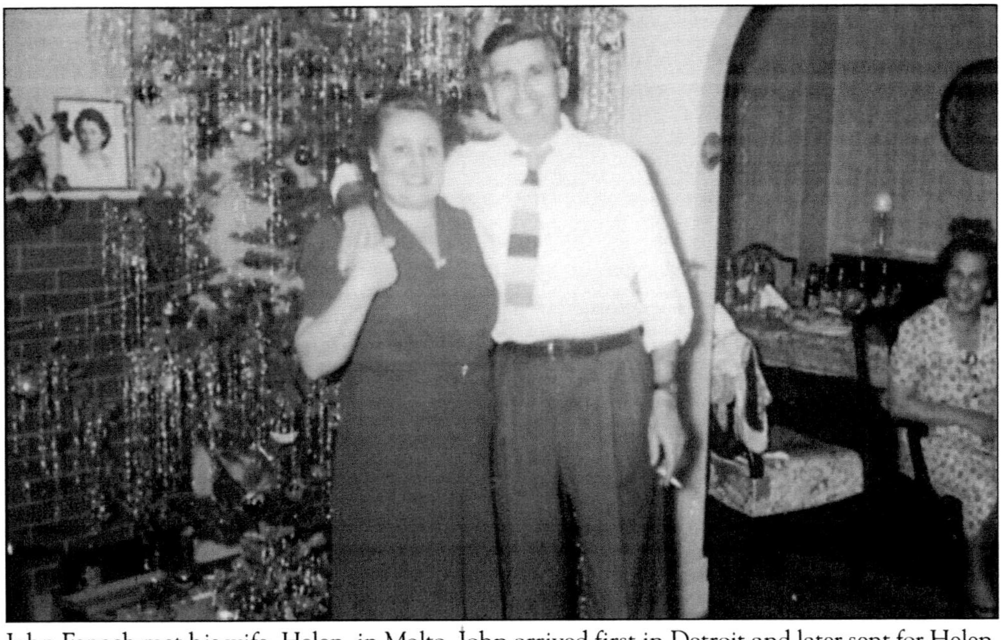

John Fenech met his wife, Helen, in Malta. John arrived first in Detroit and later sent for Helen. When she arrived, they were married in 1930. They had four children: Frances, Robert, Mary Ann, and John Jr. Frances remained in the family home after her parents died in 1968. She was awarded a landscape beautification recognition by Corktown and Detroit Edison on two occasions. She lived in the home until 1990. (Courtesy of Frances Fenech.)

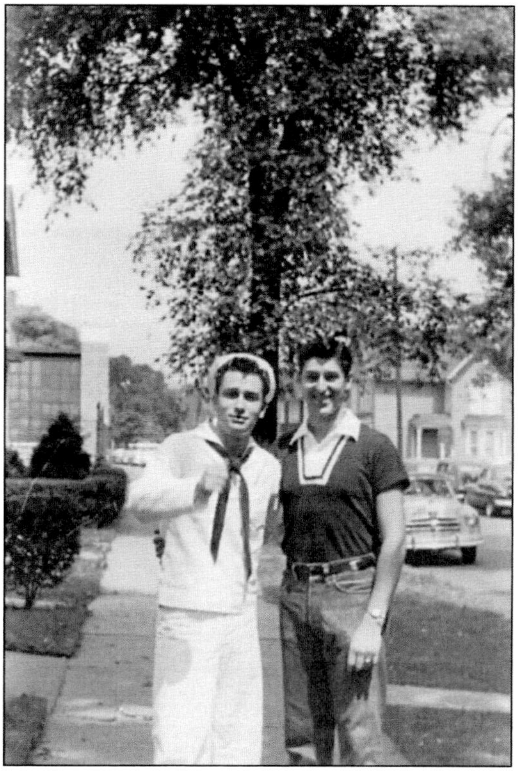

Renold Mirabitur, who served in the U.S. Navy, visits with his friend and next-door neighbor, Robert Fenech. They continued their friendship as adults, even after each had married and moved out of the city. (Courtesy of Mary and Chuck Brincat.)

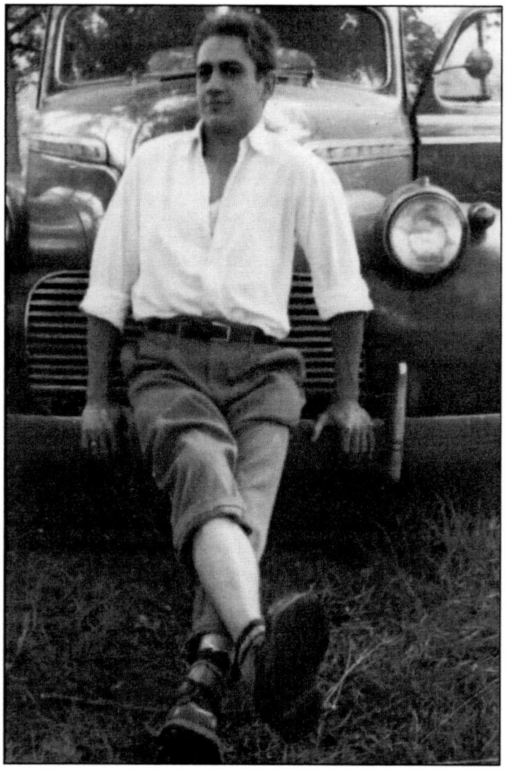

Bobby Capace relaxes at Mandon Lake. Mandon Lake was a popular area for Maltese to own summer homes. The 26-acre lake is located in White Lake Township in Oakland County. (Courtesy of Mary and Chuck Brincat.)

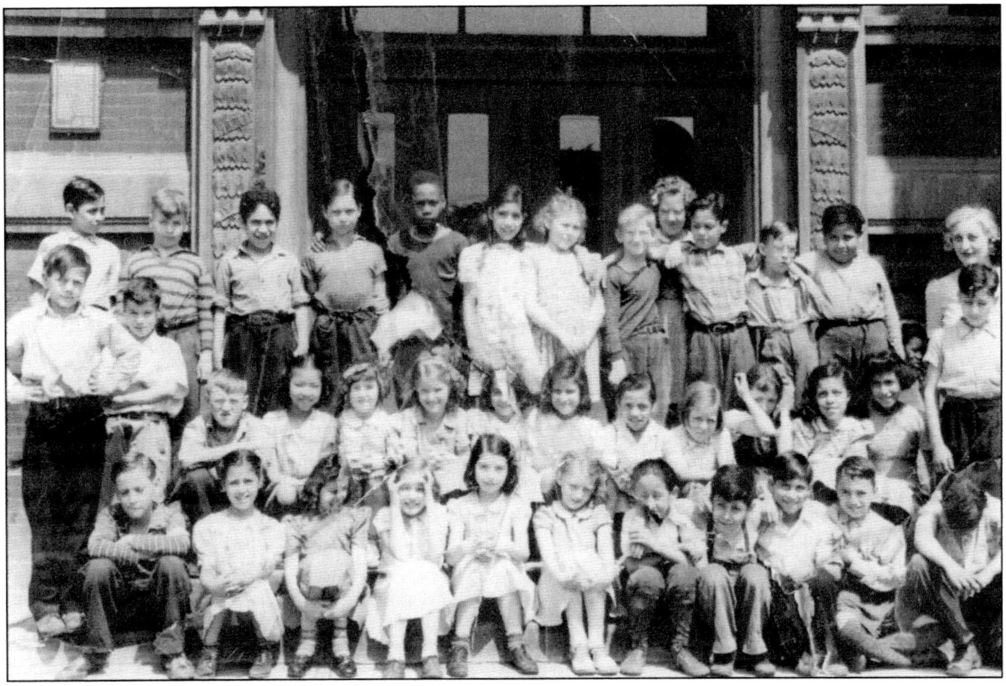

Many Maltese children attended Douglas Houghton School on Abbott Street in Corktown. This photograph is from about 1943. The school was opened in 1853 and was called the Eighth Ward School. It was renamed after Douglas Houghton, the first president of the school board. The school was demolished in the 1950s. (Courtesy of Mary and Chuck Brincat.)

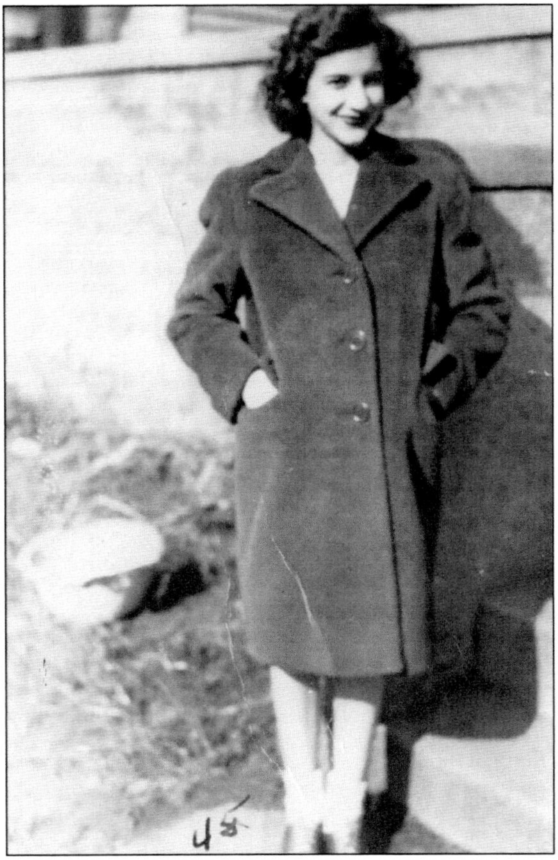

Mary Tabone lived on Church Street in Corktown. In this *c.* 1945 picture, she is posing outside her house. Even though they lived across the street from one another for a short time, Mary only started dating Chuck Brincat after he returned from the service. They were set up on a blind date together and married when she was 19 and he was 23. They celebrated their 60th anniversary on September 9, 2010. (Courtesy of Mary and Chuck Brincat.)

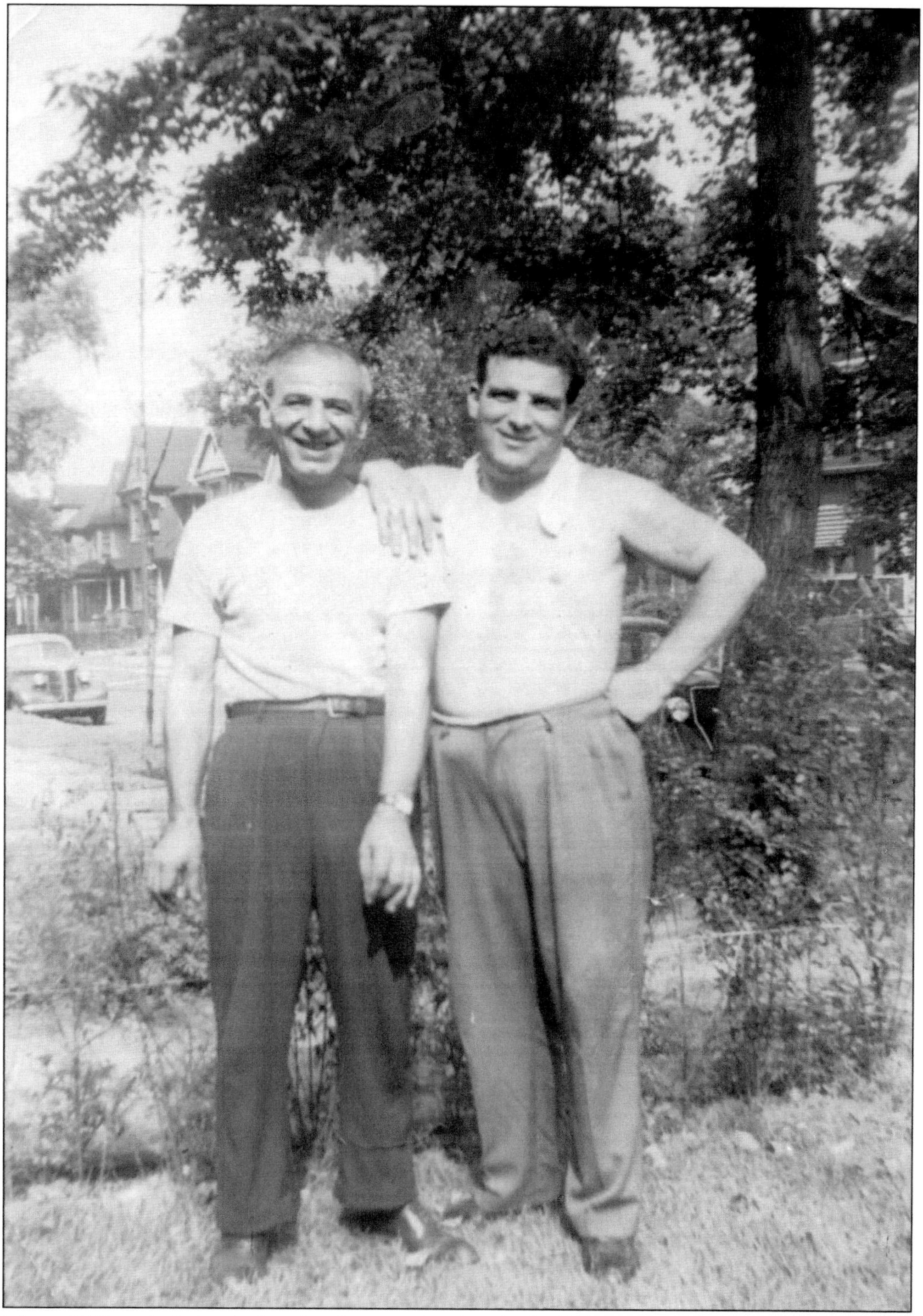

Manuel Tabone's father-in-law, Joe Lauron, lived with the Tabones on Church Street when his wife, Caroline (Micallef), died. When Joe arrived in the United States, the Lauron family name was changed; in Malta, the name was Lauro. Caroline was an accomplished seamstress in Malta. (Courtesy of Mary and Chuck Brincat.)

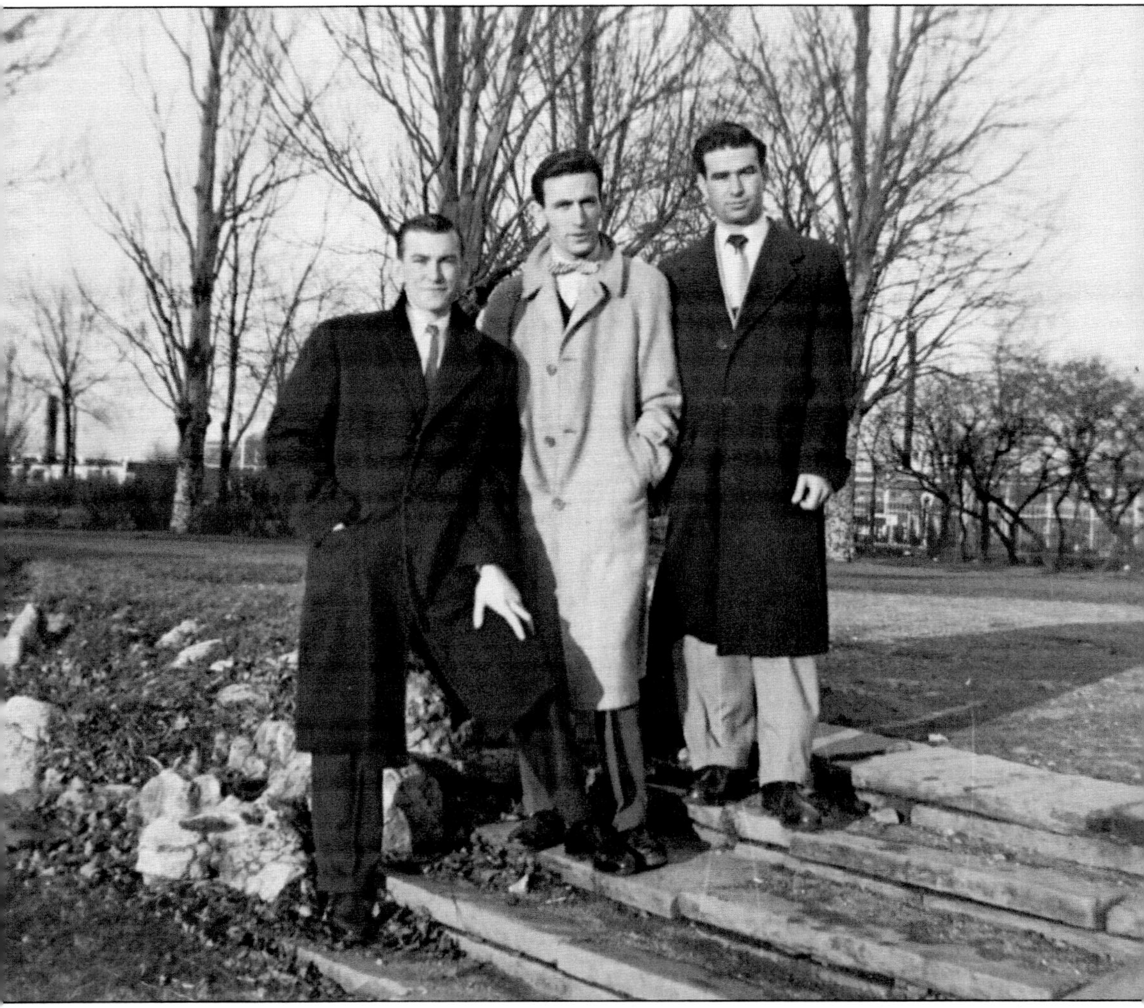

Pictured from left to right around 1950, Caesar, Tony, and Henry Pons are posing for a picture taken in a park in Windsor. Caesar Pons remained in Canada, Tony Pons moved to Detroit, and Henry Pons moved to Australia. The "down-under" country is known for its large Maltese population. Tony, a clothing salesman, was a Boy Scout leader in Canada, Detroit, and Livonia.

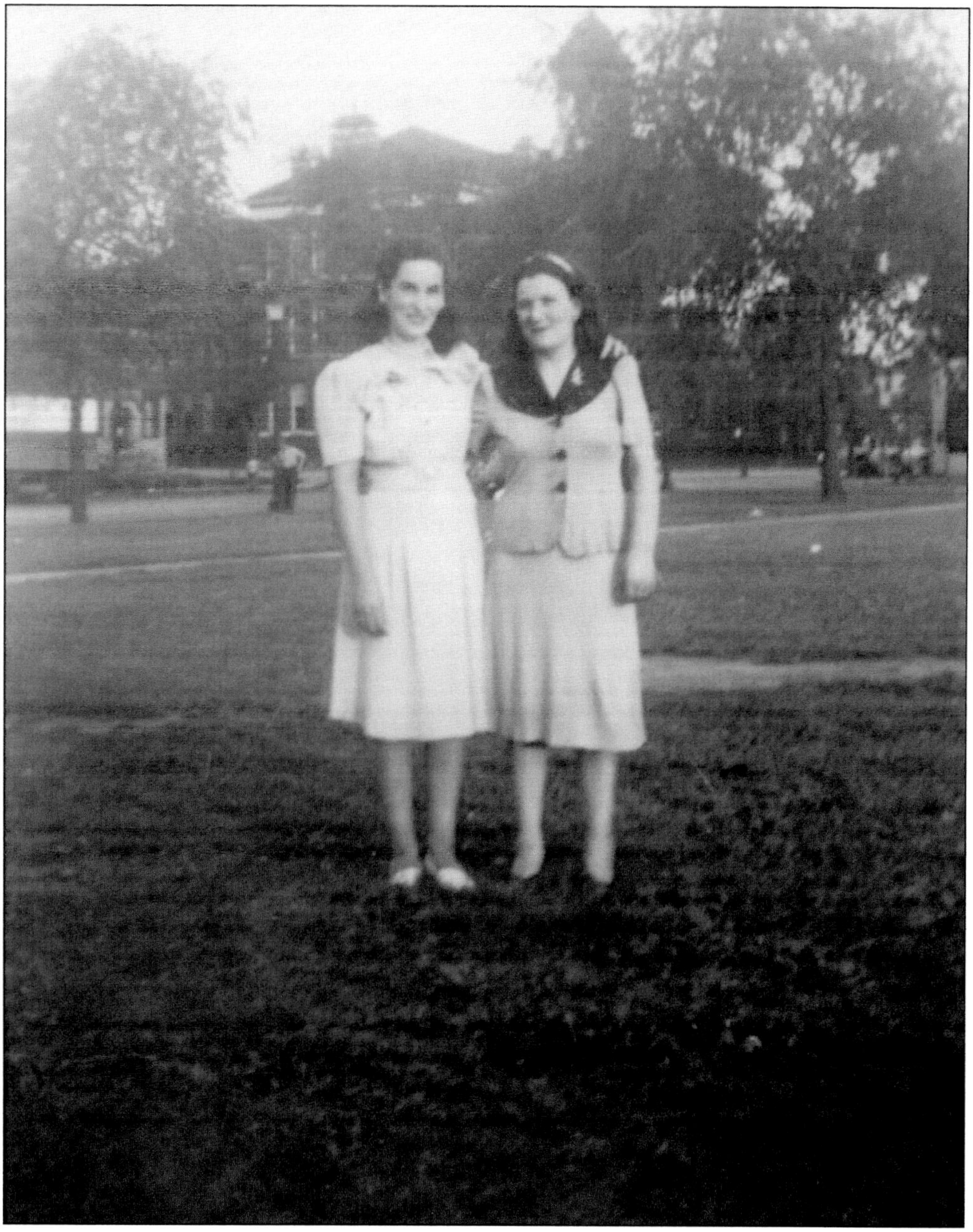

Colleen Attard (left) is with Vicki Cusheri in the park by a Detroit train station around 1945. Colleen was married to Charlie Attard, and they raised Theresa, Freddie, and Carmen. They were all born and raised in Corktown. (Courtesy of Theresa [Attard] Srock.)

Two

You Are What you Eat

The Maltese people brought their famous pastizzi from their homeland to their new country. While pastizzi is the signature Maltese dish, it is very difficult to make, so a lot of Maltese people have not learned the process or have decided it is easier to buy them ready-made. The flaky, almost pastry-like dough requires an arduous process that takes hours to prepare.

The dough is filled with ricotta cheese or meat and peas and can be used as an appetizer or main meal. A few hours have to be set aside to make the delectable food, or it can be bought at the Maltese clubs in Detroit and Dearborn.

Other favorite Maltese dishes are baked macaroni, rabbit stew, baked rice, and fish soup. For dessert, Maltese ice cream, cannolis, and sesame rings are among the most popular.

Many Maltese immigrants cooked from memory, never following a written recipe. They cooked by instinct, adjusting for variations, and it was sometimes difficult for the first and second generations to nail down recipes. Some families had the foresight to write down the recipes, but most families passed their recipes down through doing and watching.

Pastizzi

The dough:
3 cups of shortening
5 cups of flour
2 cups of cold water
1/4 teaspoon of baking powder (optional)
A dash of salt

The meat filling:
1 pound of ground beef
1 large onion, sliced thinly
1 tablespoon of tomato paste
1 small can of drained peas
1 tablespoon of grated cheese
A dash of salt, pepper, and curry powder

The ricotta filling:
2 eggs
1 pound of ricotta Parmesan cheese
1 tablespoon of grated cheese
A dash of salt and pepper
1 tablespoon of semolina (optional)
parsley to taste (optional)

Add flour, water, and salt in an electric mixer. Mix for 15 minutes or knead together by hand for approximately 20 minutes. It should feel slightly moist. Cover and let stand for one hour. Cut away 1/8 of the dough. Lightly grease the table and spread using a rolling pin until the dough is very thin; pull and stretch a little at a time. Spread a generous amount of shortening all over the top of the dough. Start at one end and roll the dough, pulling back and up while rolling. Repeat this process, adding all of the dough to the same roll. Cut the roll to about a foot. Refrigerate or freeze until ready to use. Cut the dough into 1.5-inch sections. Lay each piece with the circles facing up. Brown the beef and remaining ingredients for the meat filling. Spread out the circles and add either the ricotta or meat fillings. Bring both sides of the dough in the middle to cover the filling. Place on an ungreased cookie sheet. At 450 degrees, bake until golden brown.

Baked Macaroni

1 pound of macaroni
1 pound of ground beef
1 six-ounce can of tomato paste
1/4 teaspoon of garlic powder
2 eggs, slightly beaten
1 tablespoon of grated cheese
Hot water
A dash of curry powder (optional)

Brown the beef and add the garlic powder and tomato paste. Fill the tomato paste can with hot water twice and add to the mixture. Add the remaining ingredients and simmer approximately 30 minutes. Add two eggs to the cooked and drained macaroni. Add grated cheese. Mix well and add the sauce. Pour it all into an ungreased deep baking dish and bake at 375 degrees for about one hour or until the top is crisp. If it is not baked, this dish is Mostoccoli. For Mostoccoli, add a pound of ricotta cheese (optional) when adding the eggs.

Maltese Sesame Seed Rings
(Quaqhaq or Kak)

1 cup of butter or margarine
1 ½ cups of sugar
2 eggs
1 grated orange rind
1 grated lemon rind (optional)
2 teaspoons of vanilla
5 cups of flour
3 teaspoons of baking powder
¼ cup of milk
2 tablespoons of Anise seeds
Sesame seeds

Beat butter and sugar. Mix in eggs and add grated rind and vanilla. Then add flour, baking powder, milk, and anise seeds. The dough should be soft, not sticky. Roll the dough into 4- or 5-inch pencil-like rolls. Form a ring and press the ends together. Place the sesame seeds in a bowl and lightly press tops of the rings in the seeds. Place them on greased cookie sheets and bake at 375 degrees for about 15 minutes. (Courtesy of Stella Grima.)

Three

The Backbone of Maltese Communities

Fr. Michael Borg celebrated the first Catholic Mass of the Maltese people in Detroit on November 14, 1920. The Maltese population in Detroit, ranging between 6,000 to 7,000 people, was the largest in the nation according to a December 12, 1920, *Detroit Free Press* article.

In November 1927, Fr. Michael Cefai was assigned as the priest of St. Paul's Maltese Church. By 1950, the church had about 500 Maltese families. When the John C. Lodge Expressway was built, Fourth and Plum Streets were obliterated, and St. Paul's was forced to close.

Many of the Maltese relocated to Madonna, a historically Italian parish, located on Oakman Boulevard. By 1958, Father Cefai took his Maltese congregation to St. Boniface in the heart of their former community, which was near where Tiger Stadium was once located.

Meanwhile, in 1957, a religious order called the Missionary Society of St. Paul was founded on Malta with a mission to minister to Maltese people throughout the world. The society sent its members to the Detroit Archdiocese, where St. Bernadette Parish, located on Dix Road in Dearborn, became the new Maltese nucleus.

Fr. William Bonnici arrived at Most Holy Trinity Church on January 1, 1973, to become a chaplain of the Maltese people in Detroit. "We have a beautiful heritage," Father Bonnici said. "Maltese are all Catholic and they bring their faith with them, and that is why they wanted their own chaplain."

The first seeds of the Christian faith in Malta were planted when St. Paul shipwrecked on the island in 60 AD. St. Paul was under arrest and on his way to Rome to be judged before Caesar. Among the prisoners was the physician St. Luke, who recorded the account of the journey.

They left a harbor in Crete with the intention of making a safer harbor along the coast in which to stay the winter. The ship they were travelling in was blown off course by a storm and arrived at Qawra Point after about 14 days. It ran aground on a piece of rock that was known as TalGhazzinin. All those who had been shipwrecked reportedly spent three days at the villa of Publius, who was the chief man on the island. After staying with Publius, they moved on to Melita, the capital. In the city, Paul cured Publius's father of a fever, after which Publius was converted to Christianity. Still a prisoner, St. Paul had been confined to a cave prison, St. Paul's Grotto in Rabat, but he was still given freedom, which allowed him to evangelize and perform many miraculous cures.

After three months, they set sail again and were loaded with gifts from their Maltese friends. The Maltese built magnificent cathedrals and churches that often became the hub of towns and villages. They continued that tradition when they arrived in Detroit and started St. Paul's Maltese Church.

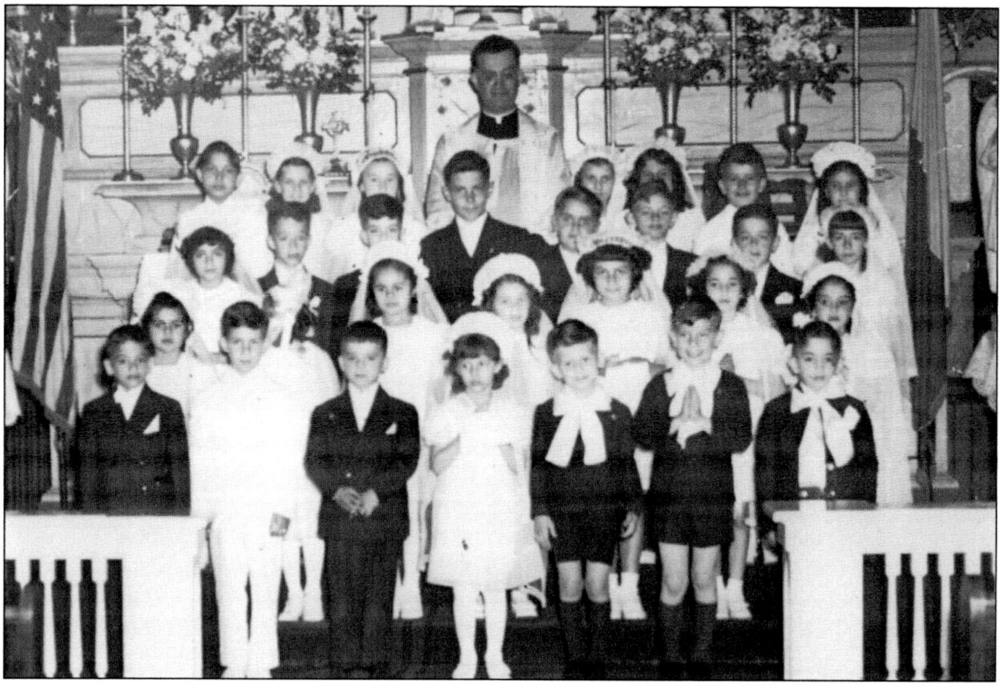

Fr. Michael Cefai is shown with young children at St. Paul's Maltese Church, which was located at the corner of Fourth and Plum Streets and several blocks west of the intersection of Grand River and Cass Streets. (Courtesy of Theresa [Attard] Srock.)

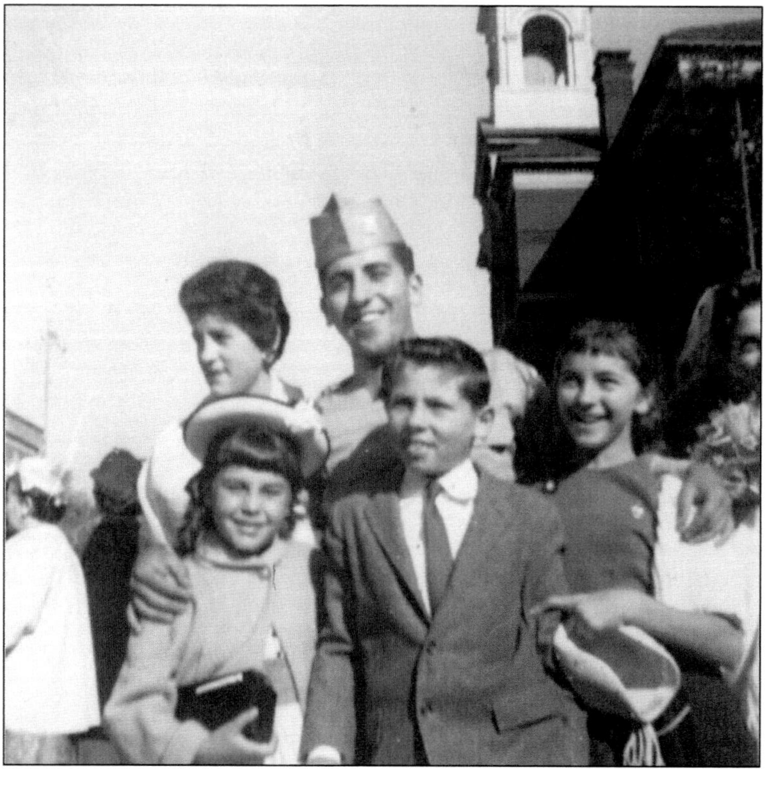

Manuel DeBono, Agnes DeBono, Delores DeBono, Diane Fenech, and Don Bonello stand outside the St. Vincent de Paul Church. Diane is Mary (DeBono) and Joseph Fenech's daughter, and Don was Jessie (DeBono) and Emmanuel Bonnello's son. (Courtesy of DeeDee DeBono.)

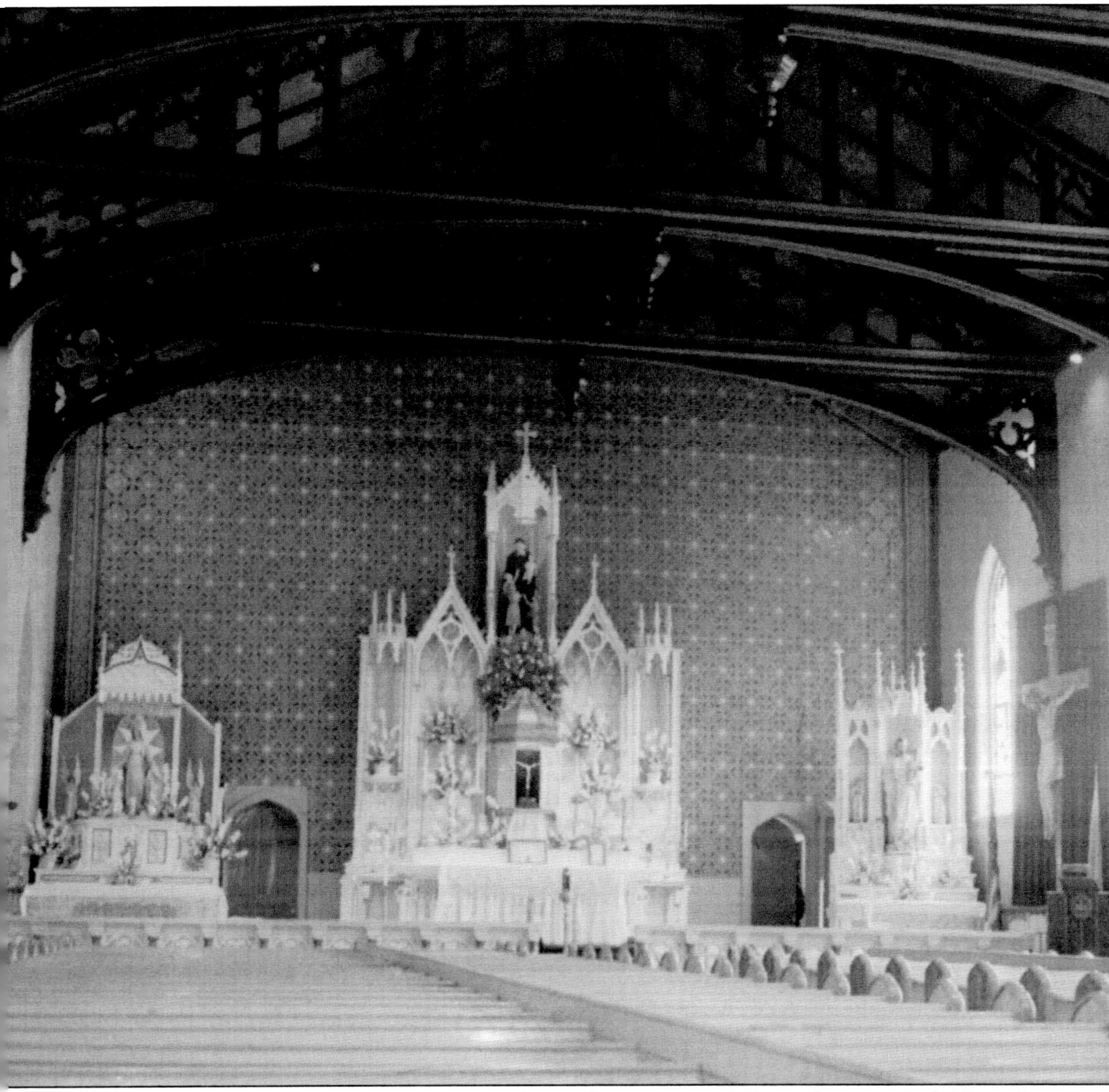

St. Vincent de Paul Church and School were located on Fourteenth Street between Dalzelle and Marantette Streets in Detroit. (Courtesy of Mary and Chuck Brincat.)

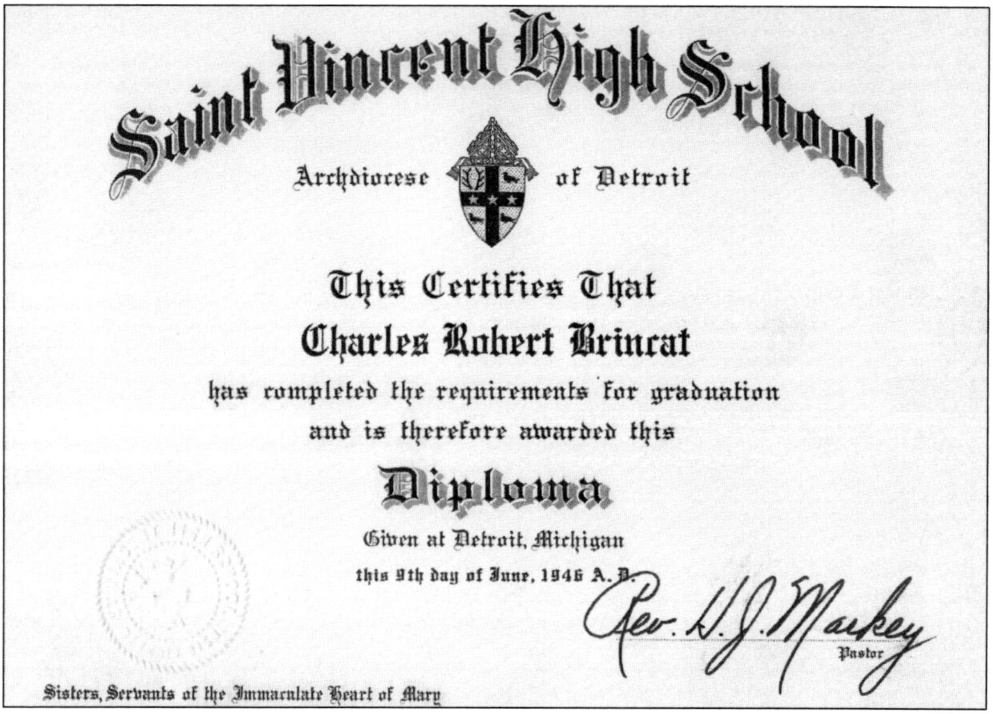

Saint Vincent High School

Archdiocese of Detroit

This Certifies That

Charles Robert Brincat

has completed the requirements for graduation
and is therefore awarded this

Diploma

Given at Detroit, Michigan
this 9th day of June, 1946 A.D.

Rev. H. J. Markey
Pastor

Sisters, Servants of the Immaculate Heart of Mary

Here is a high school diploma issued in 1950 from St. Vincent de Paul High School. The high school was opened in 1888 and consolidated with St. Boniface in 1971. (Courtesy of Mary and Chuck Brincat.)

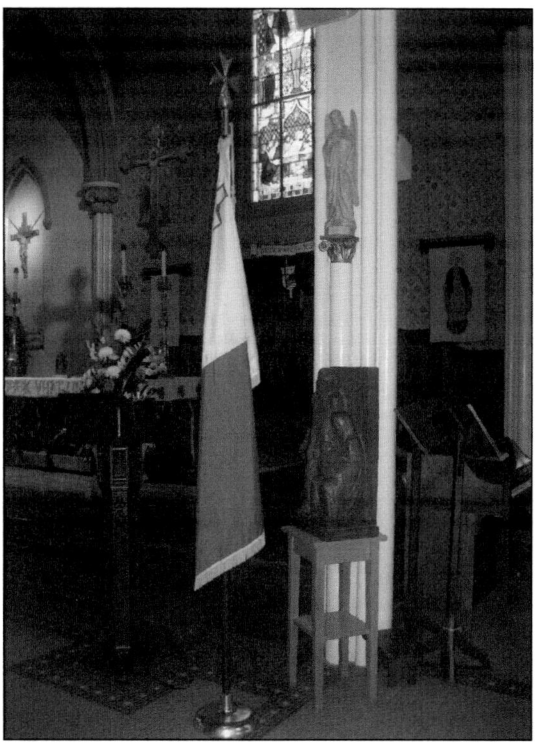

A Maltese flag stands at the front of Most Holy Trinity Church. Count Roger of Sicily gave the red and white colors to Malta in 1091. In the upper left-hand corner is the George Cross, which was awarded to Malta by King George VI for the country's bravery and gallantry during World War II. (Courtesy of Lia Andreassi.)

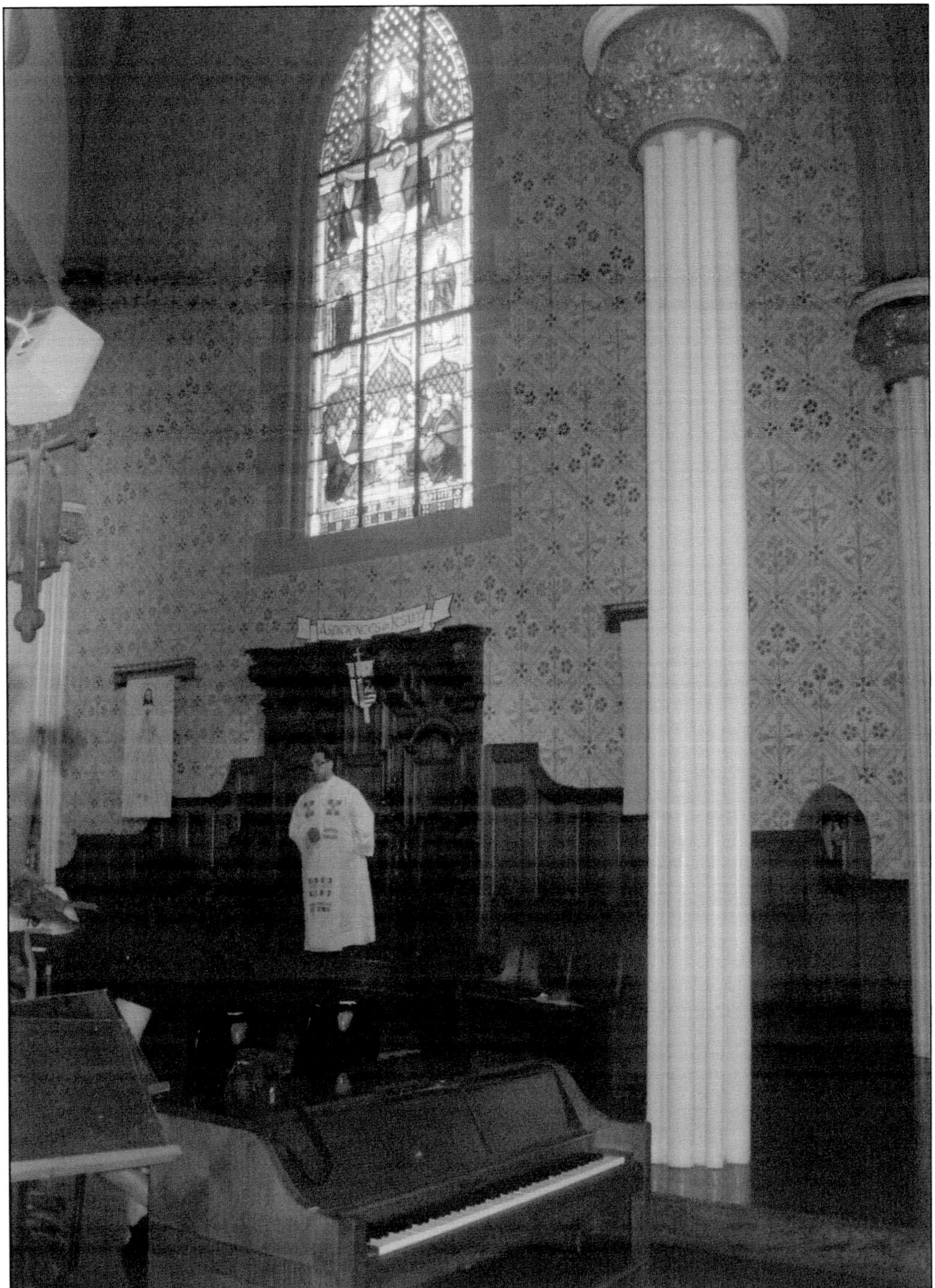

This picture was taken inside Most Holy Trinity Church in Detroit. The church was founded in 1834 and still provides Saturday and Sunday Masses as well as services for holy days of obligation. Most Holy Trinity Elementary School is on LaBrosse Street.

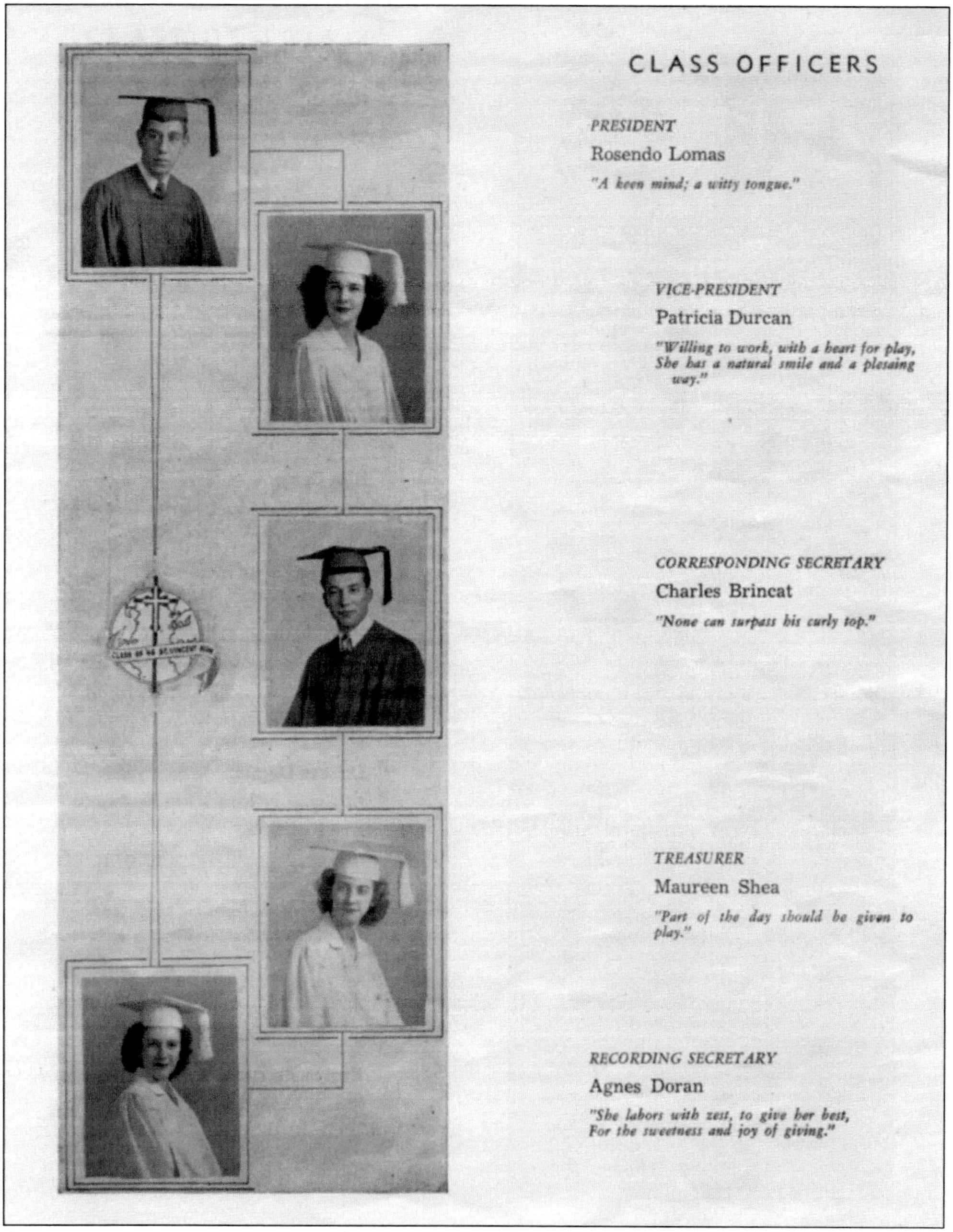

CLASS OFFICERS

PRESIDENT
Rosendo Lomas
"A keen mind; a witty tongue."

VICE-PRESIDENT
Patricia Durcan
*"Willing to work, with a heart for play,
She has a natural smile and a pleasing way."*

CORRESPONDING SECRETARY
Charles Brincat
"None can surpass his curly top."

TREASURER
Maureen Shea
"Part of the day should be given to play."

RECORDING SECRETARY
Agnes Doran
*"She labors with zest, to give her best,
For the sweetness and joy of giving."*

A commencement announcement from St. Vincent de Paul High School is shown listing heritages from many nationalities. (Courtesy of Mary and Chuck Brincat.)

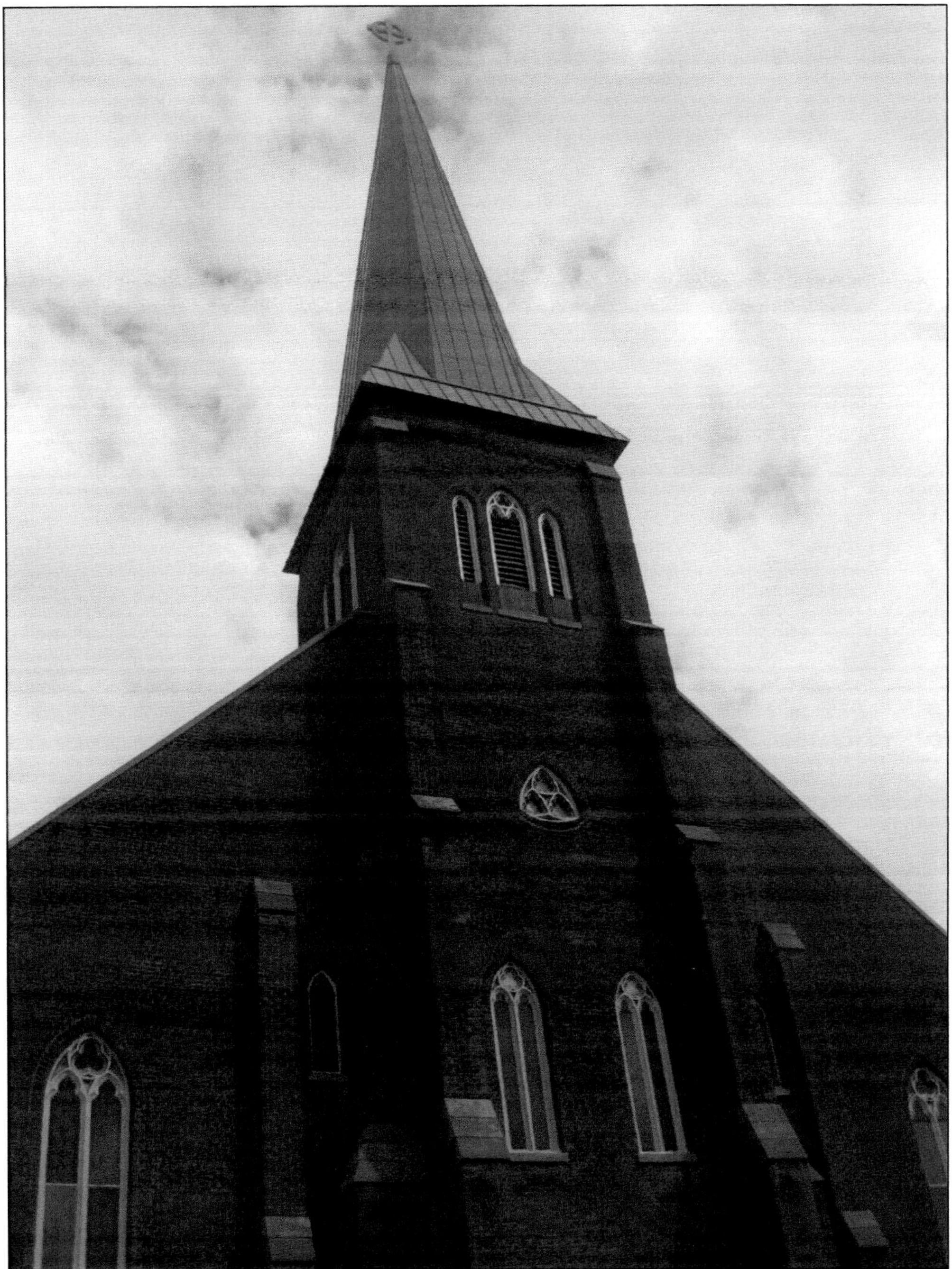

Most Holy Trinity Church was the first English-language parish in Detroit. The earliest parishioners were Irish immigrants. The city faced a cholera epidemic that began in 1832, and the church was converted into a hospital. The surrounding neighborhood is Corktown, which was named after a county in Ireland. Maltese, Mexican, and African Americans also lived in Corktown in subsequent years. Under Fr. Clement Kern (1907–1983), the church became a major center for Latino American residents in southeast Detroit. As of 2010, Masses are now offered in both Spanish and English.

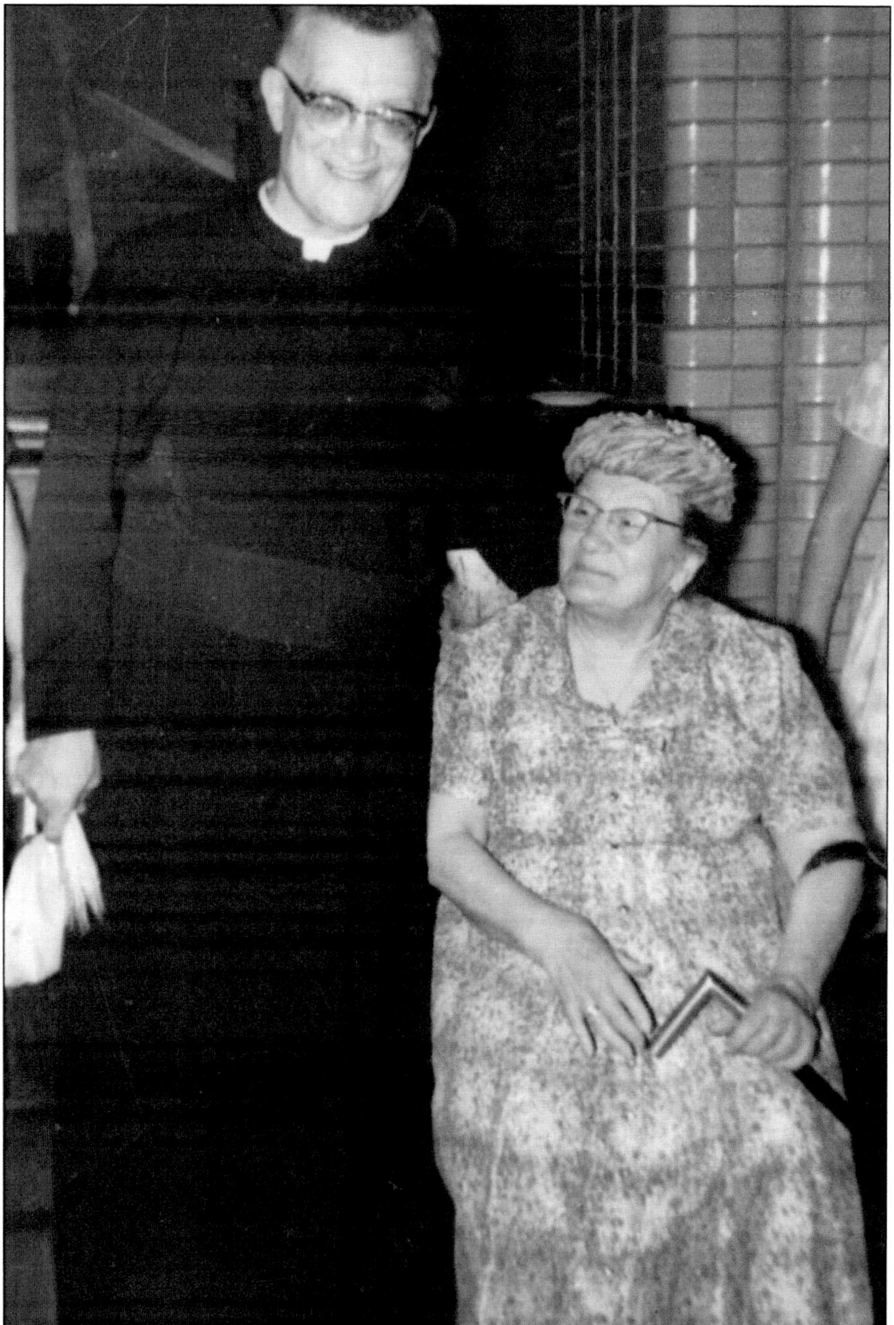

In November 1927, Fr. Michael Z. Cefai was assigned as pastor of St. Paul Maltese Church. His role became that of shepherd of all Maltese in Detroit. The parish attracted Maltese immigrants, prompting continuous growth. The peak was in 1950, when there were 500 Maltese families that belonged to the church. With the construction of the John C. Lodge Expressway, Maltese people in Detroit relocated to Madonna on Oakman Boulevard, and by 1958 Father Cefai relocated again to St. Boniface, near Corktown. (Courtesy of William LaFerle.)

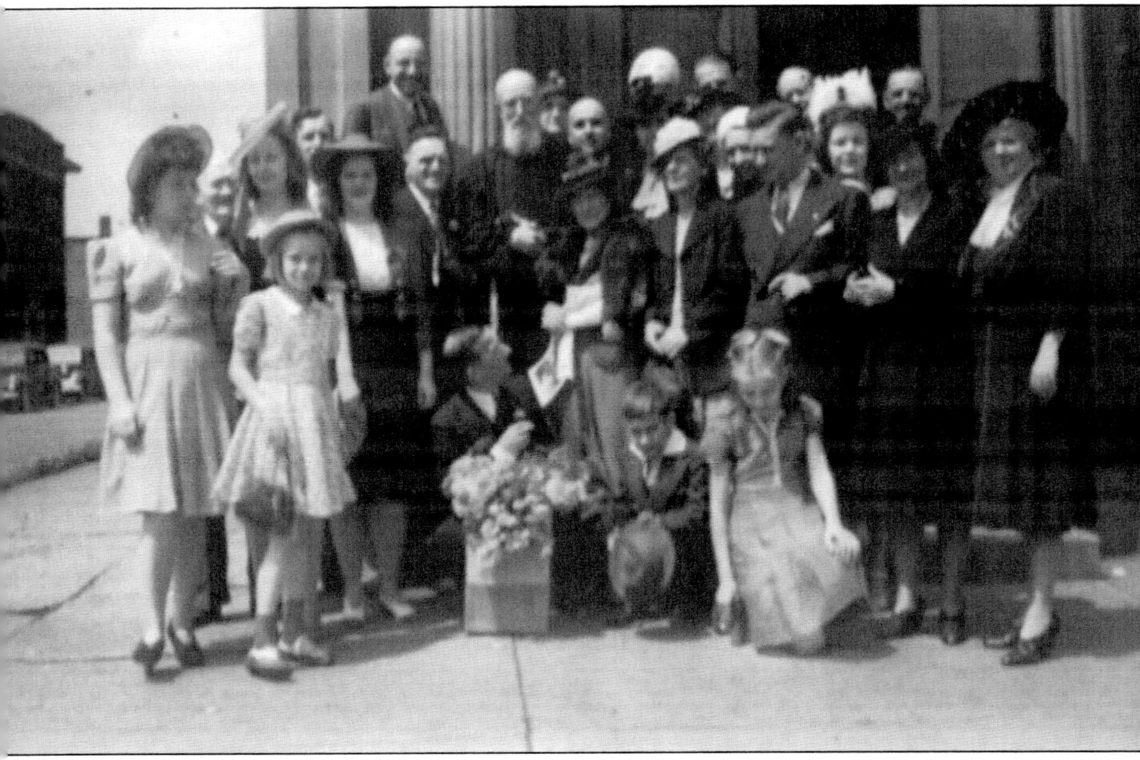

Fr. Solanus Casey poses with parishioners in front of St. Paul's Maltese Church, which was where he served the Maltese people in Detroit. The Capuchin Franciscan was born Bernard Francis Casey on November 25, 1870, in Wisconsin. He had nine brothers and six sisters, and his parents were Irish immigrants. After his ordination in 1904, he spent 20 years in New York in both Harlem and Yonkers. In 1924, he was assigned to St. Bonaventure Monastery in Detroit, where he worked for 20 years. Father Solanus died at age 86 on July 31, 1957, at the same time and on the same day of his First Holy Mass 53 years earlier. Father Solanus was named Venerable on July 11, 1995 by Pope John Paul II. Supporters hope he will be named Blessed before finally being named Saint. (Courtesy of William LaFerle.)

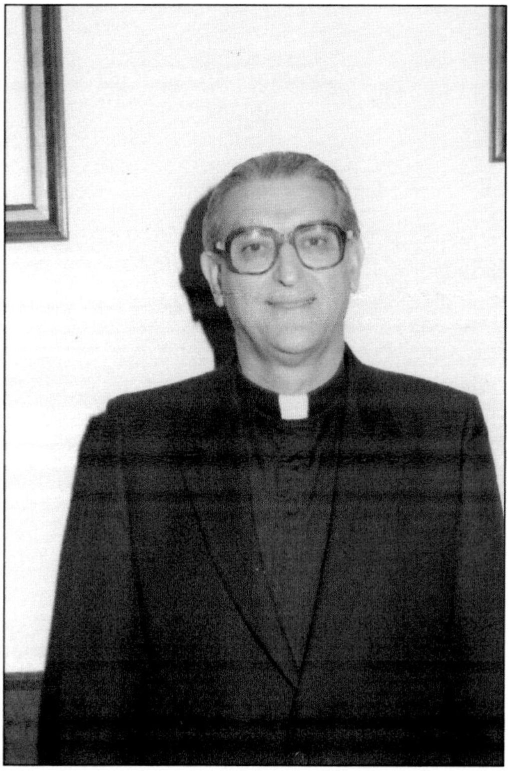

During the 30 years Fr. Robert Cini lived in Detroit as chaplain for the Maltese Community, he was also the pastor of St. Bernadette in Dearborn from January 1, 1978, to June 30, 1998, and pastor of Our Lady of Mount Carmel in southwest Detroit from July 1, 1998, to October 19, 2008. Both parishes are now closed: St. Bernadette on June 30, 1998, and Our Lady of Mount Carmel on October 17, 2008. (Courtesy Fr. Robert Cini.)

Fr. William Bonnici arrived at Most Holy Trinity Church on January 1, 1973, to become a chaplain of the Maltese people in Detroit. "We have a beautiful heritage," Fr. Bonnici said. "Maltese are all Catholic and they bring their faith with them, and that is why they wanted their own chaplain." He followed Fr. Michael Borg and Fr. Michael Cefai as chaplain in the Maltese community in Detroit. "The Maltese people began intermarrying people of other nationalities and moving out of Detroit," said Father Bonnici, who went on to serve at many churches throughout Michigan.

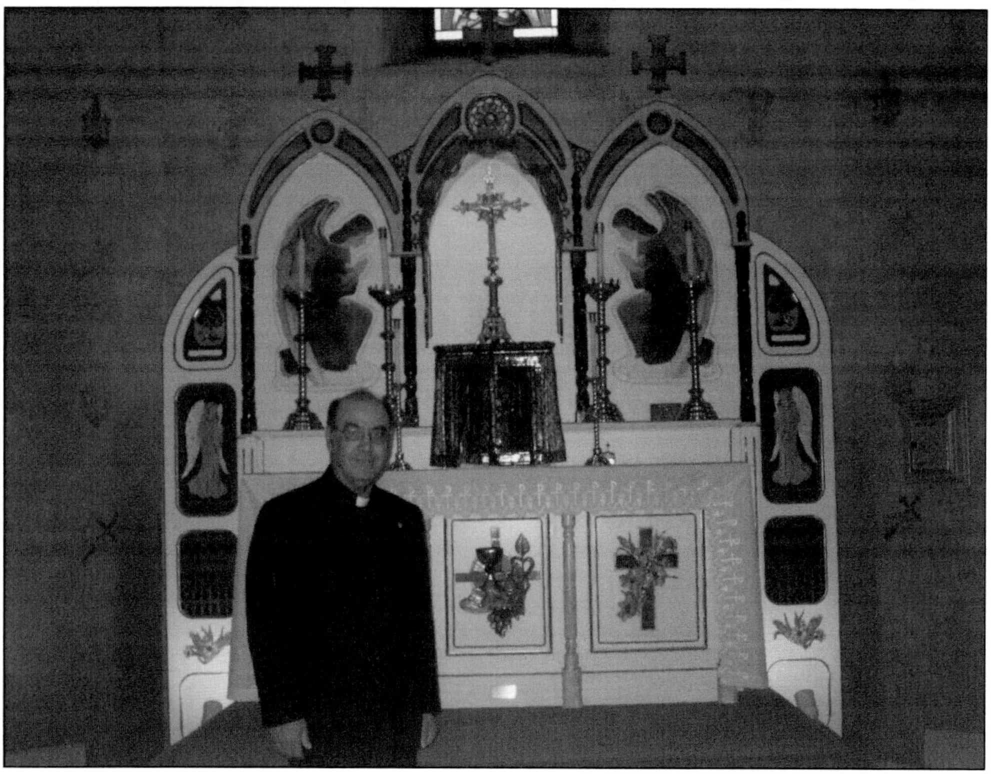

Fr. Joseph Mallia is pastor of St. Frances Cabrini in Allen Park. He is also the chaplain at the Maltese American Community Club in Dearborn. This charismatic leader was born in 1962 in Malta, which was where he lived until his family moved to Corktown in 1965. His family moved to Allen Park a year later. Father Mallia attended 12 years of school at St. Cabrini and entered the seminary in 1980. He was ordained in 1992. He served as associate pastor at St. Joseph Church in Lake Orion, St. Michael's Church in Sterling Heights, and St. Martin DePorres Church in Warren. He became pastor of St. Kenneth Church in Plymouth and came back to his home parish, St. Cabrini, in 2003. In 2007, he was appointed canon in Malta, which is an honorary title with the Church of the Immaculate Conception in Malta. "The Maltese community was unique from other ethnic groups in that when they came to this country, many came with experience in the dry docks, and they came speaking English," Father Mallia said. "They were easily assimilated and they could easily get jobs at the factories because they came with a trade. They came with the hope of one day going back. Some did and most stayed." (Courtesy of Father Mallia.)

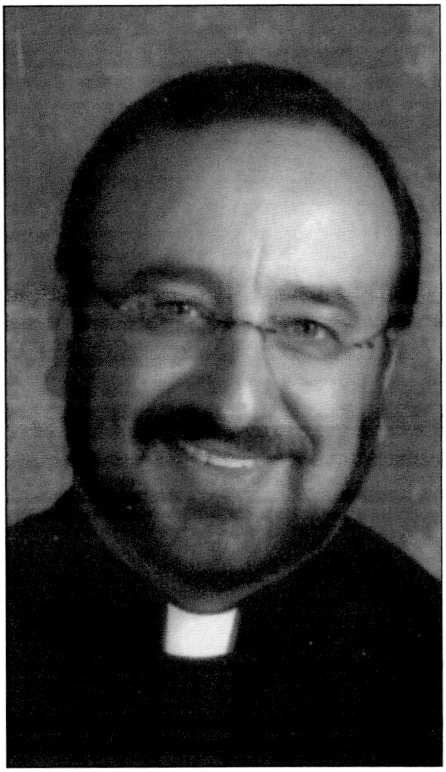

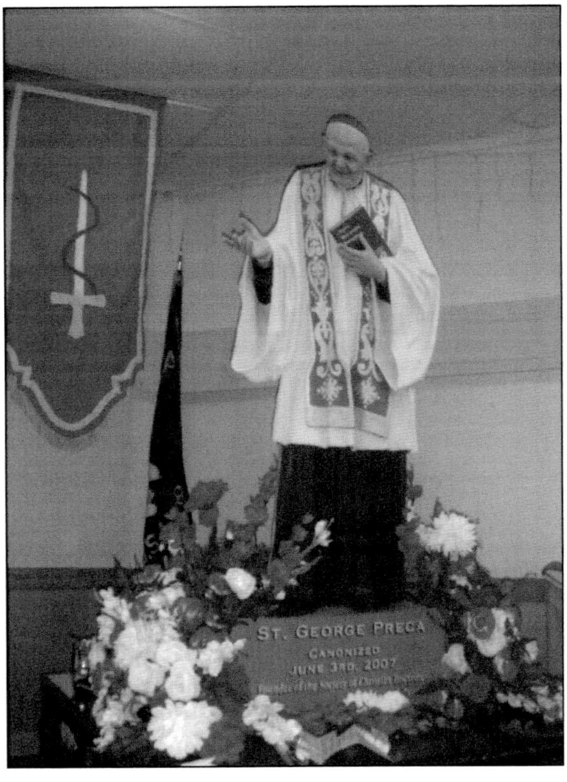

St. Dun George Preca became the first Maltese saint when he was canonized on June 3, 2007, by Pope Benedict XVI. St. George Preca founded the Society of Christian Doctrine, a society of lay catechists in Malta. He is affectionately known as "Dun Gorg" and is popularly referred to as the "Second Apostle of Malta" after Saint Paul of Tarsus. His feast day of May 4 is celebrated annually at the Maltese club in Dearborn. (Courtesy of Paul Borg.)

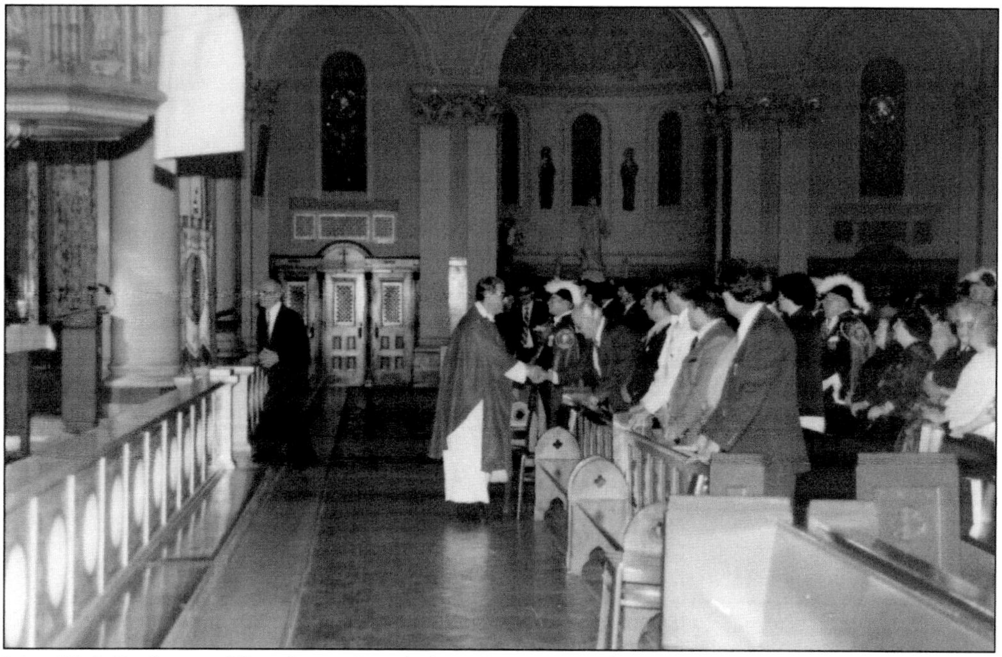

Most Holy Redeemer Church was founded in 1880. Located at 1721 Junction Avenue, the church is part of the West Vernor-Junction Historic District. It was once estimated as the largest Roman Catholic Church parish in North America. In 2010, the parish still has an elementary school, but its associated high school is closed. (Courtesy of Fr. Robert Cini.)

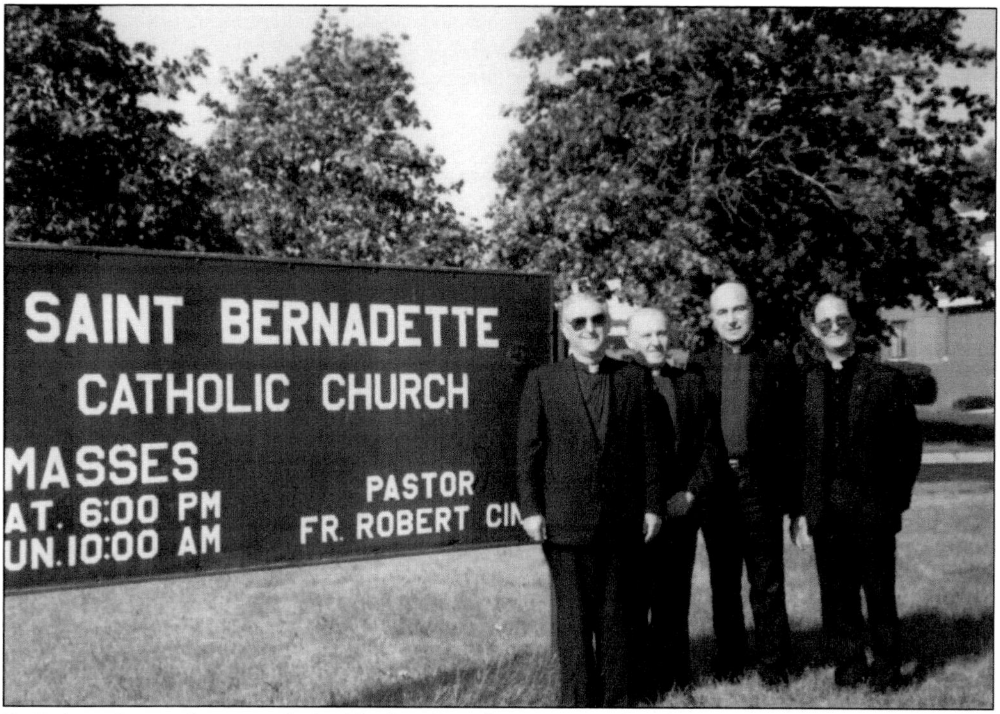

Fr. Robert Cini is shown with Archbishop Joseph Merceica of Malta and his accompanying clergy at St. Bernadette Parish in Dearborn. (Courtesy of Fr. Robert Cini.)

Here is the crowning ceremony of the Blessed Mother statue at St. Vincent de Paul Church. Statues of the Blessed Mother are often crowned in May, which is considered Mary's month in the Roman Catholic Church. August 15 is the feast day of the Assumption of the Blessed Mother into heaven and is celebrated as a special holiday in Malta. The Roman Catholic Church holds that Mary, Jesus' mother, was taken—body and soul—into heaven.

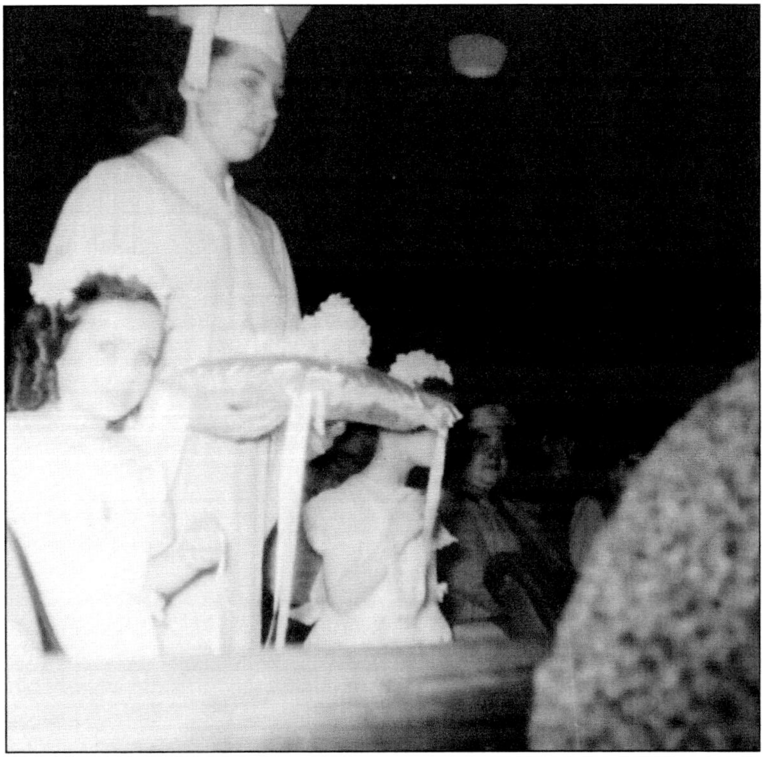

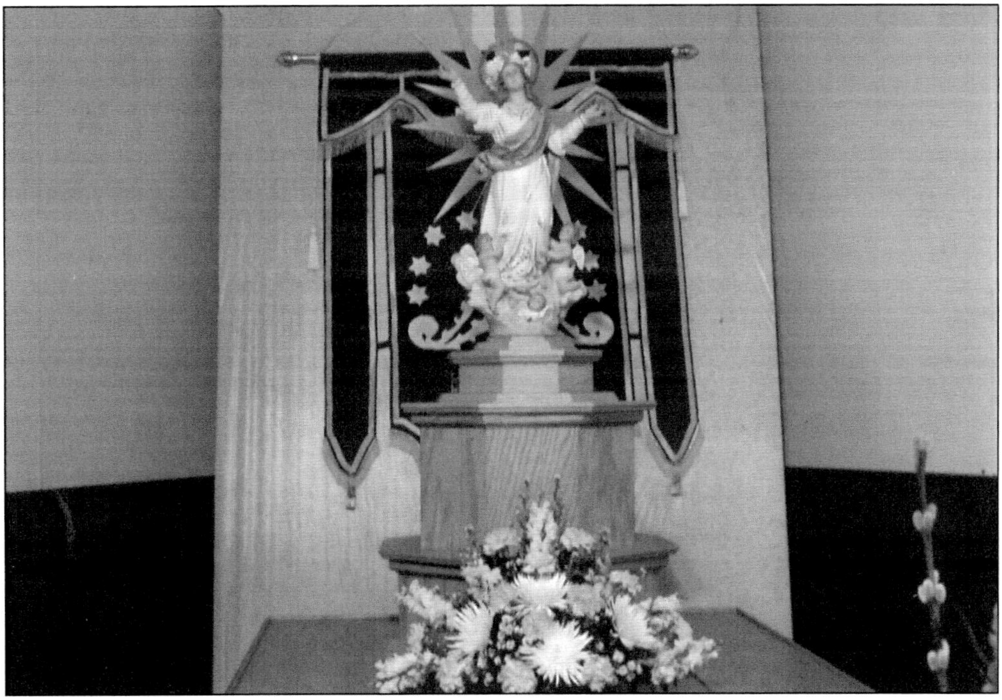

This statue of the Blessed Mother at the Dearborn Maltese club was built by Maltese artist Michael Camilleri and was placed in a ceiling-to-floor case. It is brought out on feast days and carried through the club to honor the Blessed Mother.

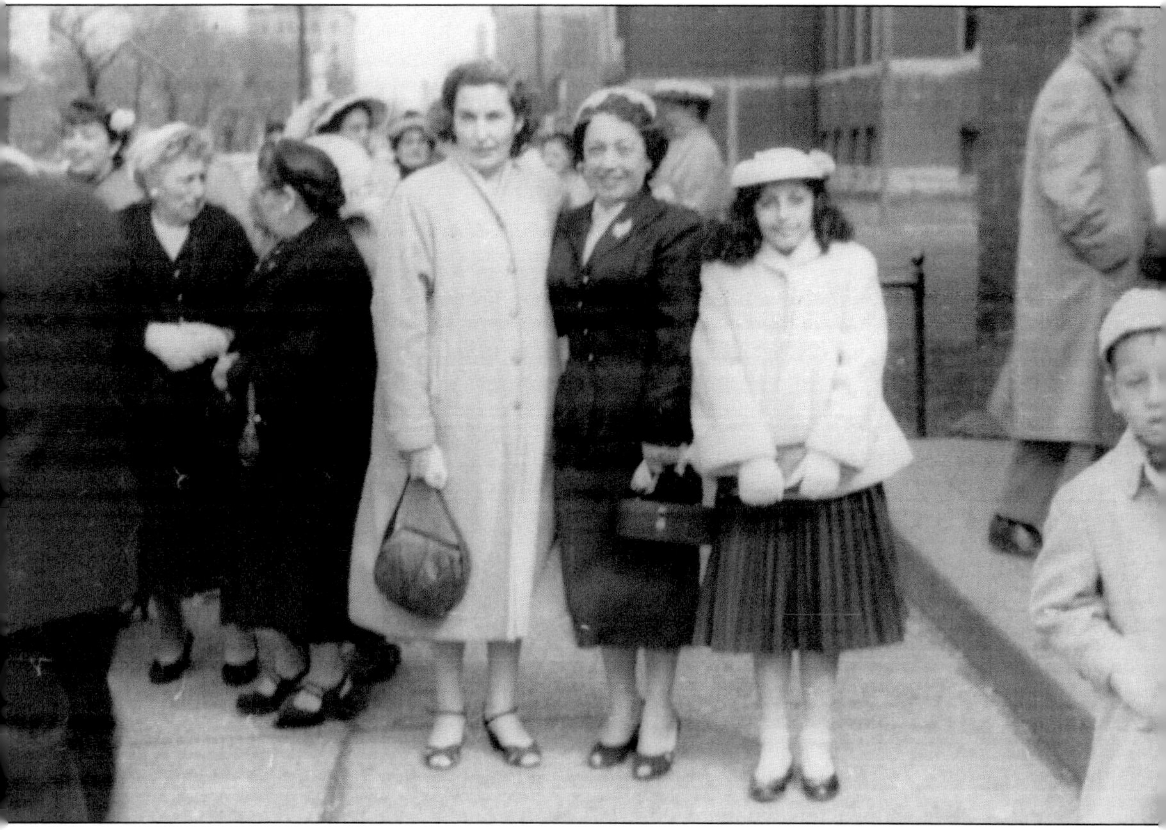

Colleen, Dolores, and Antoinette Attard stand outside Most Holy Trinity Church. When Dolores and her husband, Paul, came to Detroit with their five children, they lived for a short time with Colleen and her family. Colleen was a stay-at-home mother known for her wonderful Maltese and American meals.

Four

Maltese Become Entrepreneurs

Maltese immigrants also integrated themselves into Detroit life by opening businesses. Probably the most prominent Maltese business was the Maltese American Finance Corporation. On November 25, 1922, the corporation held a meeting called by secretary Anthony Vella, who explained the running of the organization and distributed copies of its rules to those who attended the meeting. The corporation, which dealt in land contracts guaranteed by the U.S. government, had 541 shareholders. Maltese immigrants were offered a special program that allowed them to return to Malta, either for an extended stay or to retire, and leave their assets with the corporation to be looked after by the corporation's experts.

Other Maltese entrepreneurs opened their own businesses, like Borg Studios, which was operated by Emmanuel Borg. He was a pioneer in the photography business and was always searching for new processes and techniques. Revered in the photography business, he also wrote an article for *National Geographic* about photographic techniques.

With more money to spend, most immigrants also started restaurants. Many Maltese men were either single or their wives lived in Malta. When they came to Detroit, they were forced to cook their own meals unless they ate out. So Different Restaurant was at 972 Michigan Avenue at Fifth Street. The newspaper *Il Malti-American* advertised that So Different Restaurant offered excellent food "taken in the company of other Maltese." The Melita Bakery at 2511 Fifth Street soon followed after the opening of the Melita Lunch restaurant. Offering special Maltese-style bread, the bakery was especially popular with the Maltese in Detroit.

Some other small-business owners included Grech and Brincat, who opened a thriving shop on Howard Street that bore the name of General Grocers.

John Vella opened his School of Dancing at 1355 Howard Street. Anthony De Guara tailored, cleaned, and pressed clothes at his Sixth Street and Porter Street shop. De Guara changed his name slightly, but his advertisements made it clear that he was Maltese and that he hoped that his countrymen would patronize his shop.

Joseph Vella opened Bagley Trumbull Market in the 1930s, and the business remained open and in the family for 70 years.

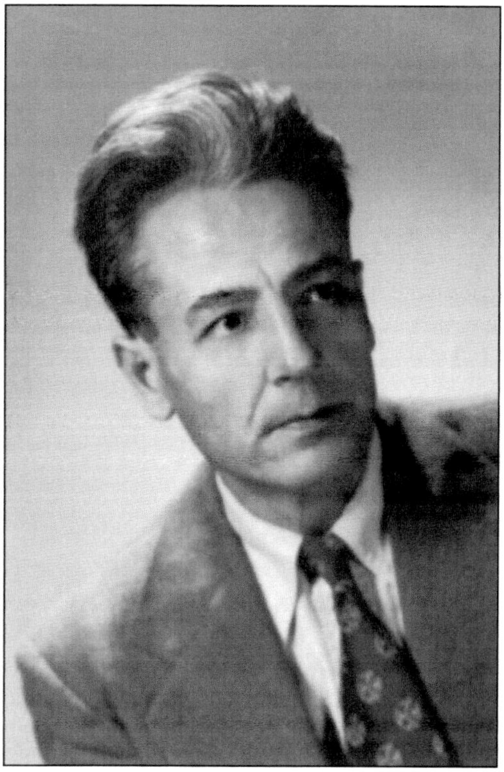

Emmanuel Borg owned Borg Studios in Corktown. Borg was originally from Sliema, Malta. He and his family, which included his parents and 11 brothers and sisters, traveled to Detroit to make a new start. He spent countless hours in the library researching various photographic techniques to perfect his art. Borg was well known for his portrait and wedding photographs. He also worked at transferring images onto porcelain. (Courtesy of Tess Vella.)

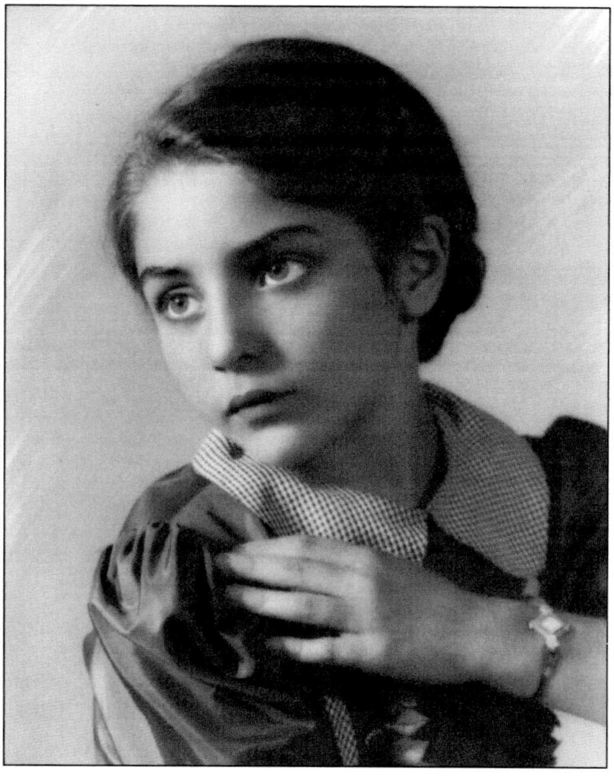

Ten-year-old Tess (Haley) Vella often modeled for Emmanuel Borg for his work at Borg Studios. Vella had her wedding in Corktown but later moved to Livonia, where she raised eight children. From her eight children, she has a total 23 grandchildren and one great-grandchild. (Courtesy of Tess Vella.)

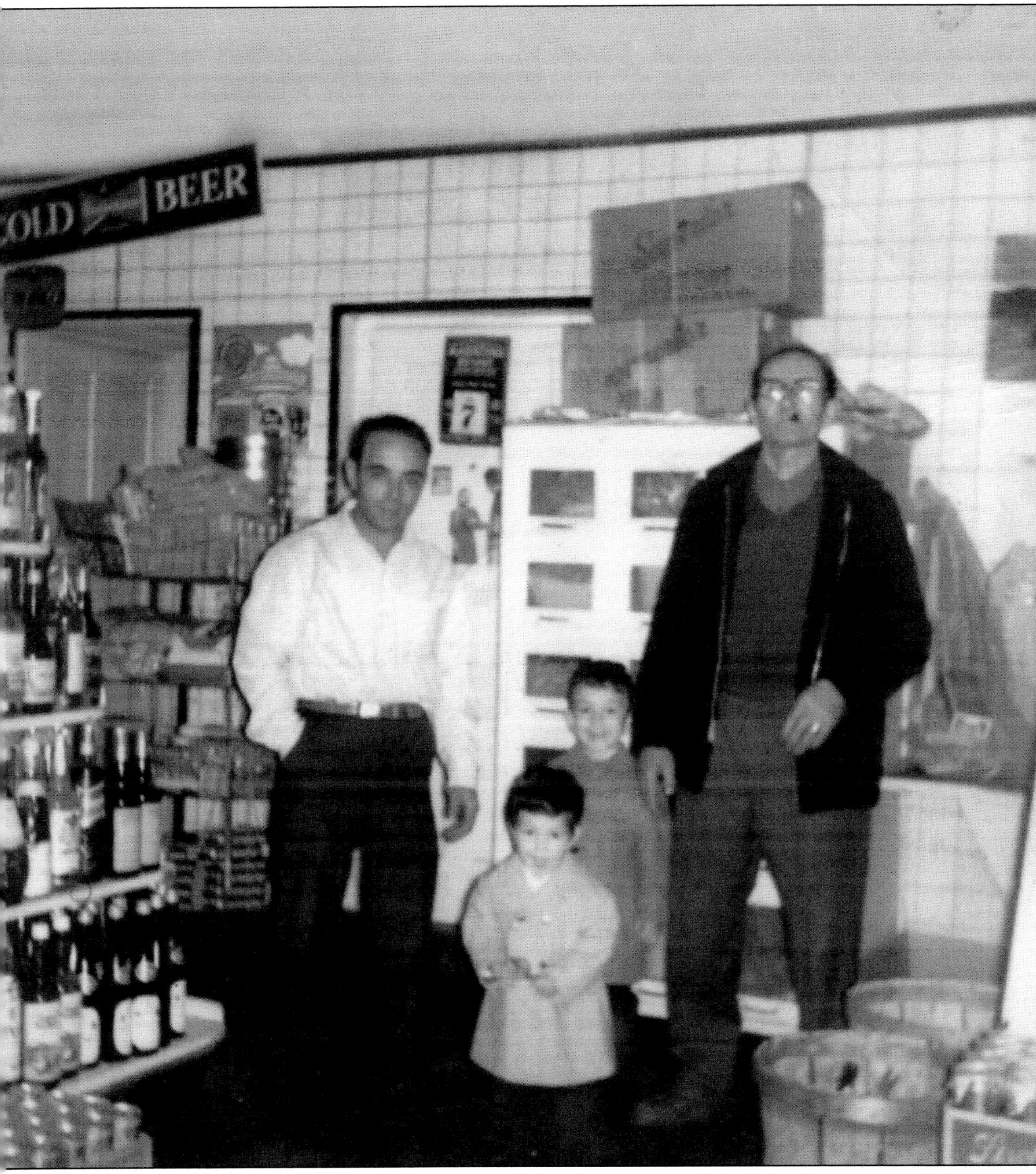

Joseph Vella (far right) opened Bagley Trumbull Market in the 1930s. Felix Formosa and his children, Anthony and Felix Jr., are also pictured. Operated by family members, the business remained open for more than 70 years. (Courtesy of Josephine Formosa.)

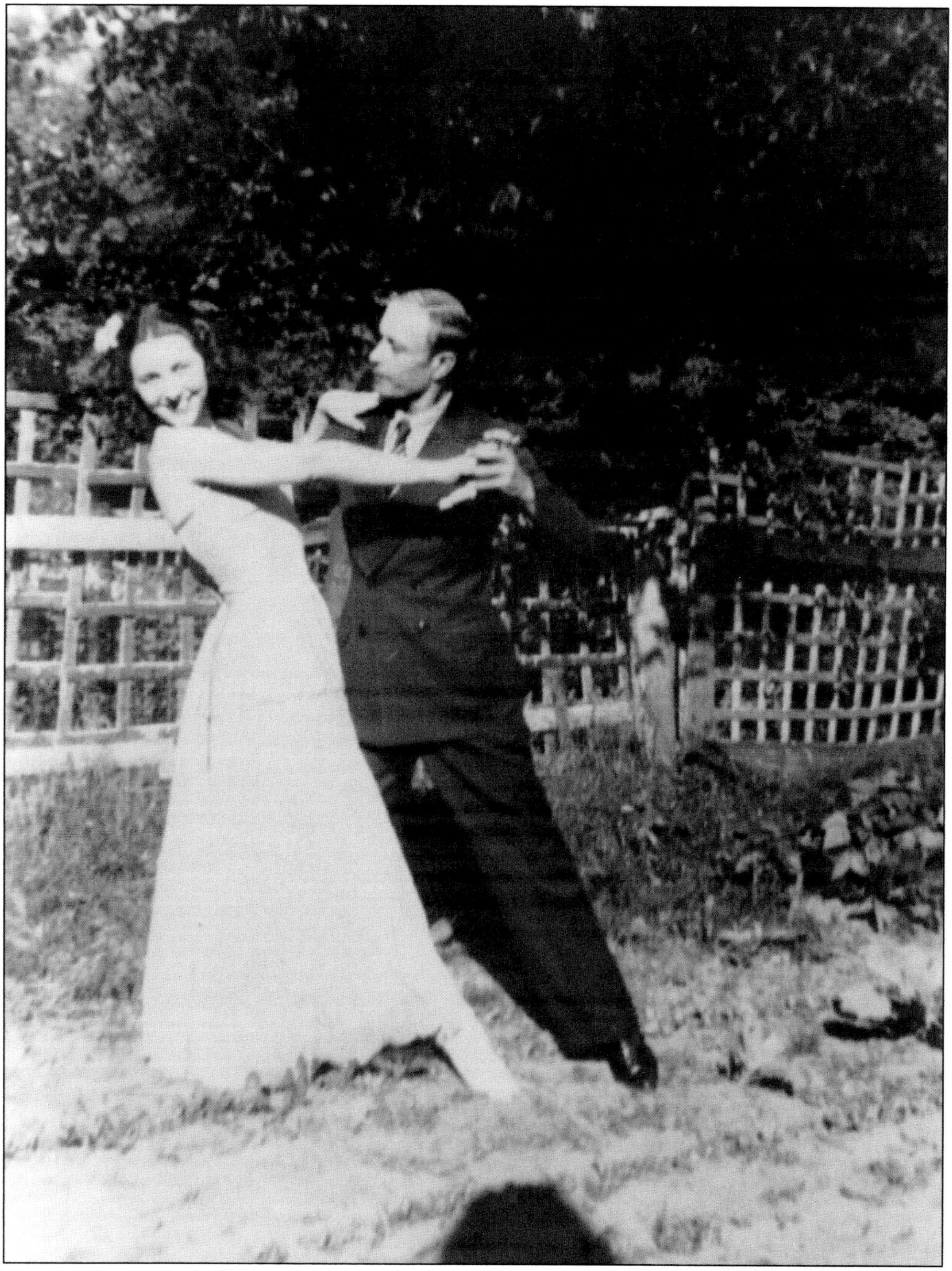

Joe Vassallo taught ballroom dancing to Maltese people in the late 1940s and early 1950s. Joe was a champion ballroom dancer and won many trophies for his performances. (Courtesy of Terise Attard Okasinski.)

Five

Maltese Get a Kick out of Soccer

Maltese in Detroit brought their favorite sport from Malta, and some of the soccer teams in Detroit even date back to the late 1930s. A few of the team names were St. Mary's, the Maltese Falcons, and the Melita American Dearborn Soccer Club.

Frank Borg and Paul Scicluna were known for promoting soccer throughout the metropolitan Detroit area, not only among the Maltese but also among soccer players of all nationalities and ages. "My nana had 13 children after World War II," explains Mario Scicluna, a professional soccer player who currently lives in Redford. "My uncle was Paul Scicluna, we call him the Godfather of Michigan Soccer," Mario Scicluna said. Paul coached at Bentley High School in Livonia, Catholic Central High School in Detroit, and Eastern Michigan University. A field at Eastern Michigan University is named after Paul.

"After we started youth soccer, we founded Total Soccer indoor facilities, so kids could play all year long," Mario Scicluna said. The Scicluna family is also involved in WAZAFC, which sponsors soccer sports teams and trains young people throughout the state ("waza" in Japanese means "technique"). Mario and his two brothers, Valentino and Dominic, have played soccer professionally around the world. "I grew up eating raviolis and kicking a soccer ball around," Mario Scicluna said.

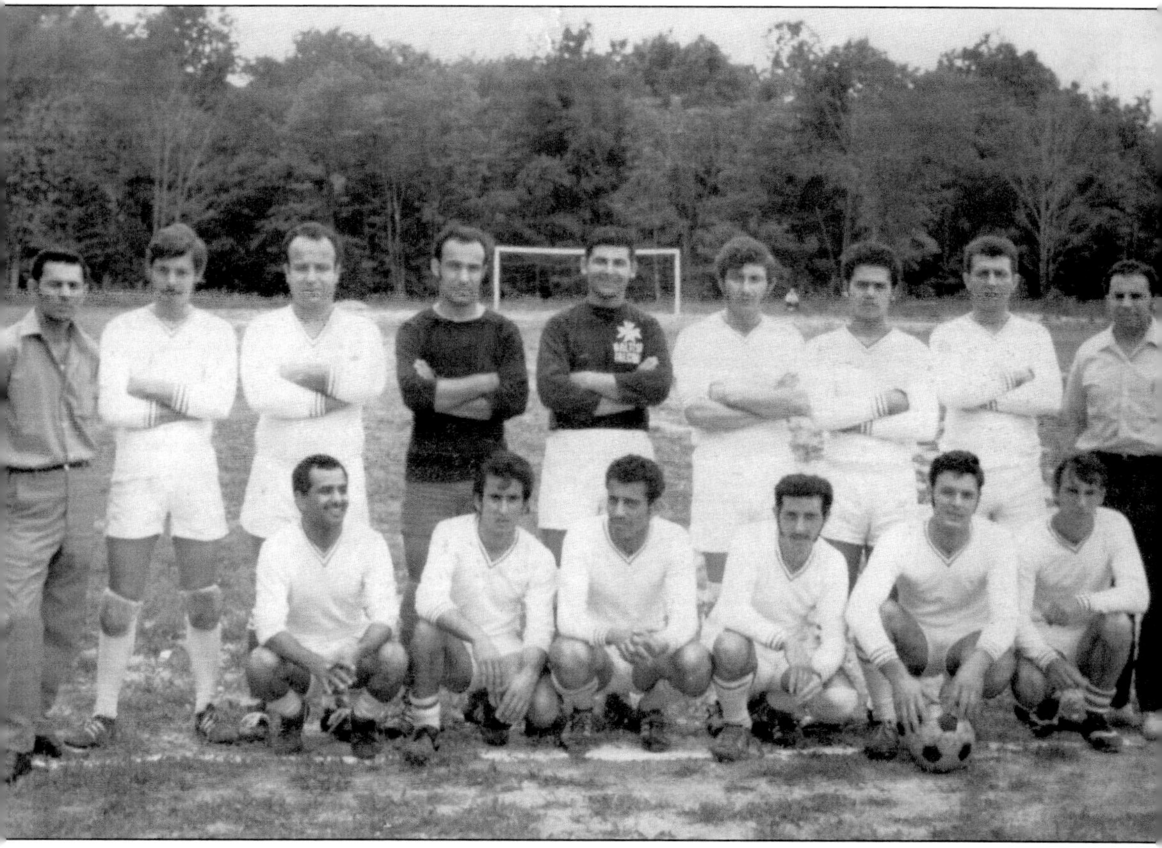

The Detroit District Soccer champions of 1968, the Maltese Falcons, included (first row) Ahmin Musa, Carmel Vassallo, Fens Kohari, John Caruana, and Alex Muscat; (second row) Sam Agius, Jimmy Curmi, Frank Borg, Mario Borg, George Camilleri, Dino Mocha, Petras Stafos, Paul Vassallo, and Carmello Agius. Some of the players were of other nationalities. (Courtesy of John Caruana.)

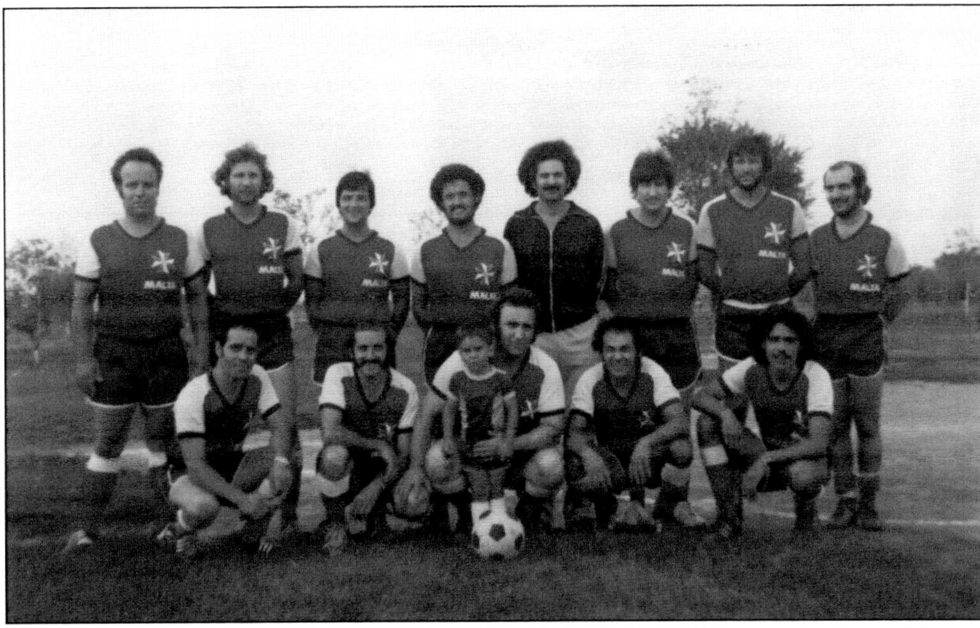

The Maltese Falcons Soccer team in 1966 included Frank Borg, Mico Apolos, Jimmy Muscat, Dominic Stenko, Tony Caruana, Joe Mizzi, John Caruana, Sam Borg, Michael Borg, Reno Catania, and Joe Catania. (Courtesy of John Caruana.)

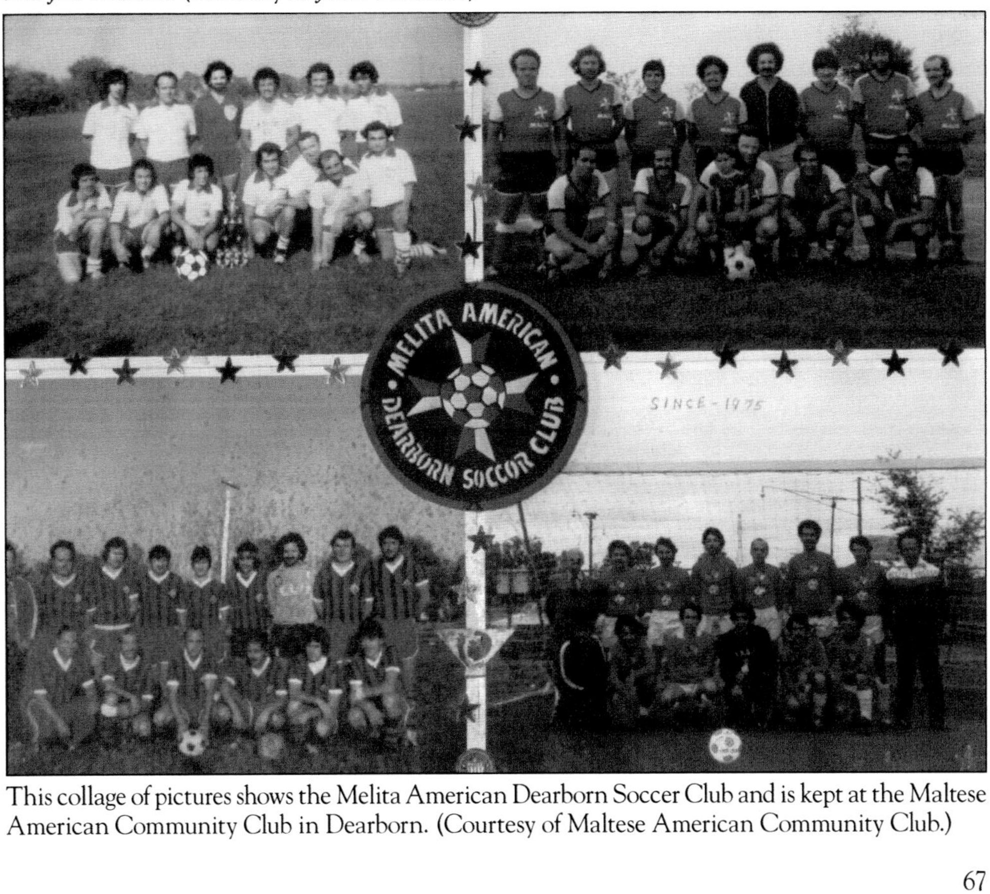

This collage of pictures shows the Melita American Dearborn Soccer Club and is kept at the Maltese American Community Club in Dearborn. (Courtesy of Maltese American Community Club.)

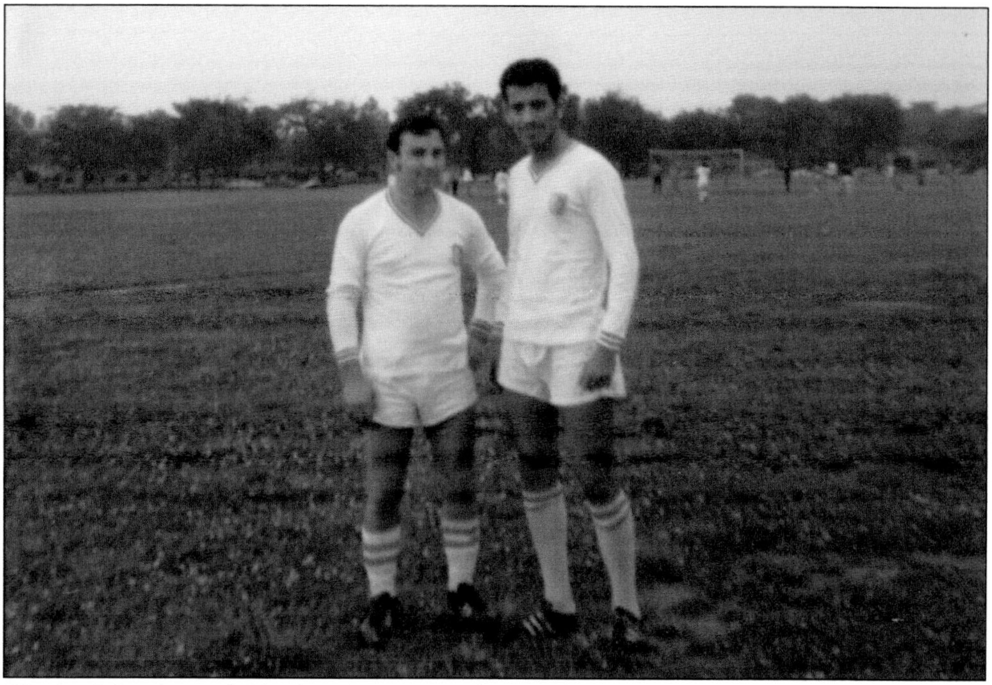

Charlie Schembri and Charlie "Goose" Cauchi, members of the Maltese Falcons, practiced at Patton Park in Detroit in 1965. Maltese soccer players in Detroit often used the park for games. (Courtesy of Charlie Schembri.)

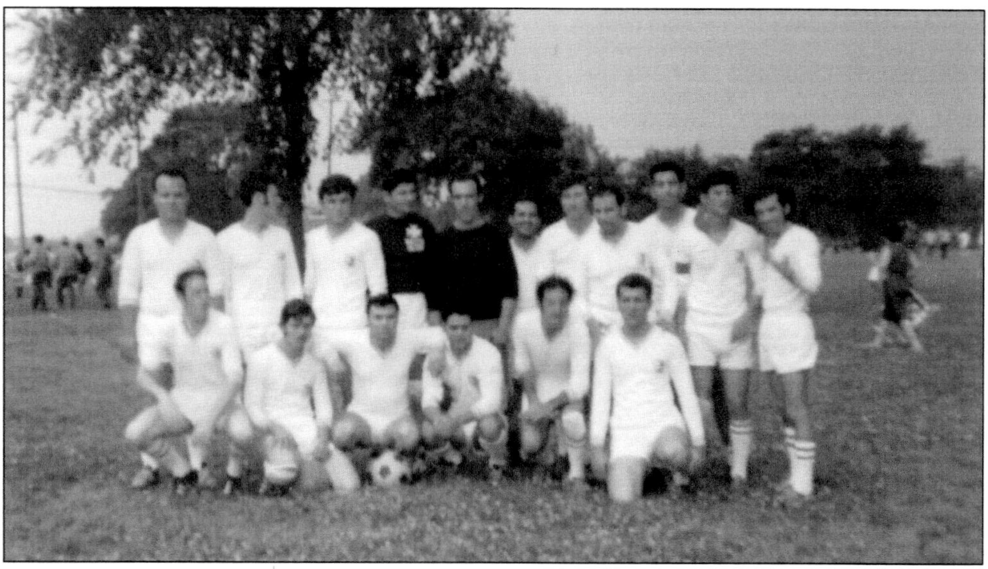

This is the Maltese Falcon Soccer team. Maltese soccer clubs in Detroit have a long history. John B. Spiteri, a prominent member of the banking circles in Detroit, formed the first true Maltese club, the Sons of Malta, located on Howard and Third Streets, about 1922. The club's primary purpose was to provide a Maltese soccer team for people to join. It went on to participate in the Detroit American Soccer League, captured the league's championship on more than one occasion, and was for many years later hailed as the toast of all Detroit soccer clubs, according to Larry Zahra, Maltese consul in Detroit.

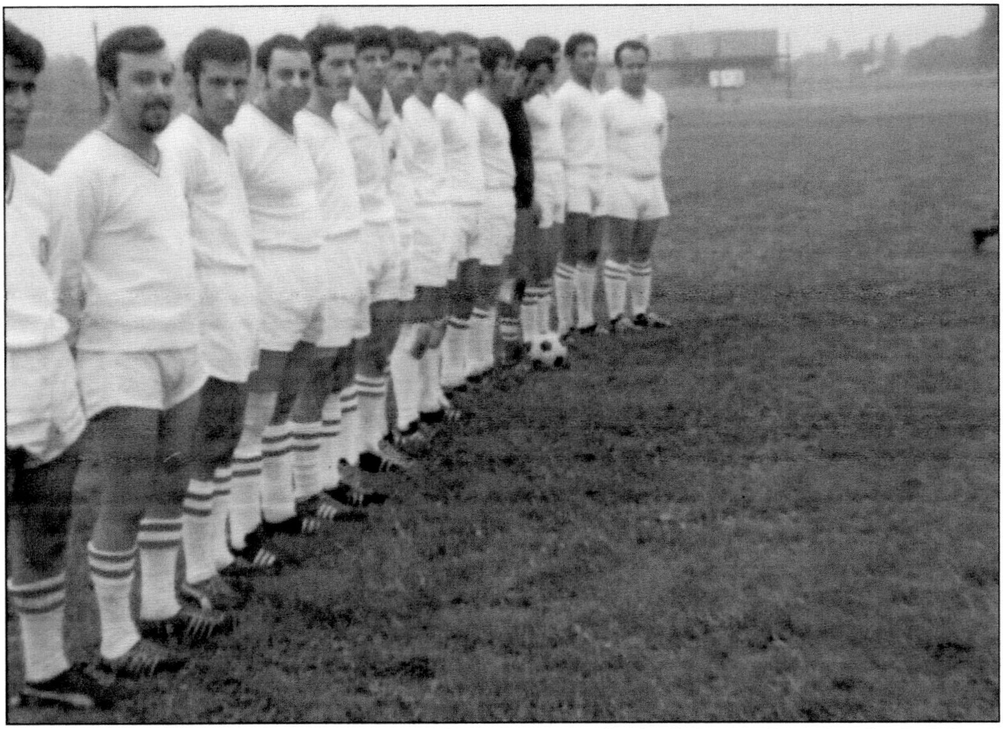

In 1928, the Ramblers were formed on Fifth Street, near Elizabeth Street. In 1930, the St. Mary's Club was started. The Ramblers could not find enough Maltese players to form a team, so they recruited Scottish, English, and Swedish players. The Maltese soccer team went on to become B Division champions and A Division semifinalists of the Detroit American Soccer League in 1934. Trophies, which are still on display at the Maltese American Benevolent Society, Inc., in Detroit, show the many successes reaped by the various Maltese soccer clubs of old Detroit. One of the first soccer teams in Detroit (below, around 1945) was the St. Mary's Maltese soccer team. (Above courtesy of Charlie Schembri; below, Paul Borg.)

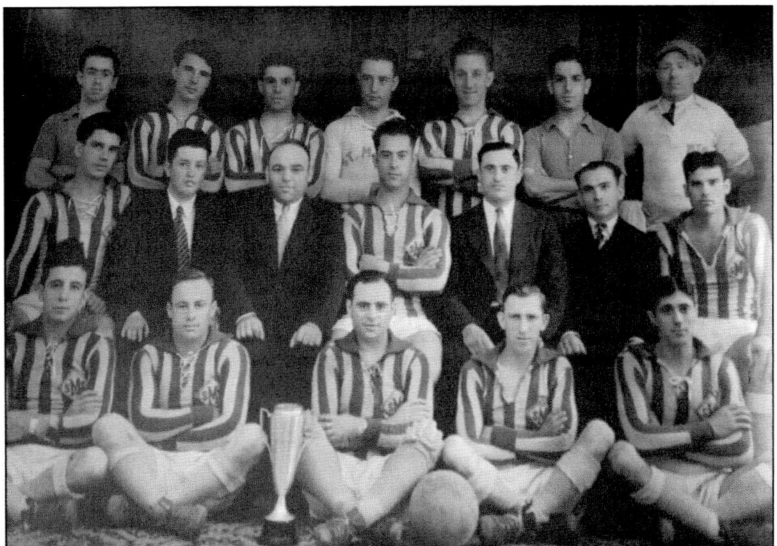

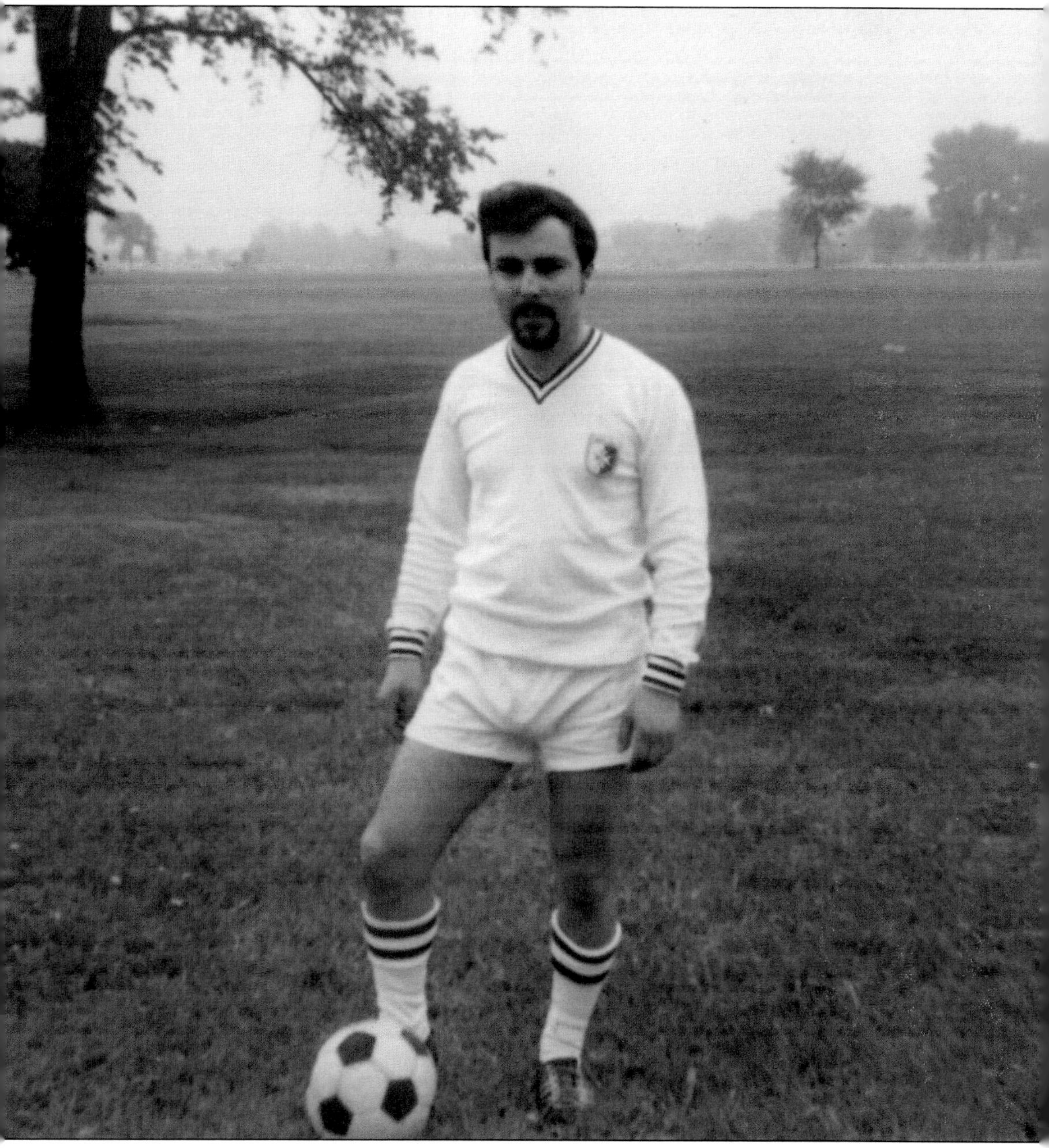

Charlie Schembri was a player for the Maltese Falcon soccer team in Detroit. (Courtesy of Charlie Schembri.)

Six

The Maltese's Place in the History of Corktown

Irish immigrants came to Detroit's shores, and ultimately Corktown, during the Great Irish Potato Famine of the 1840s. Many of these immigrants were from County Cork, which gave birth to the name Corktown. Historically the neighborhood included Third Street to the east, Grand River Avenue to the north, Twelfth Street to the west, and Jefferson Avenue and the Detroit River to the south.

By the turn of the 20th century, new groups of immigrants arrived, notably the Maltese, many of whom were lured by factory jobs in the automobile industry. Mexicans, among others, later came to the area.

Legend has it that three men from Malta settled in the community, and when they told their family and friends back home about Detroit, others followed. The Corktown community began to suffer in the 1950s and 1960s, as there was the highway construction as well as Maltese families beginning to move to the suburbs. While some Maltese remain in the Corktown area today, others have moved to different neighborhoods in the city or followed suit to the Detroit suburbs.

Corktown's remaining residential section is listed on the National Register of Historic Places and is designated as a City of Detroit Historic District. The original buildings are Federal-style, detached homes and row houses, which were built by Irish settlers. In later years, Victorian houses with Italianate, Gothic, and Queen Anne influences were added. Today the district includes about 300 housing structures and some 2,000 people.

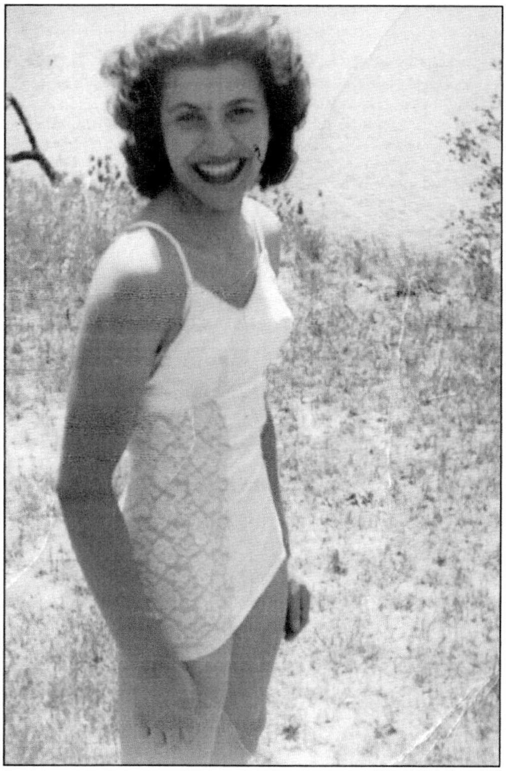

Mary Tabone poses for the camera at Mandon Lake, which was where many Maltese had summer cottages. Some people loved the area so much that they decided to live there full-time. (Courtesy of Mary and Chuck Brincat.)

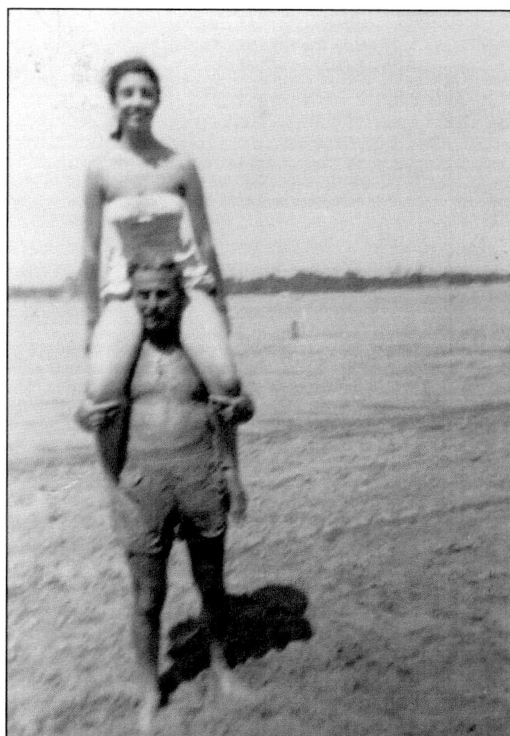

Terise Attard and Joe Attard are shown around 1950 at Belle Isle in Detroit. This was where many people gathered on weekends to take in scenic views, swim, and walk the paths. (Courtesy of Terise Attard Okasinski.)

In 1934, Chuck Brincat had his First Holy Communion at Holy Trinity. He attended elementary school at Holy Trinity. (Courtesy of Mary and Chuck Brincat.)

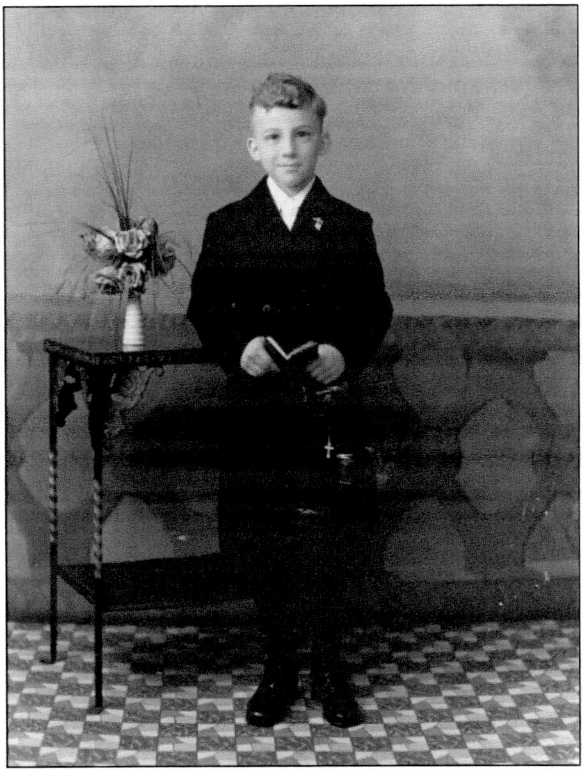

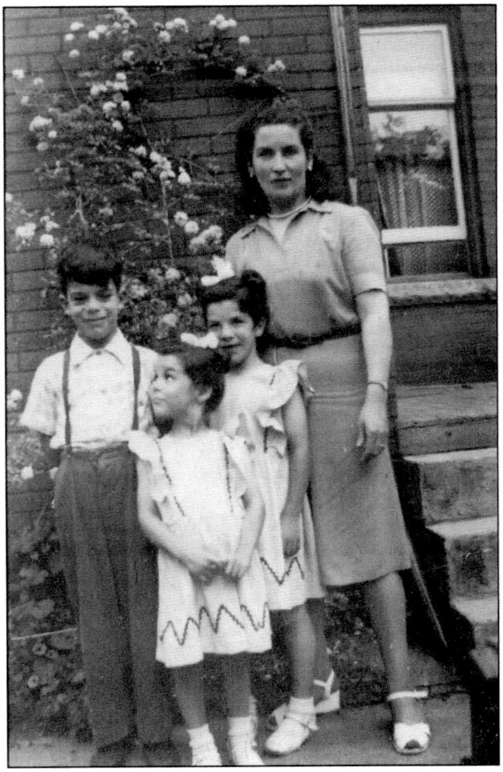

Facing Michigan Avenue, Colleen Attard is shown around 1947 with Fred, Carmen, and Theresa on Eleventh Street. The Attard family lived on Eleventh Street for about 12 years and then moved a few miles away to Vernor Highway and Trumbull Street, near Corktown. (Courtesy of Theresa [Attard] Srock.)

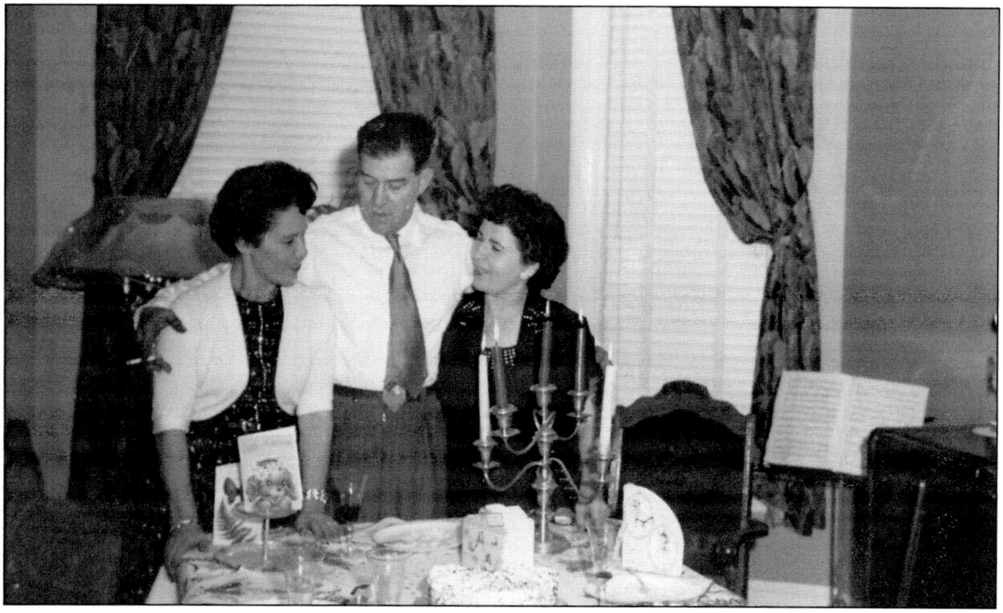

Agnes Mallia and John Felice and Elsie Felice are shown at the Felice home at 1814 Church Street in the 1950s. Elsie's sister Agnes was visiting from New York City. (Courtesy of Norma Jean Philip.)

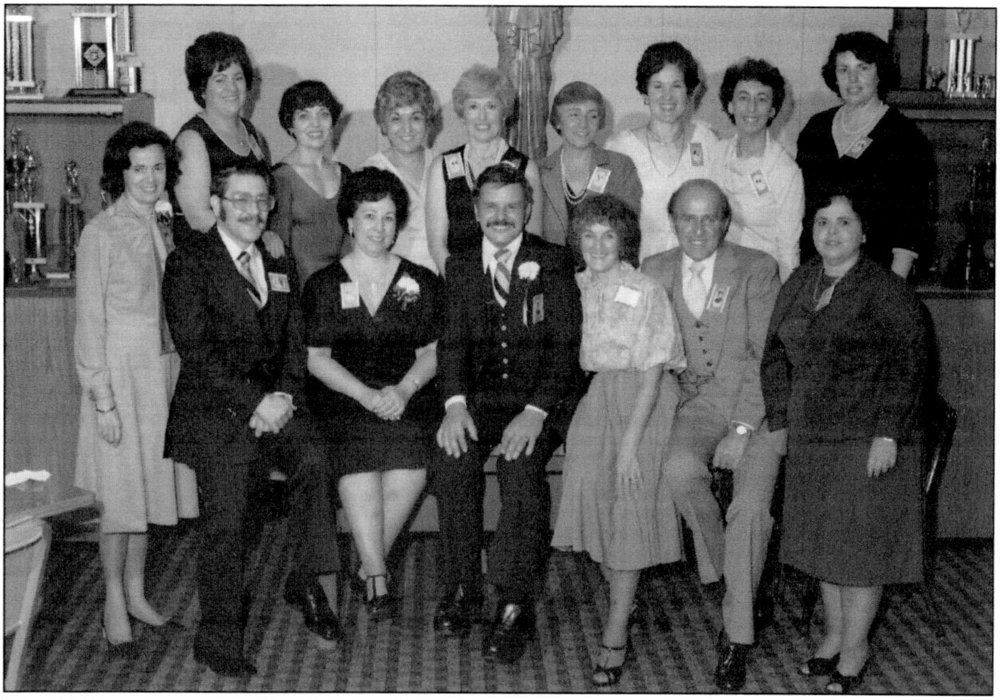

The 40th-year reunion of Maltese students from St. Vincent High School in Detroit is pictured here; they graduated in 1949. They are from left to right (front row) Angeline Cozzo, John Vella, Carmella Bonnici, Walter Cortis, Margaret Saliba, Charles Vella, and Stella Bonnici; (back row) Mary Apap, Margaret Muscat, Carmen Fenech, Frances Fenech, Carmen Zahra, Carrie Abel, Helen Cauchi, and Mary Vella. There were 64 students in the class. (Courtesy of Tess Vella.)

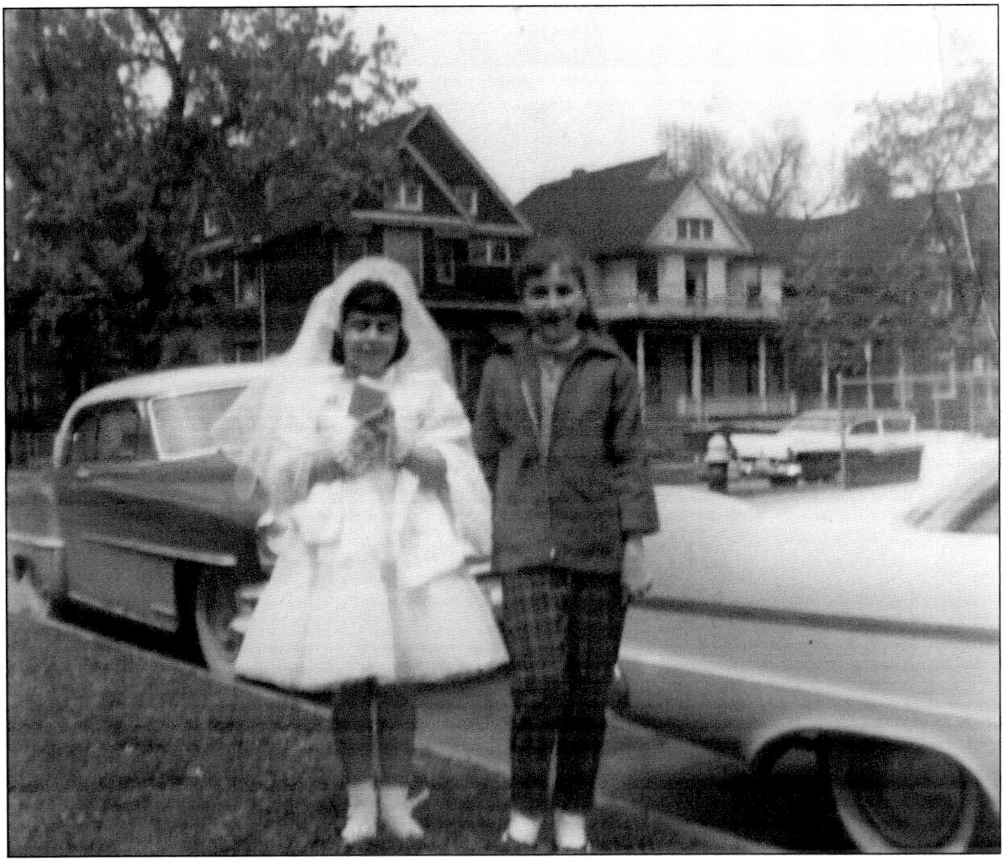

DeeDee DeBono (right) and her niece Diane Fenech are pictured around 1955. (Courtesy of DeeDee DeBono.)

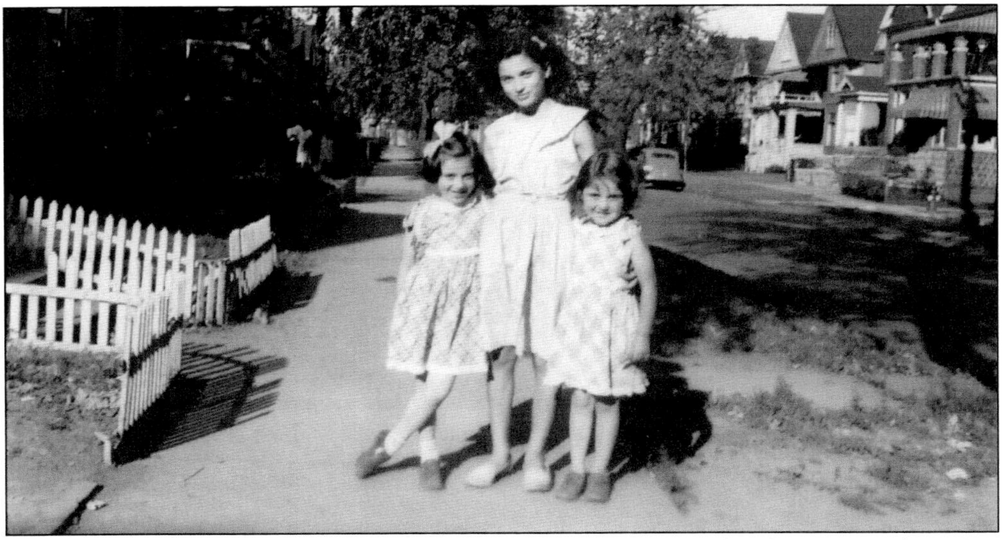

Gloria Felice, Doris Mallia, and Norma Felice are shown at 1814 Church Street in the 1950s. Gloria and Norma are sisters, and Doris is their cousin, who at the time was visiting with her family from New York City. (Courtesy of Norma Jean Philip.)

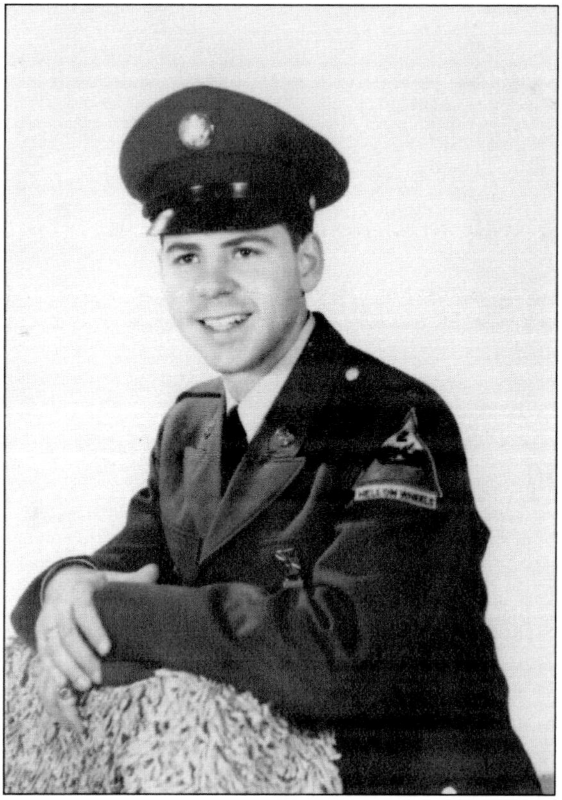

Leon Bonnici served in the U.S. Army around 1959. He went on to marry Kathleen Riordan, and they raised five children. (Courtesy of Stella Grima.)

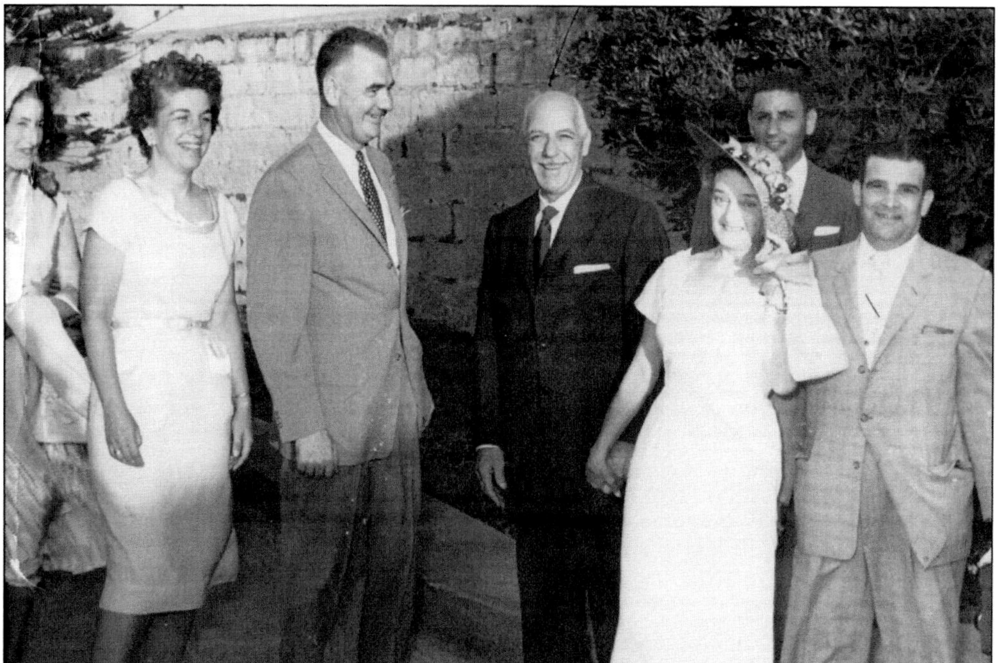

Joseph Calleja (center, with the black suit), a Maltese Hollywood movie star, is joined in this picture with his Maltese friends.

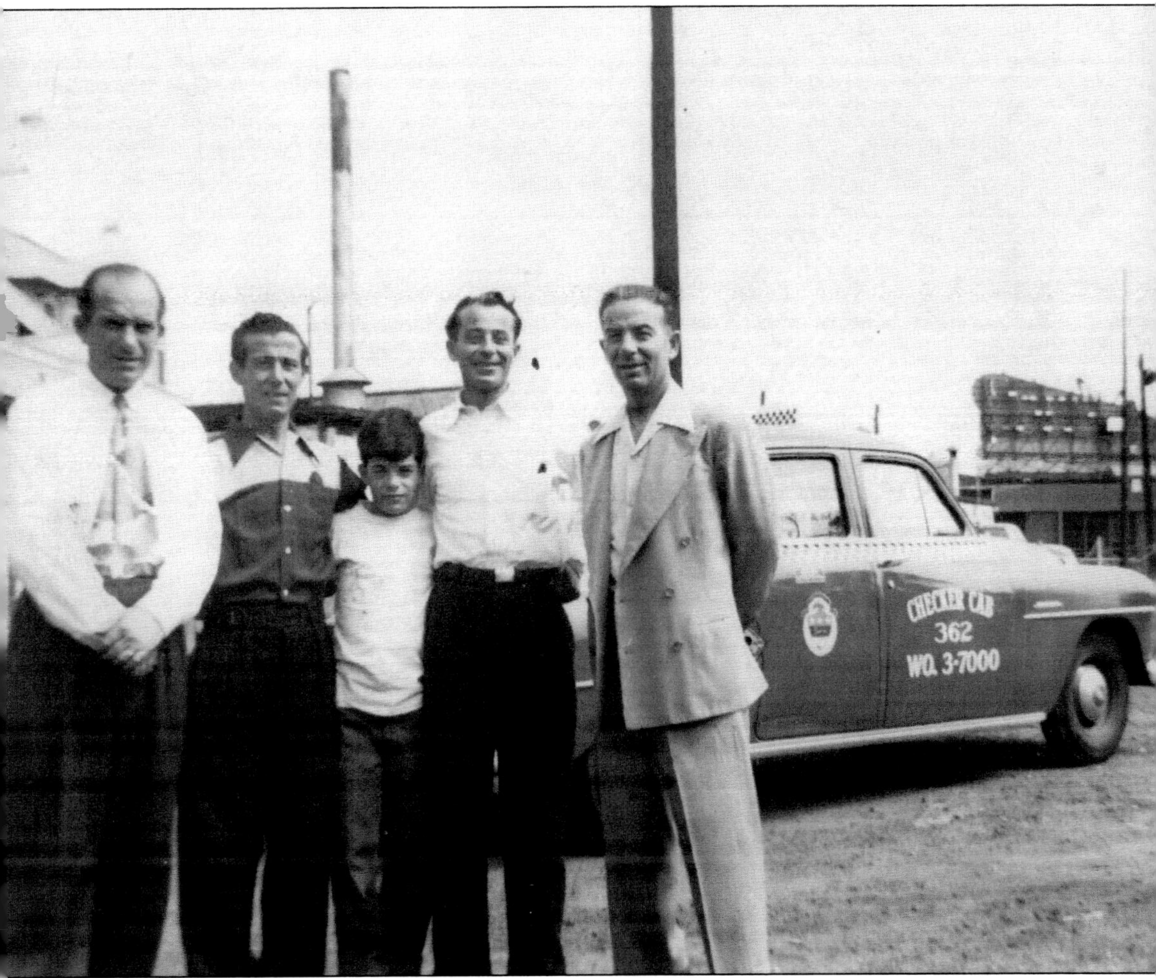

Pictured from left to right, an unidentified man and Ninu, Freddie, and Cataldo Attard pose in front of a cab in Detroit. Cataldo was a bartender at the Statler Hotel in Detroit and retired from the landmark location.

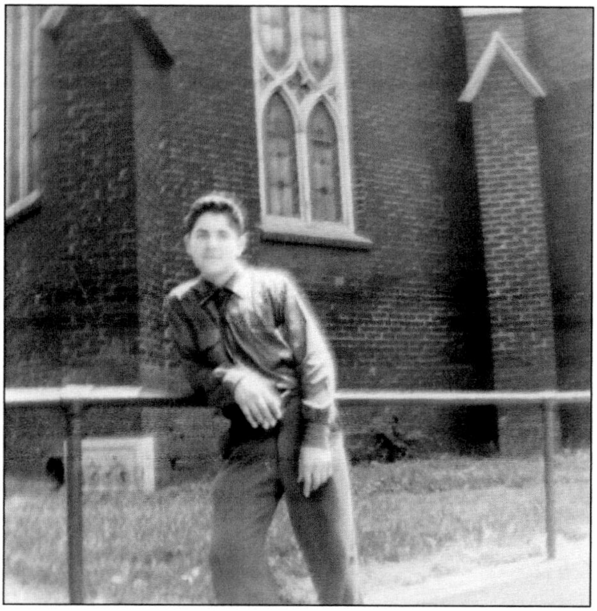

John DeBono is pictured outside St. Vincent de Paul Church around 1955. John is the youngest of six boys. He married and had four children.

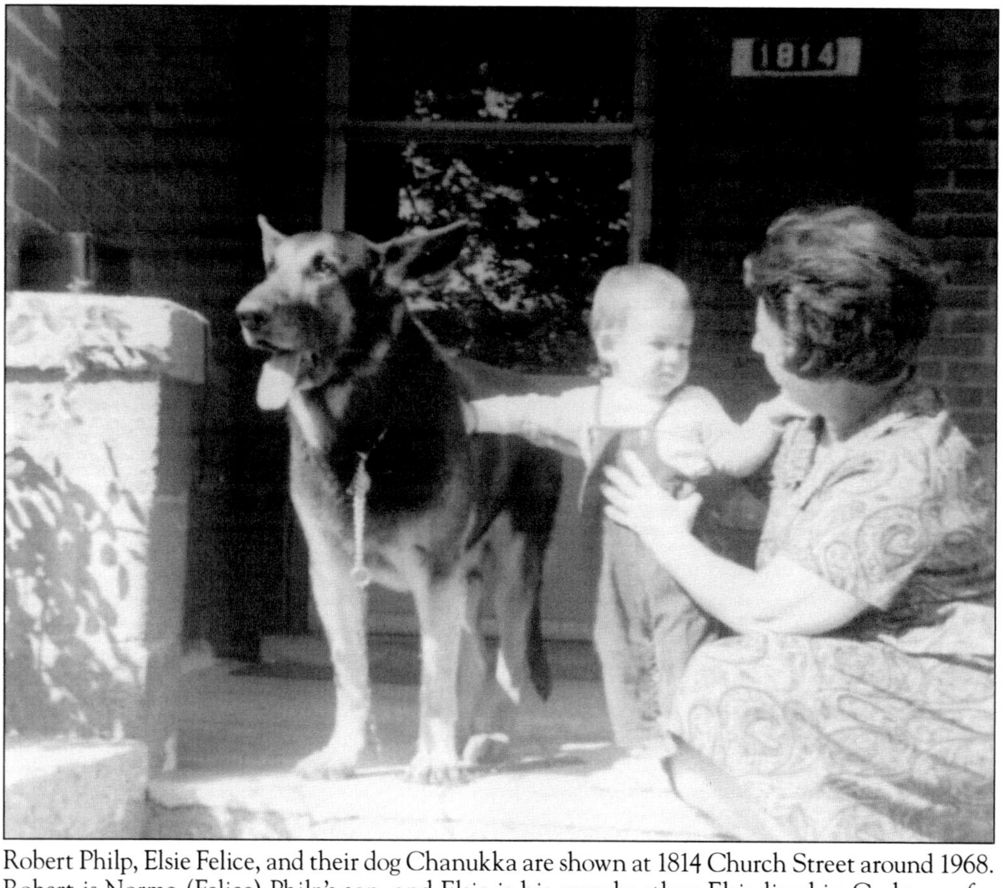

Robert Philp, Elsie Felice, and their dog Chanukka are shown at 1814 Church Street around 1968. Robert is Norma (Felice) Philp's son, and Elsie is his grandmother. Elsie lived in Corktown for more than 50 years. (Courtesy of Norma Jean Philip.)

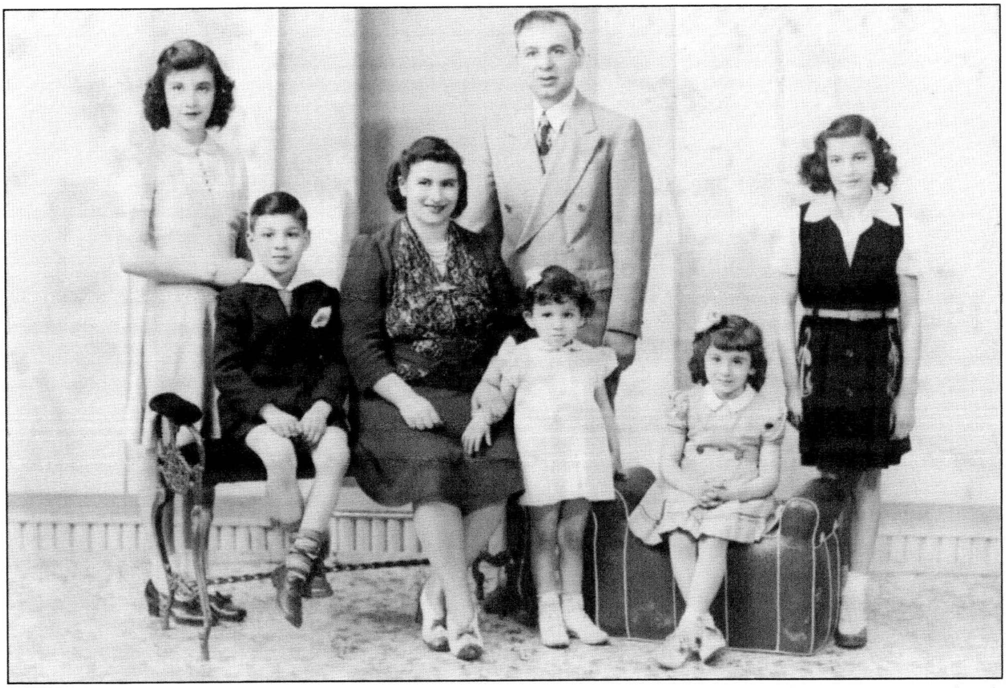

The Tabone siblings pose for the camera around 1944. They are Lena "Caroline," Mary, Michael, Evelyn, and Joan Ann. They were all born in the Corktown area. Lena had three children; Michael served in the Korean War and had four children; Mary had seven children and worked as an office manager for a food broker; Joan Ann had two children; and Evelyn had three children. (Courtesy of Mary and Chuck Brincat.)

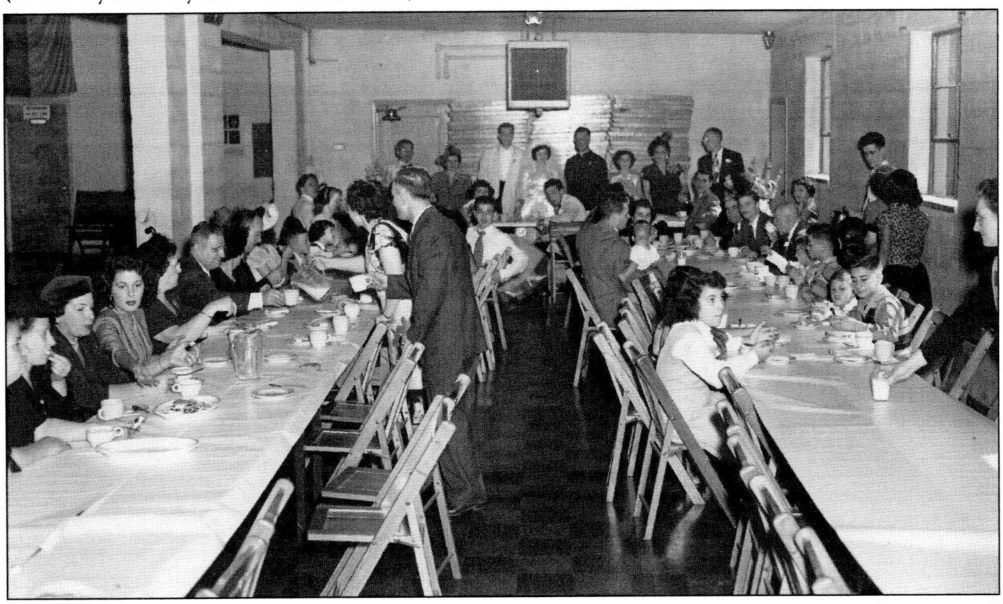

Here is Chuck and Mary Brincat's wedding reception on September 9, 1950, at St. Clement Hall on Michigan Avenue at Twenty-fourth Avenue. They had seven children: Linda, Charles Robert Jr., Brian, Gary, Kenneth, David, and Mark. Brian was actively involved in renovating Corktown properties. (Courtesy of Mary and Chuck Brincat.)

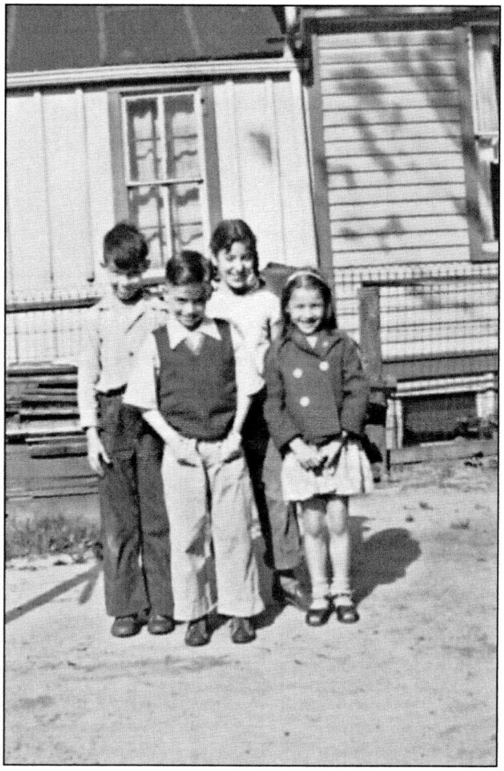

Joe Zammit, Mary Ann Fenech, and Mickey and Julie Capace are in the backyard of Mary Ann's home on Leverette Street. They were cousins and lived next door to each other. Sometimes while the children played, their moms would open the windows to converse with each other. (Courtesy of Frances Fenech.)

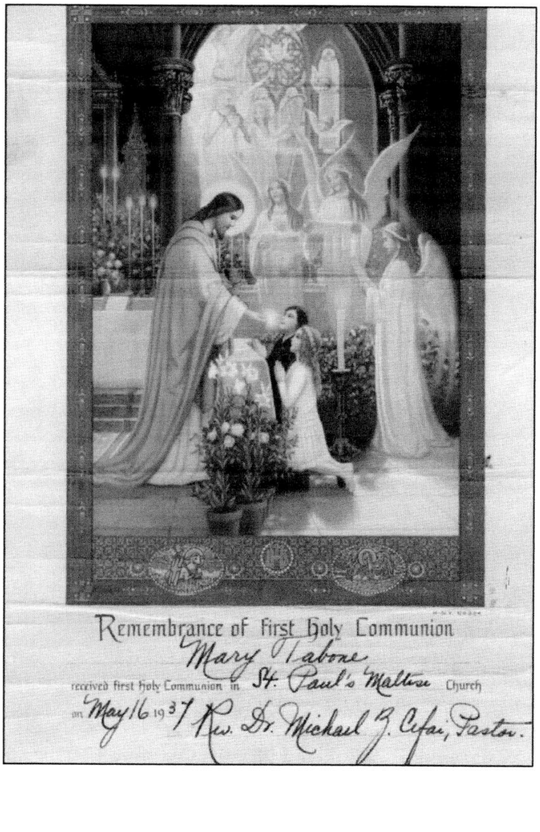
Remembrance of First Holy Communion
Mary Tabone
received first Holy Communion in St. Paul's Maltese Church
on May 16 1937 Rev. Dr. Michael J. Cefai, Pastor.

Here is Mary Tabone's 1934 First Holy Communion document from St. Paul's Maltese Church. It was signed by Maltese pastor Fr. Michael Cefai. (Courtesy of Mary and Chuck Brincat.)

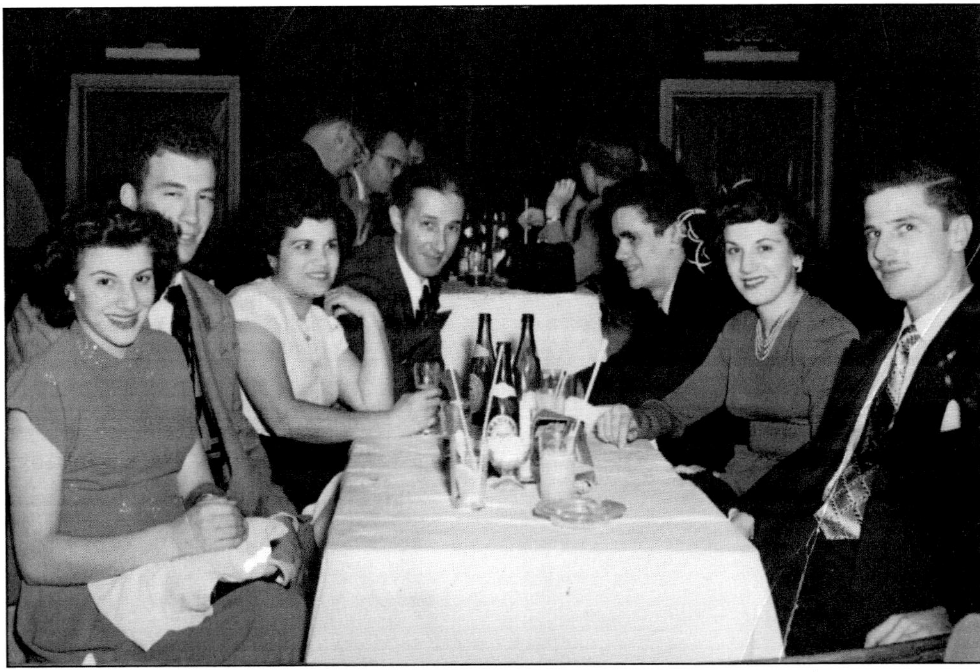

Mary and Chuck Brincat, Rose and John Baluci, Romeo Marsh, and Lena and Charles Smith are shown at the Elmwood Casino in Canada around 1950. (Courtesy of Mary and Chuck Brincat.)

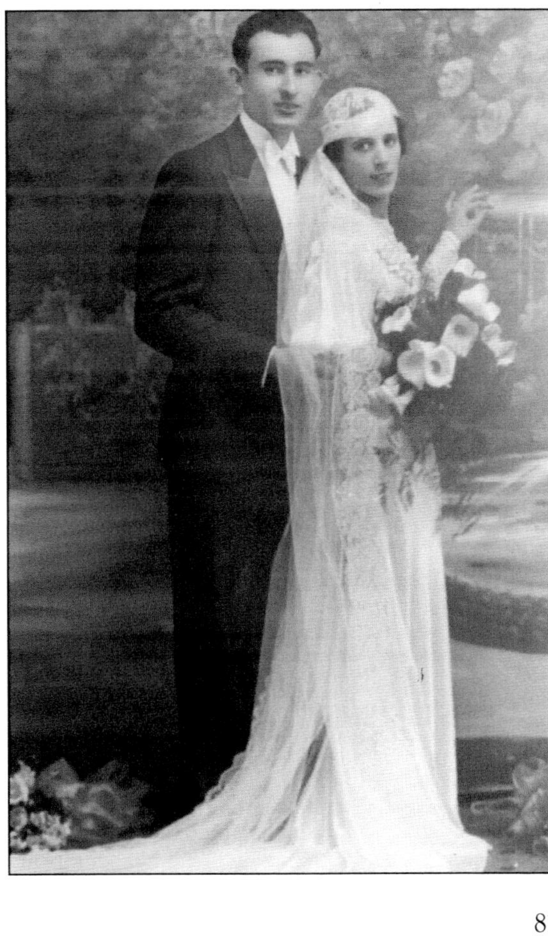

Carmen and Joseph Vella were married September 29, 1934, in St. Paul's Maltese Church in Detroit. Carmen was 12 when she moved from Malta to Montreal, where she lived for three years before moving with her family to Detroit. When Joseph arrived in Detroit, he was 19 years old. Carmen and Joseph had six children, five girls and one boy; their son died at the age of five years old. Joseph Vella was the oldest of five children and sponsored each of his siblings when they came to the United States. (Courtesy of Josephine Formosa.)

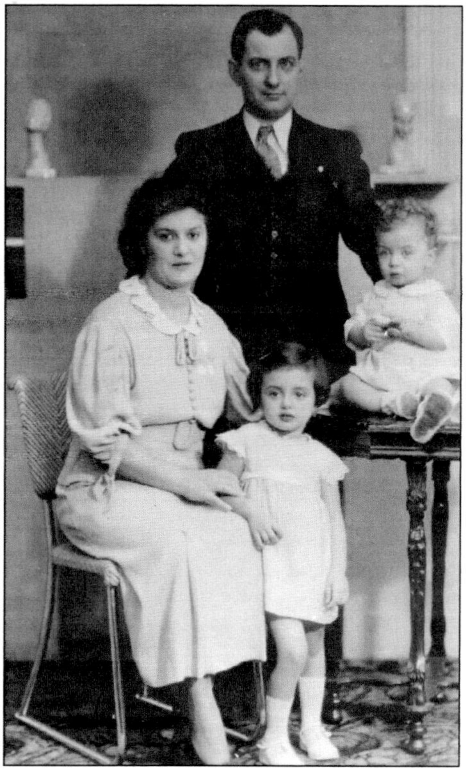

William Jr., Mary, Carmen, and William LaFerle lived on the west side of Detroit. William came to Detroit in 1919, and Carmen came in 1922; they were married in 1925. The elder William loved woodworking and was employed as an electrical engineer at Chrysler Motor Company. (Courtesy of William LaFerle.)

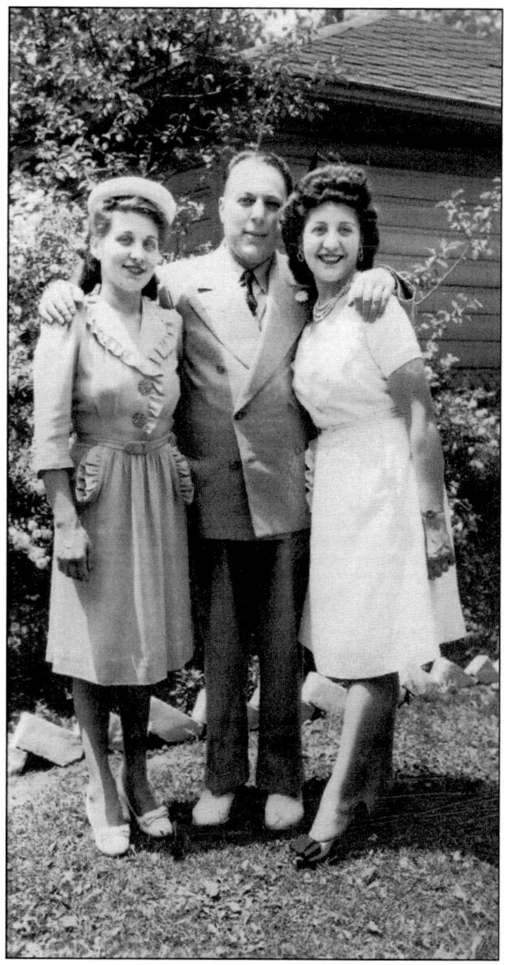

Jessie DeBono and Mary DeBono are shown with their friend Tony Vella. Mary had five children, and Jessie had six kids. (Courtesy of DeeDee DeBono.)

Philip Meilak and John Fenech are shown in cowboy suits around 1950. (Courtesy of Frances Fenech.)

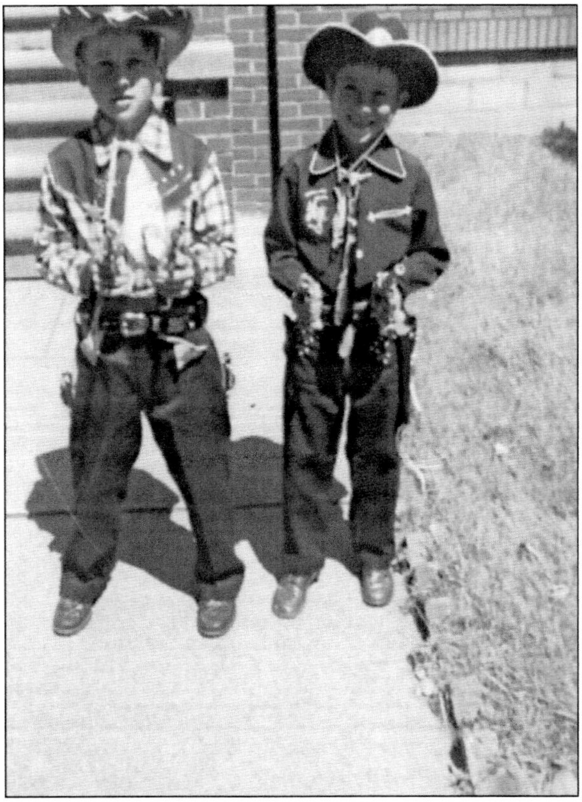

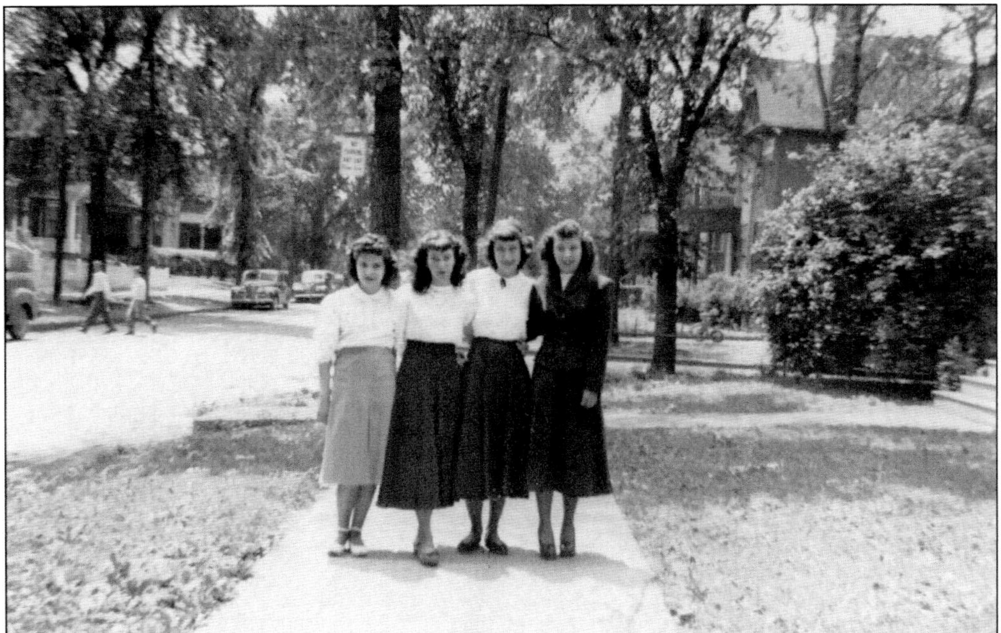

Louise Tabone, Lena Cassar, Helen Brincat, and Esther Cassar are shown on Leverette Street around 1949. Lena and Esther were sisters, and Louise and Helen were so close to them growing up that they felt like sisters. (Courtesy of Lena Cunningham.)

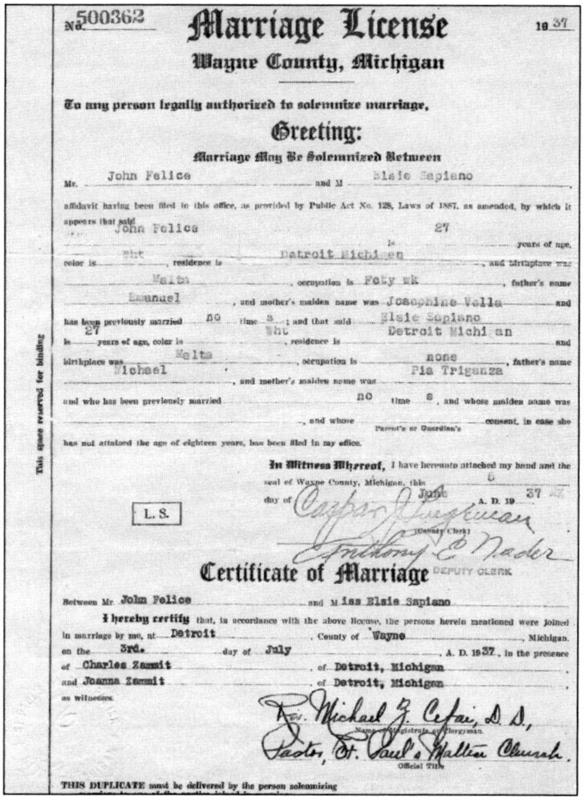

No. 500362 **Marriage License** 19 37

Wayne County, Michigan

To any person legally authorized to solemnize marriage,

Greeting:

Marriage May Be Solemnized Between

Mr. John Felice and M Elsie Sapiano,

affidavit having been filed in this office, as provided by Public Act No. 128, Laws of 1887, as amended, by which it appears that said John Felice is 27 years of age, color is Wht, residence is Detroit Michigan, and birthplace was Malta, occupation is Fcty wk, father's name Emanuel, and mother's maiden name was Josephine Vella and has been previously married no time s; and that said Elsie Sapiano is 27 years of age, color is Wht, residence is Detroit Michigan and birthplace was Malta, occupation is none, father's name Michael, and mother's maiden name was Pia Triganza and who has been previously married no time s, and whose maiden name was ______, and whose Parent's or Guardian's consent, in case she has not attained the age of eighteen years, has been filed in my office.

In Witness Whereof, I have hereunto attached my hand and the seal of Wayne County, Michigan, this 6 day of June A. D. 19 37

L. S.

Caspar J. Lingeman (County Clerk)

Anthony E. Nader DEPUTY CLERK

Certificate of Marriage

Between Mr. John Felice and Miss Elsie Sapiano

I hereby certify that, in accordance with the above license, the persons herein mentioned were joined in marriage by me, at Detroit, County of Wayne, Michigan, on the 3rd. day of July, A. D. 1937, in the presence of Charles Zammit, of Detroit, Michigan, and Joanna Zammit, of Detroit, Michigan, as witnesses.

Rev. Michael G. Cefai, D. D., Name of Magistrate or Clergyman.

Pastor, St. Paul's Maltese Church. Official Title

THIS DUPLICATE must be delivered by the person solemnizing

This space reserved for binding

This is the marriage license between John Felice and Ersillia Sapiano. They met in Malta and were married on July 3, 1936, in Detroit at St. Paul's Maltese Church by Fr. Michael Cefai. They had four children: Ronald, Alfred, Gloria, and Norma. (Courtesy of Norma Jean Philip.)

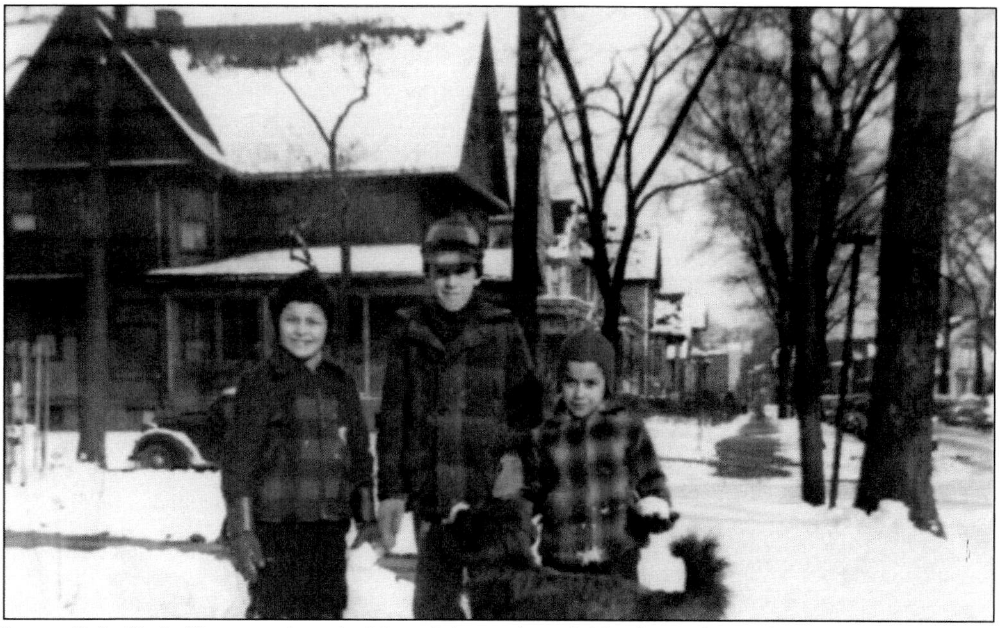

James Gale (far left), an unidentified friend (center), and Charles Gale are shown with a dog. The Gale brothers were the oldest of five children born to Rita and James Gale. For the majority of their lives, they lived in Corktown and later moved with their family to the west side of Detroit about the time they were teenagers. (Courtesy of Linda Morasso.)

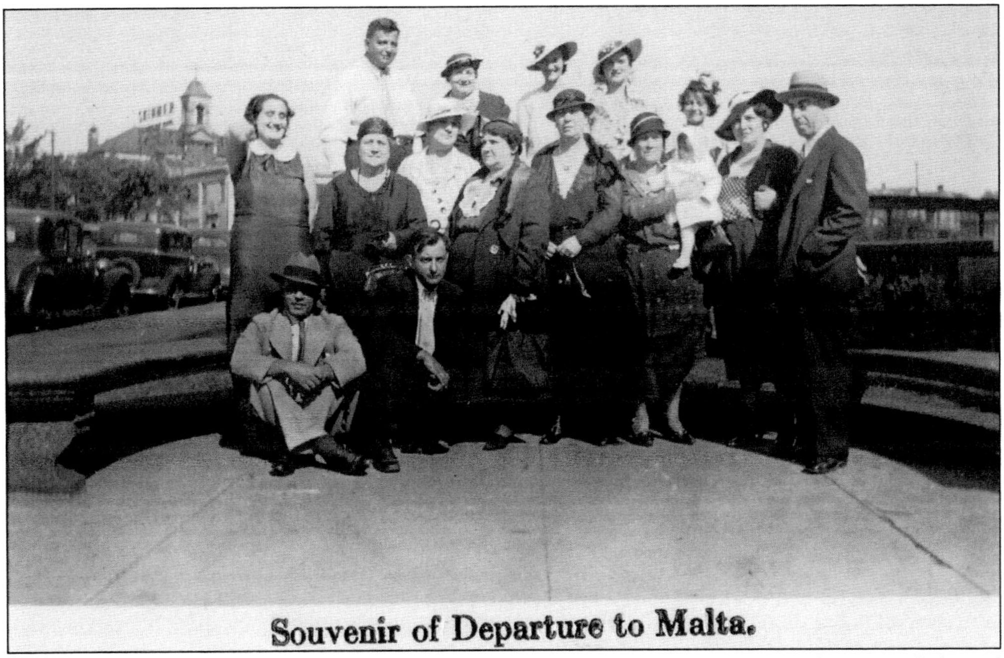

Maltese people are shown here departing from Detroit to return to Malta, where it is believed that some were going home to visit, while others were going to stay there permanently.

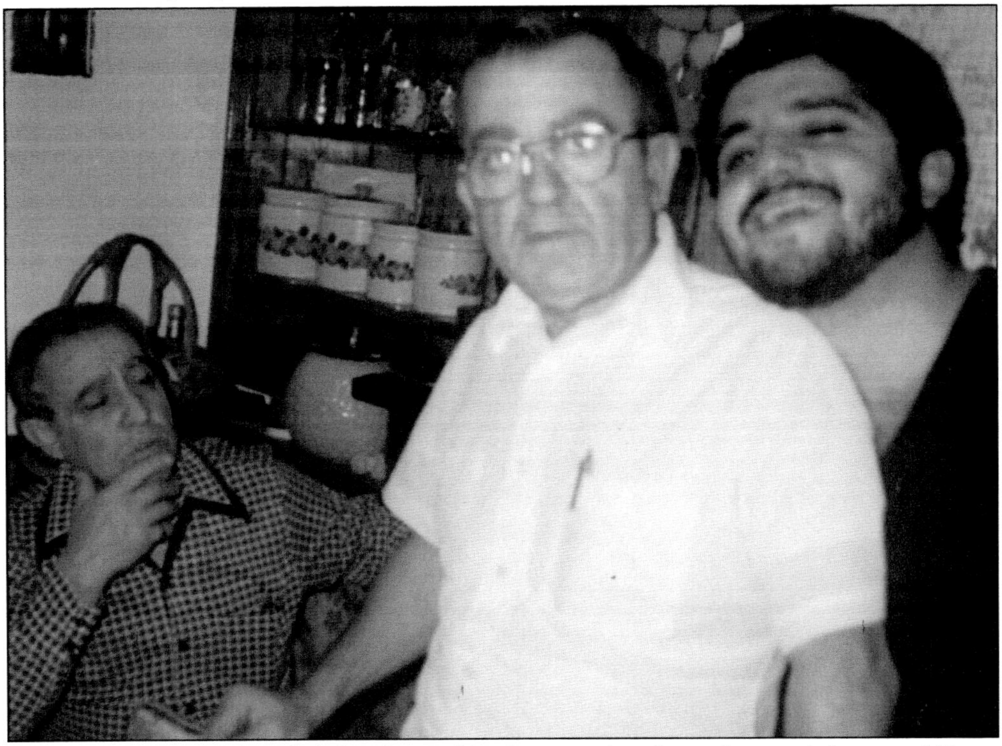

From left to right, Paul Bush (who changed his last name) is shown here with Louis and Norm Buhagiar at Thanksgiving in 1979. Norm is Louis's oldest son, and Paul is Louis's brother. Louis was the fifth youngest among 20 siblings. (Courtesy of Lisa Norwood.)

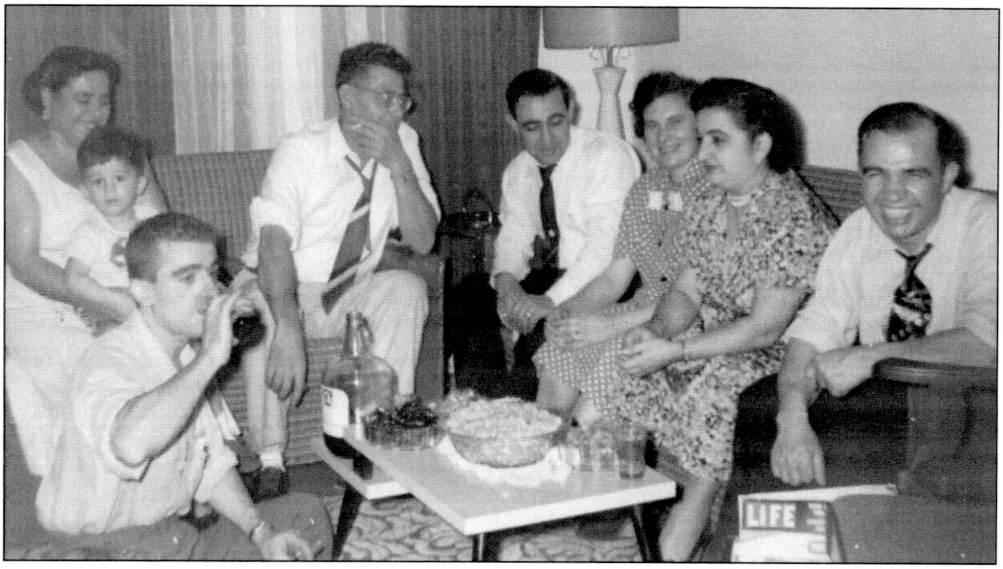

Louis Buhagiar, Martha Buttigieg, Paul Bush, Melda Bush, and Jo and Tony Micallef are shown among others at a 1950s Christmas party. Extended family members celebrated holidays together. (Courtesy of Lisa Norwood.)

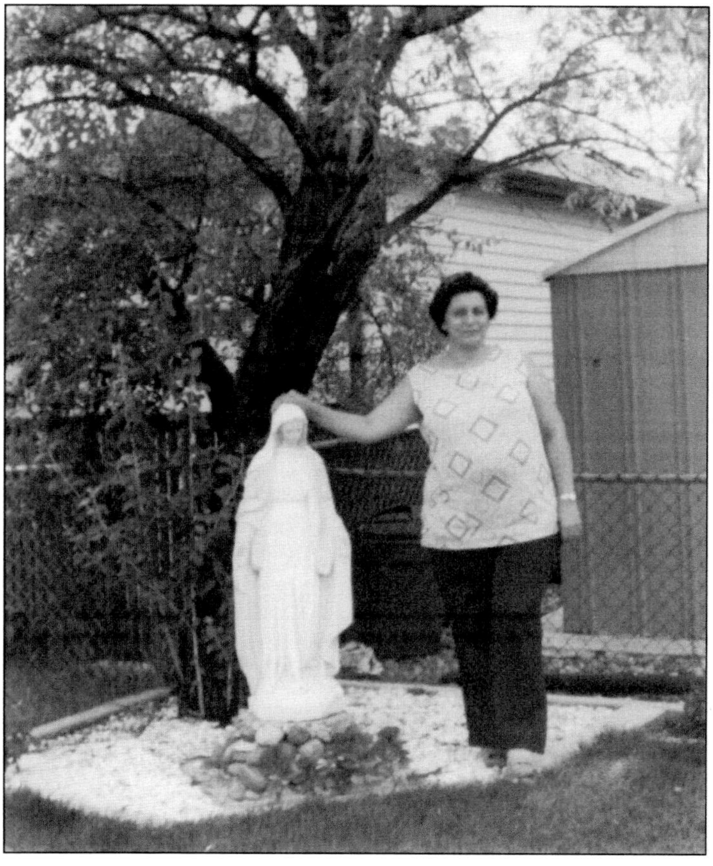

Mary Buhagiar poses here around 1980 with a statue of the Blessed Mother in her Dearborn Heights backyard. Devotion to the Blessed Mother is common among Maltese immigrants and their descendants. (Courtesy of Lisa Norwood.)

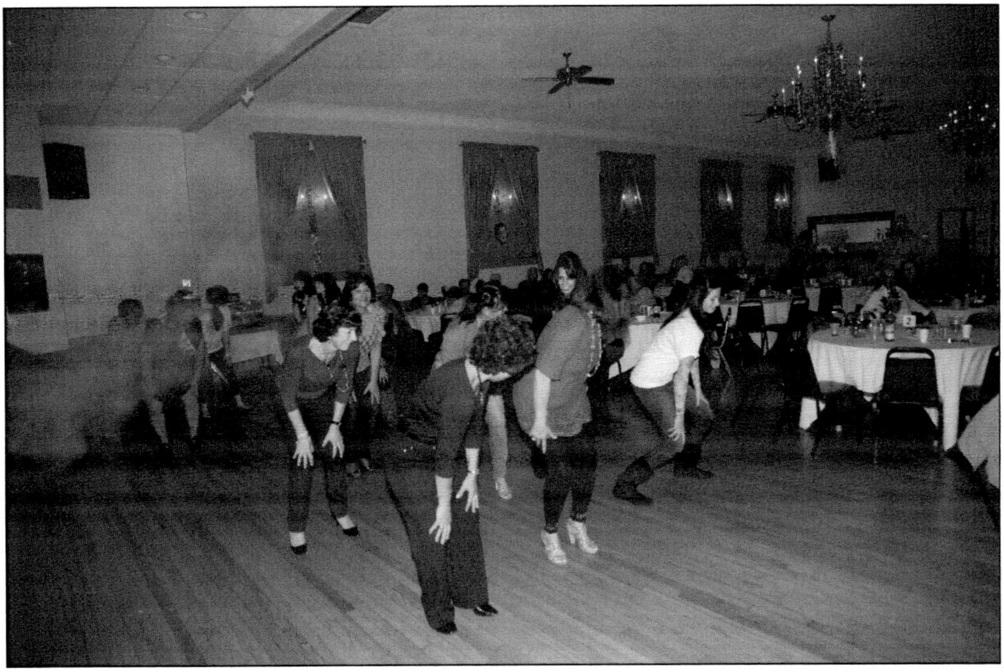

Members of the Maltese American Community Club in Dearborn, with their guests, celebrate Halloween 2010 at the club. (Courtesy of the Maltese American Community Club.)

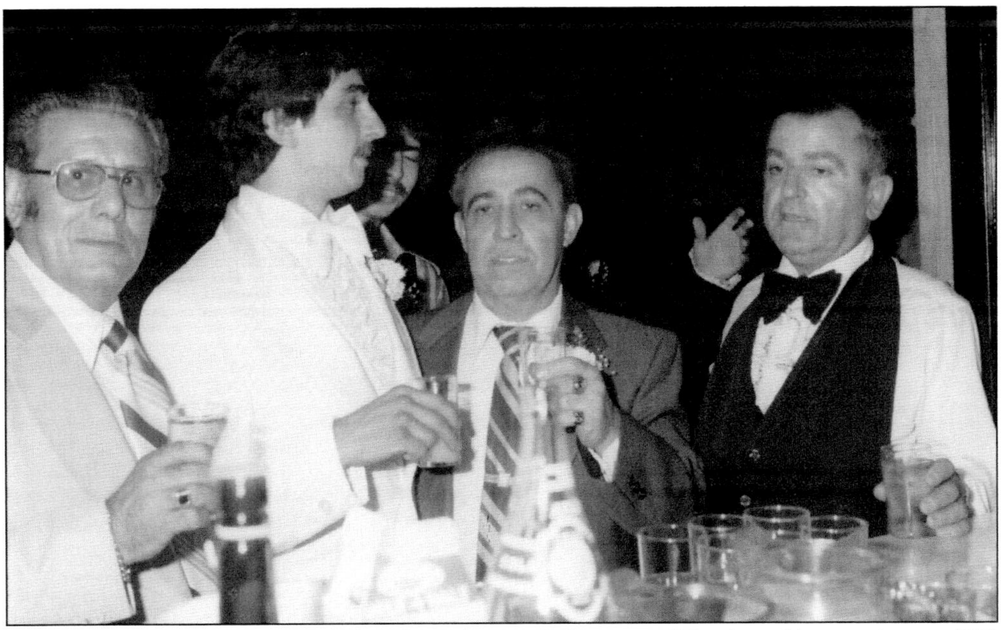

Joe Bonnici, Silvio Buhagiar, Paul Bush, and Louis Buhagiar at Silvio's wedding in August 1979 in Dearborn Heights. Paul Bush is Louis's brother, and Joe was a friend of Louis's in Malta. The families remained close when they left Malta. (Courtesy of Lisa Norwood.)

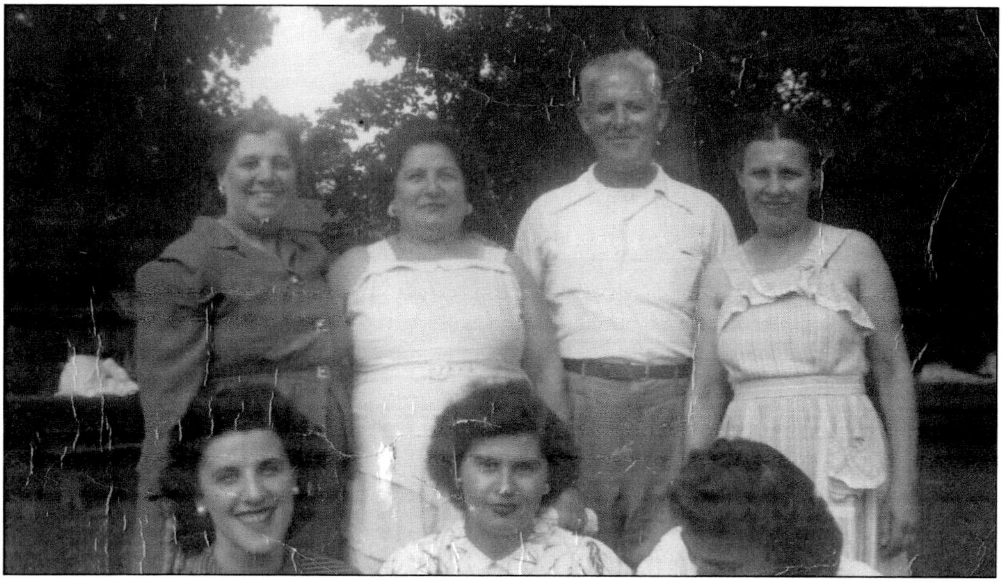

This is a picture of Agnes DeBono, Grazio DeBono, Venuta Saliba, Lena Saliba, Jessie Xerri, Ester ? and Mary ? .

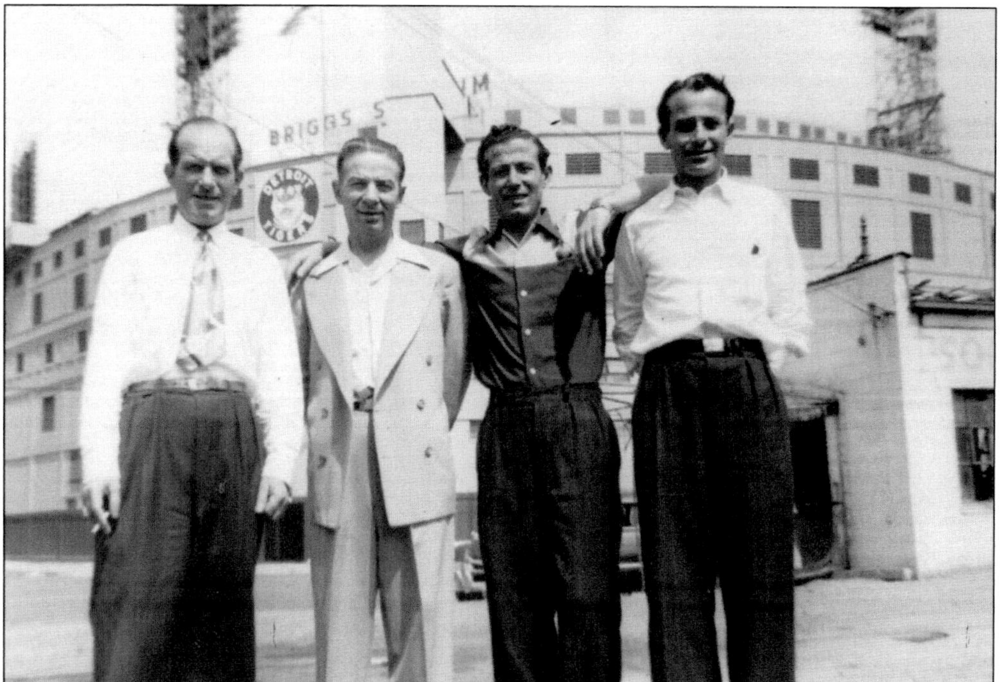

From left to right, an unidentified man and Charles, Ninu, and Fred Attard are shown outside Briggs Stadium, also known as Navin Field and finally Tiger Stadium, which was located in Corktown. The stadium was torn down in stages with the final demolition in 2009. Since then the Tigers have played at Comerica Park, also in Detroit.

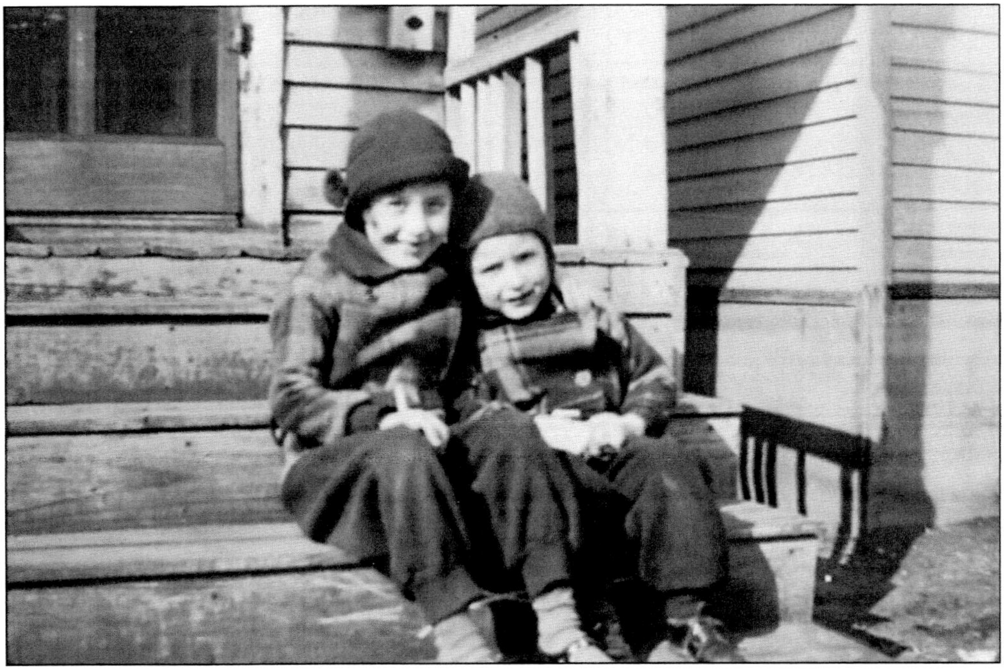

Siblings Frances and Robert Fenech are shown sitting on their porch on Labrosse Street around 1938. (Courtesy of Frances Fenech.)

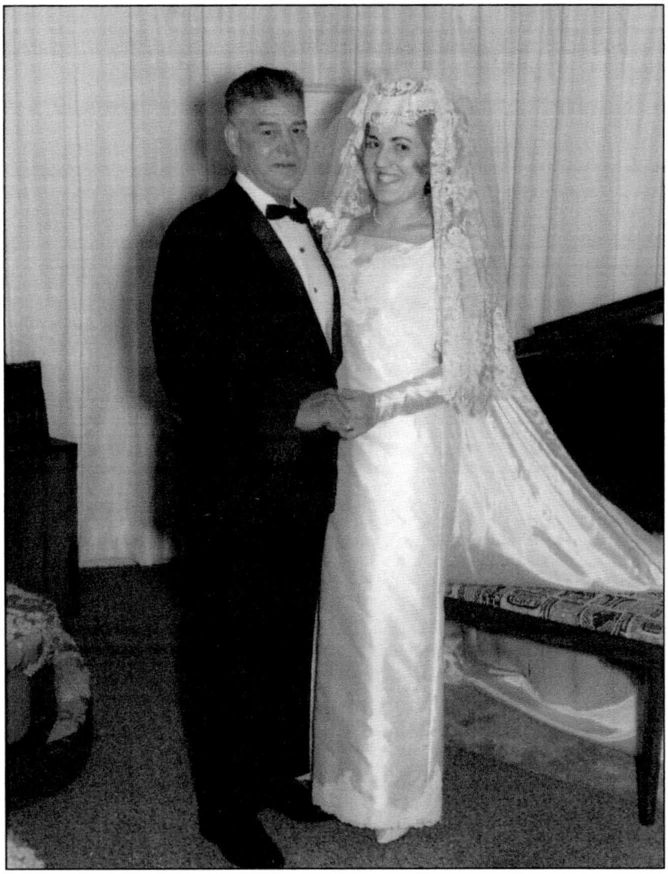

John Felice and his daughter Norma Jean Felice are shown in the parlor of their home at 1814 Church Street on October 21, 1966. (Courtesy of Norma Jean Philip.)

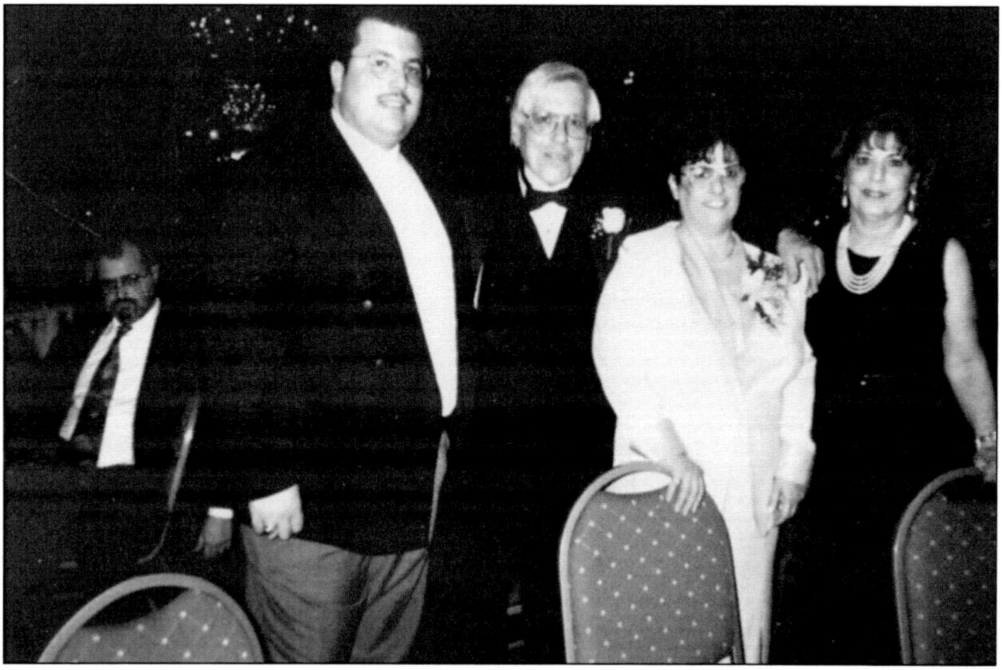

Kevin Knott, John and Silvia Fenech, and Mary Ann Knott are shown at the wedding of John and Silvia's son Christopher in 1998.

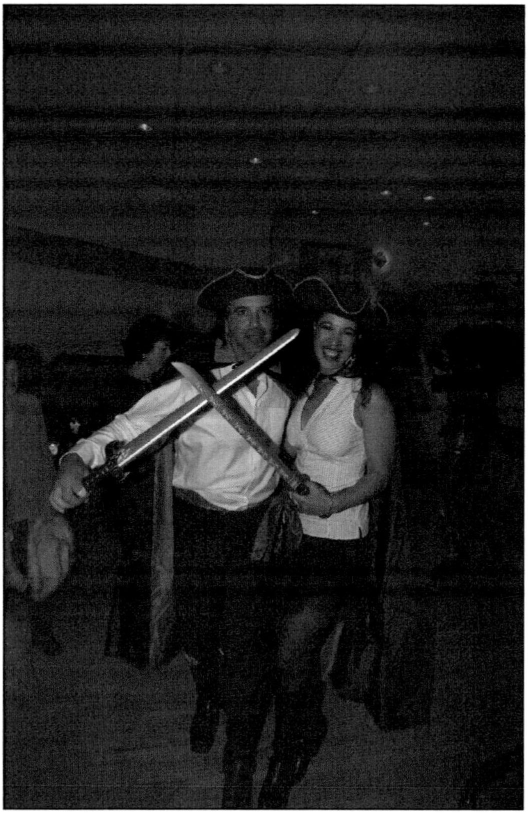

Dewain and Wendi Diacono pose at the Dearborn Maltese club during the 2010 Halloween party. (Courtesy of the Maltese American Community Club.)

Mary DeBono was married to Joseph Fenech, and they had five children: Diane, Bob, Ronnie, Joseph, and Billy. (Courtesy of DeeDee DeBono.)

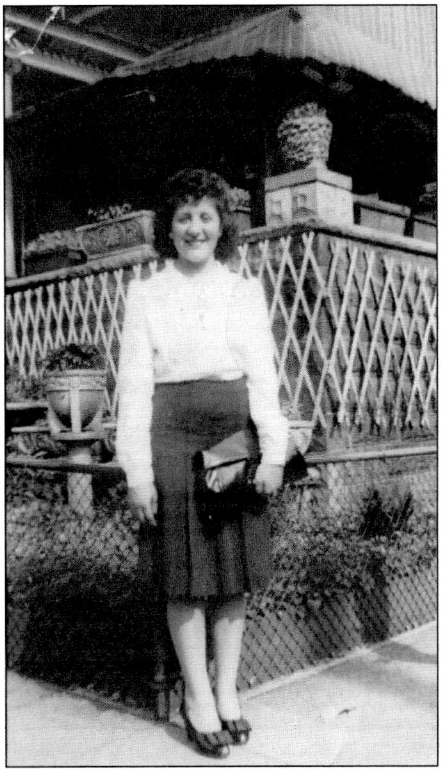

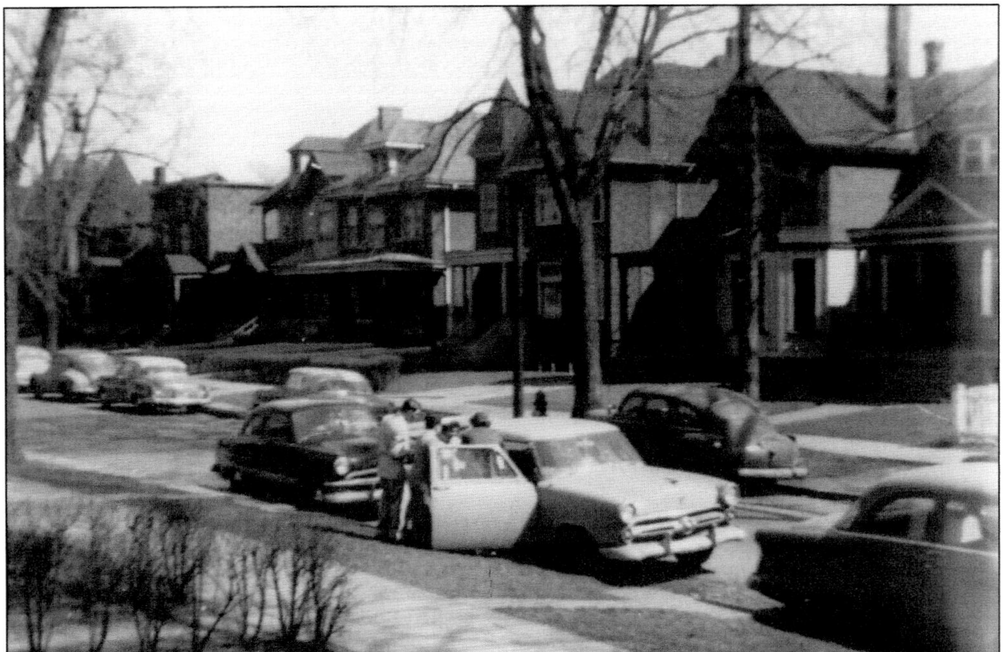

This picture shows Leverette Street in the early years of Maltese living in Corktown; originally Irish and German immigrants lived in the community. In later years, other ethnic groups to have moved to the area have been Mexican and African American.

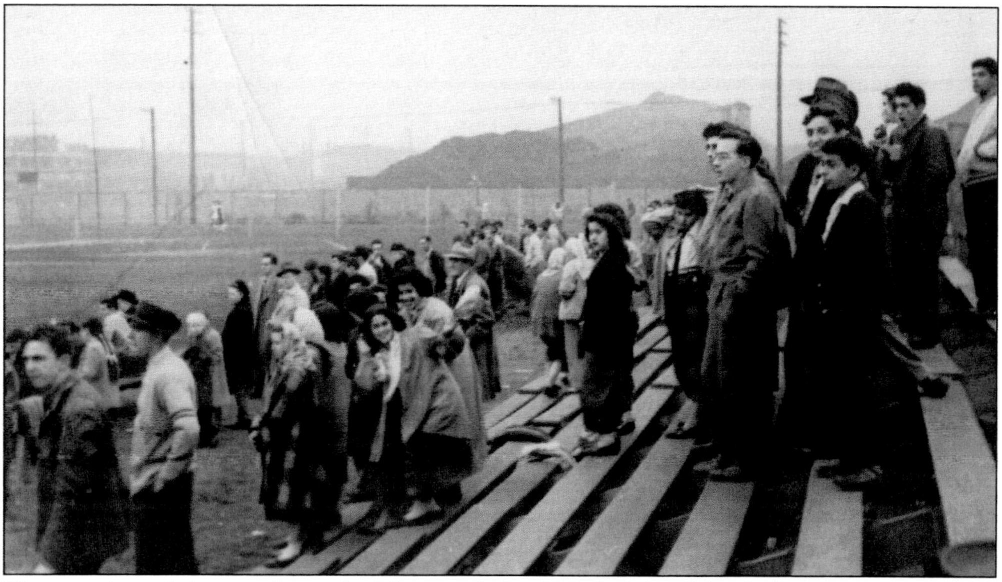

This is a shot of the stands at a St. Vincent de Paul High School football game around 1948. (Courtesy of Tess Vella.)

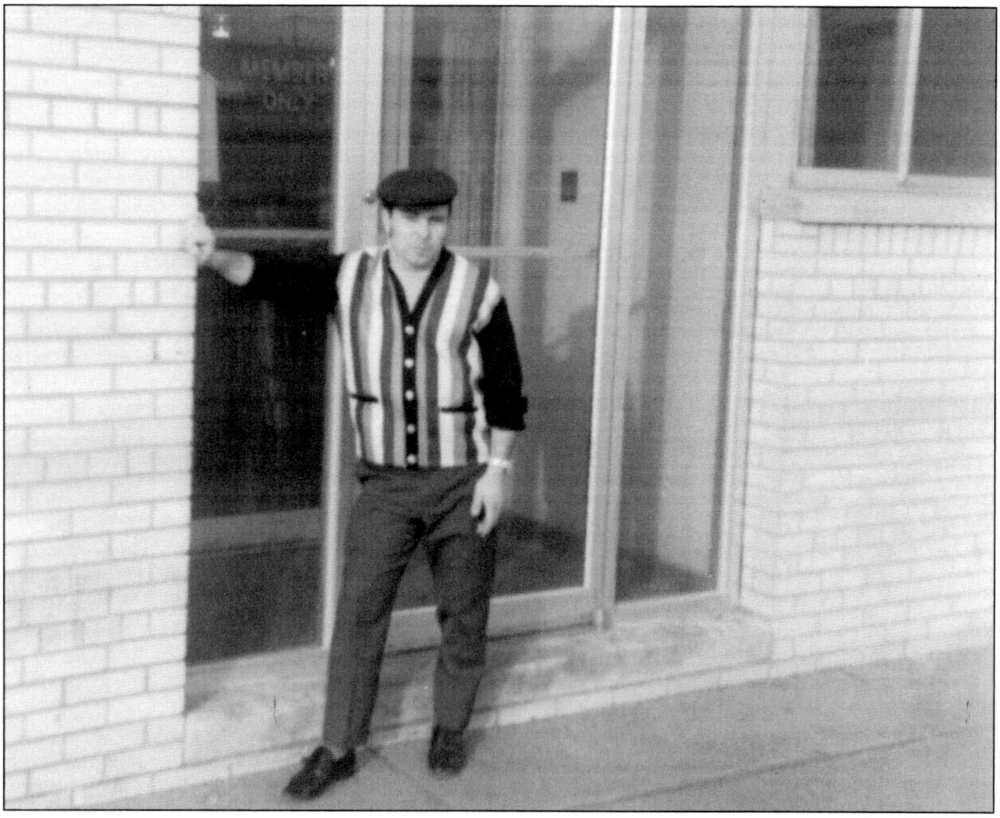

Charlie Schembri stands outside the Maltese club around 1963. Many Maltese immigrants went to the Detroit club to socialize, especially when they first arrived in the United States. (Courtesy of Charlie Schembri.)

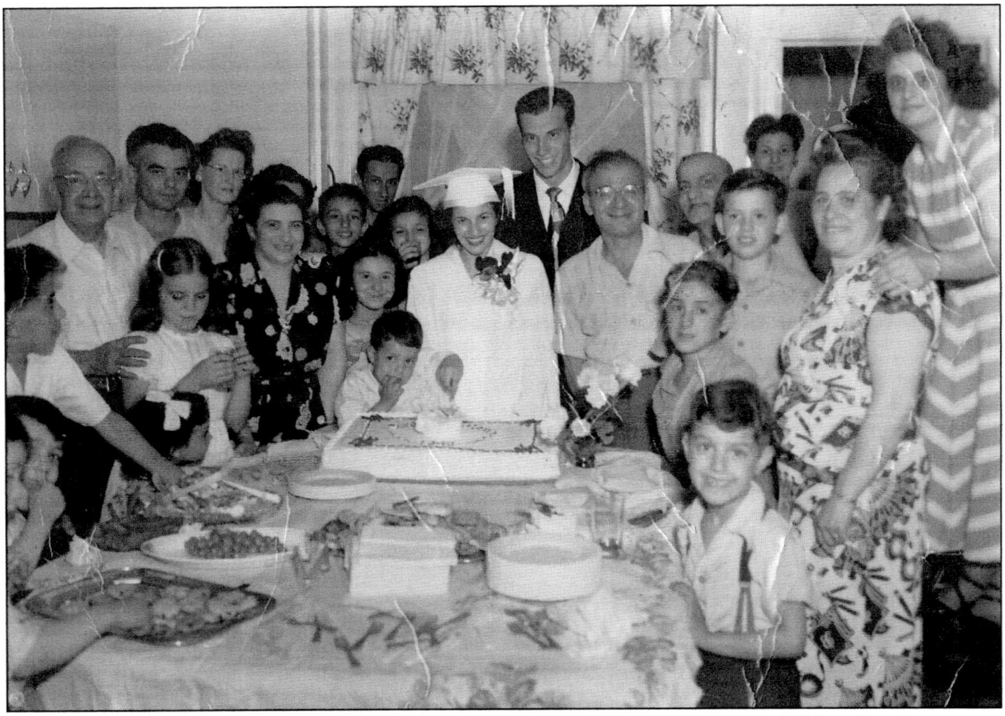

In 1949, Mary Tabone graduated from Detroit Girl's Catholic Central. Her family is seen here celebrating the event with a party at her home in Corktown. (Courtesy of Chuck and Mary Brincat.)

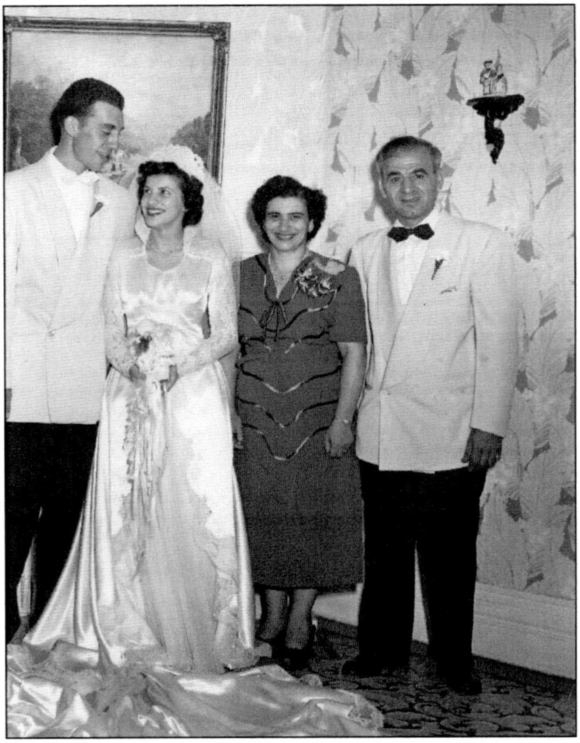

Chuck and Mary Brincat are shown at 1649 Church Street with Mary's parents, Mary and Manuel Tabone. The Tabones lived in the Corktown home for more than 35 years. (Courtesy of Chuck and Mary Brincat.)

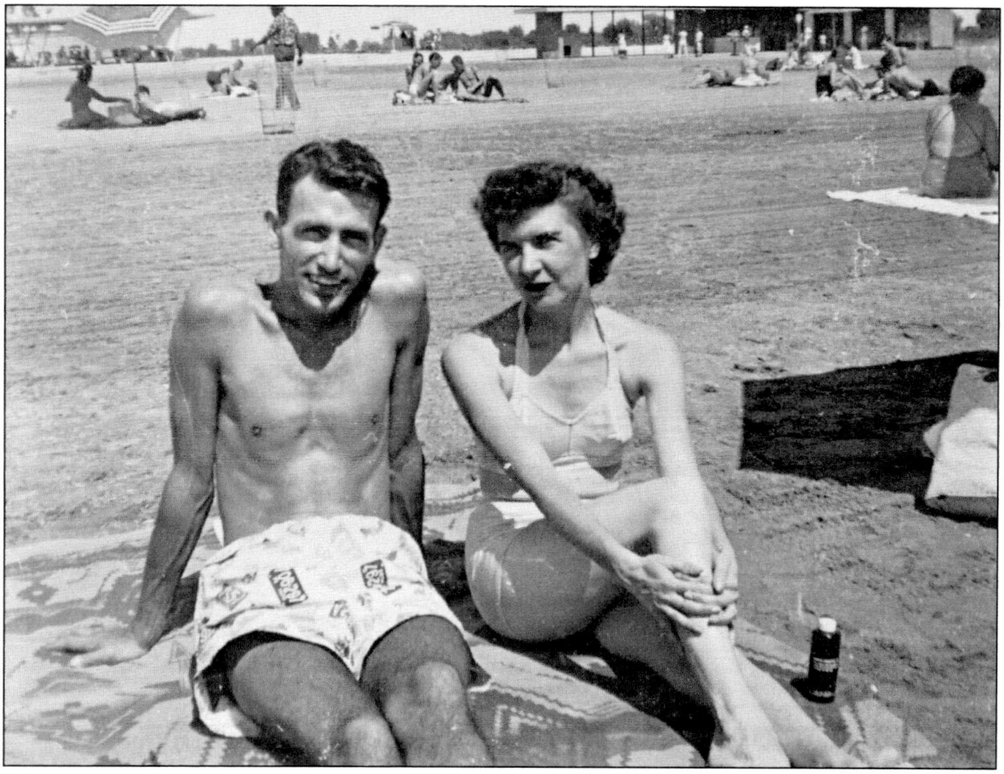

Tony Pons and his wife are shown on a beach in Michigan. (Courtesy of Tony Pons.)

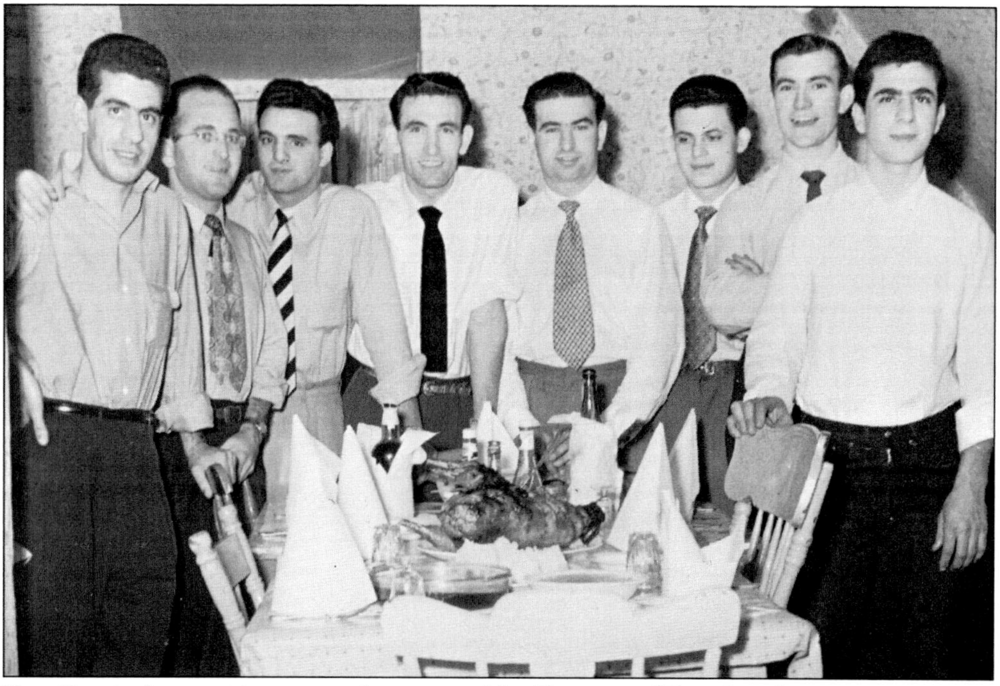

Tony Pons is shown with a group of men at a table. (Courtesy of Tony Pons.)

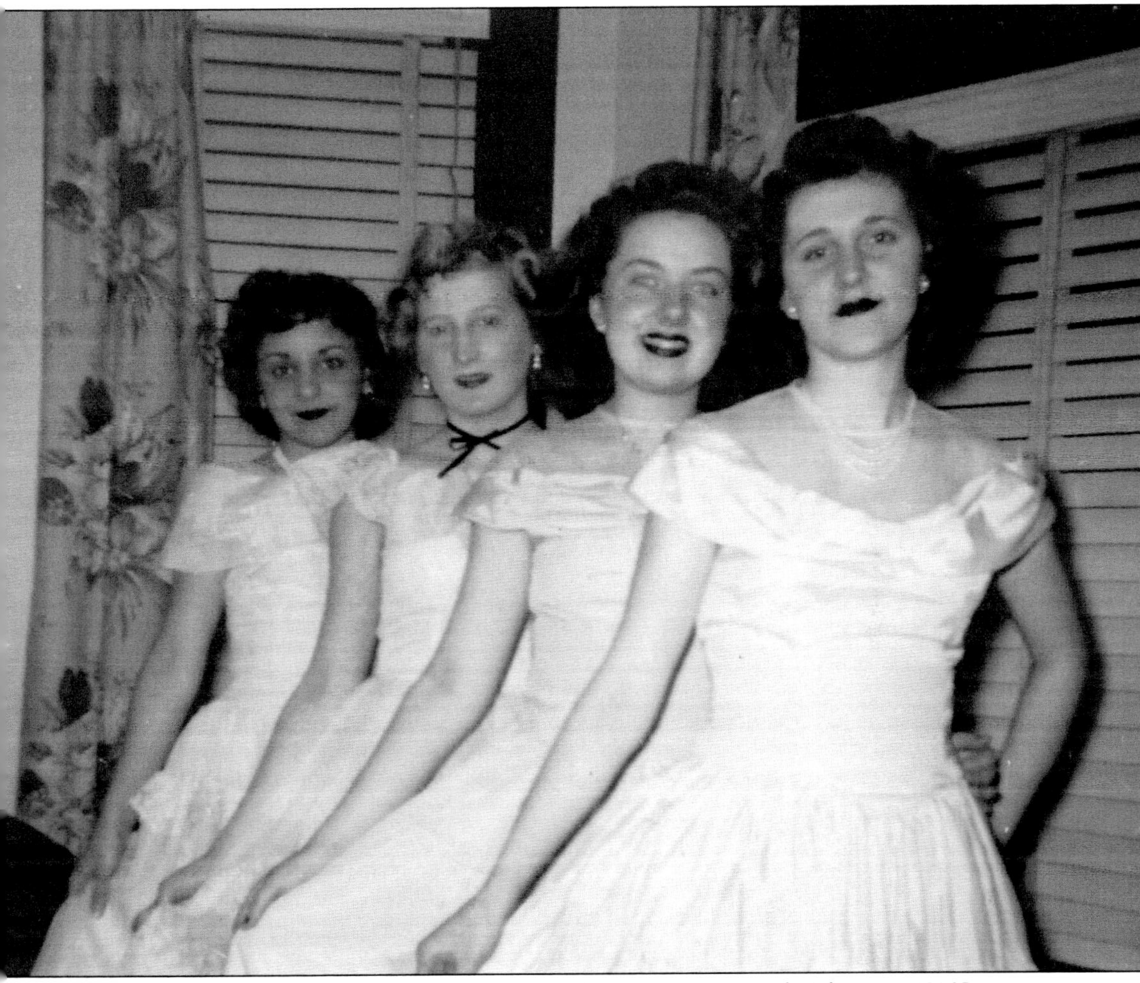

Tess Haley, Rose Adams, Eileen Murphy, and MaryEllen Rotz pose in Haley's home at 1816 Leverette Street after a St. Patrick's Day play at St. Vincent de Paul School. (Courtesy of Tess Vella.)

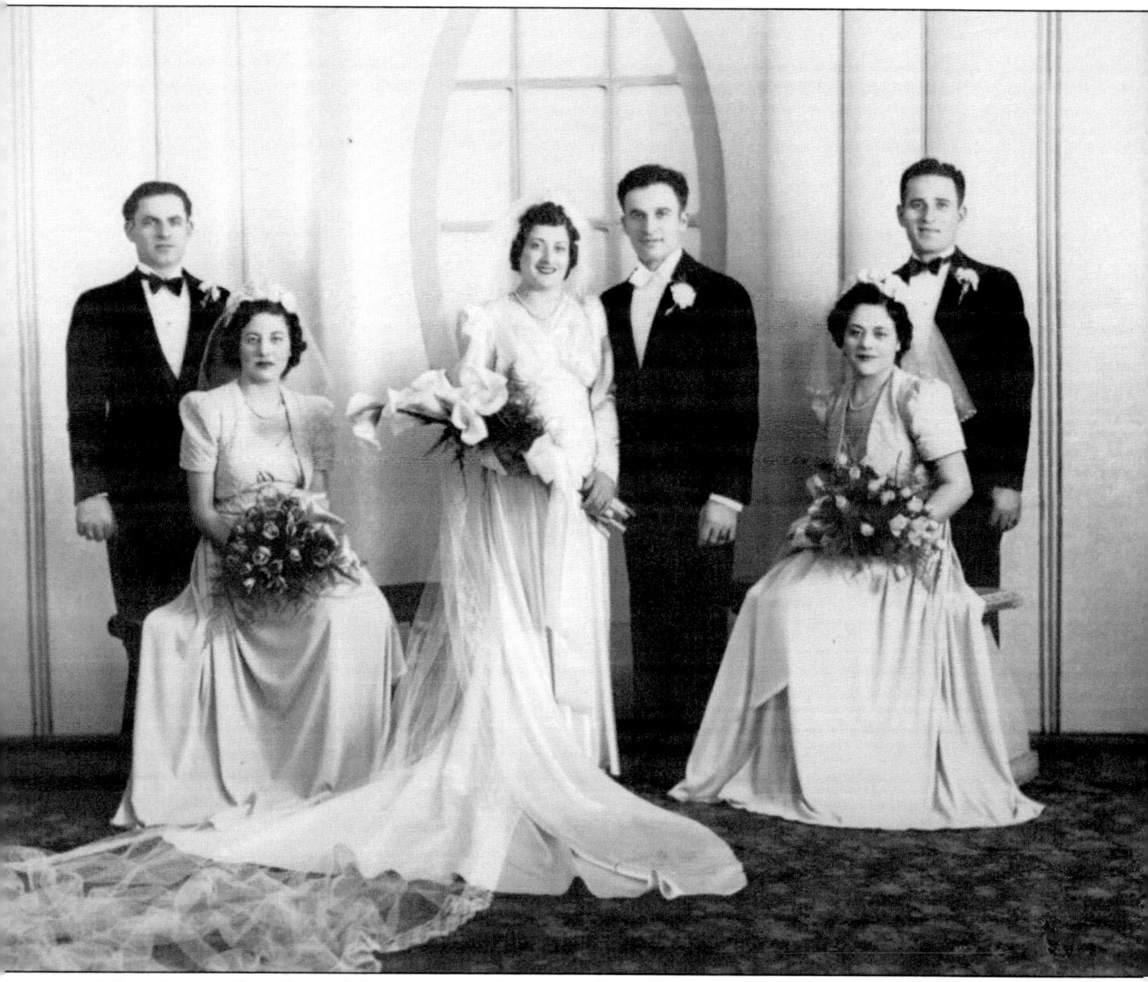

Here is a studio shot of the marriage between Rita Borg and James Gale. The picture shows an unidentified person, Melita Borg, Rita and James, Judith Merceica, and George Gale. (Author's collection.)

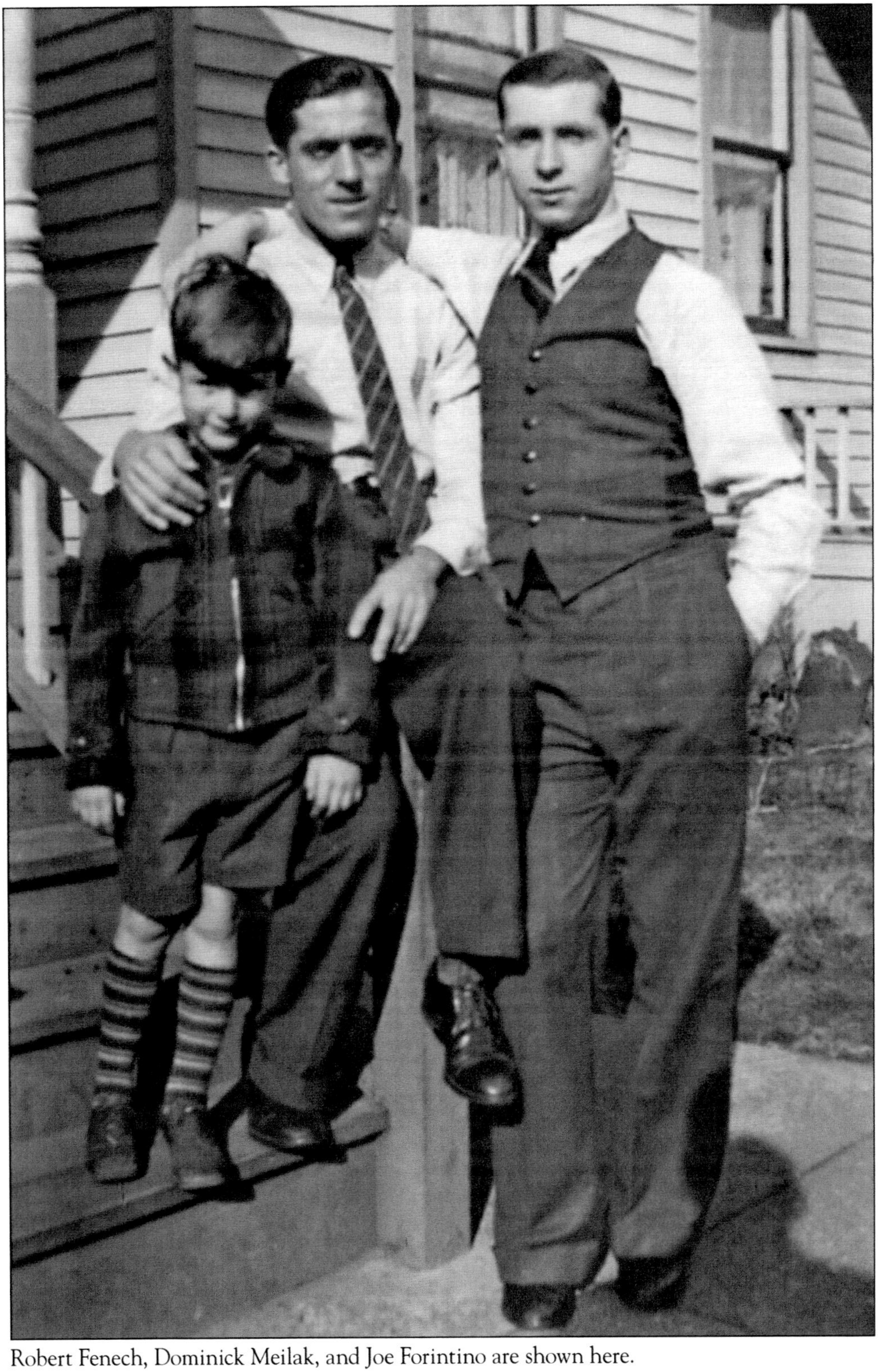

Robert Fenech, Dominick Meilak, and Joe Forintino are shown here.

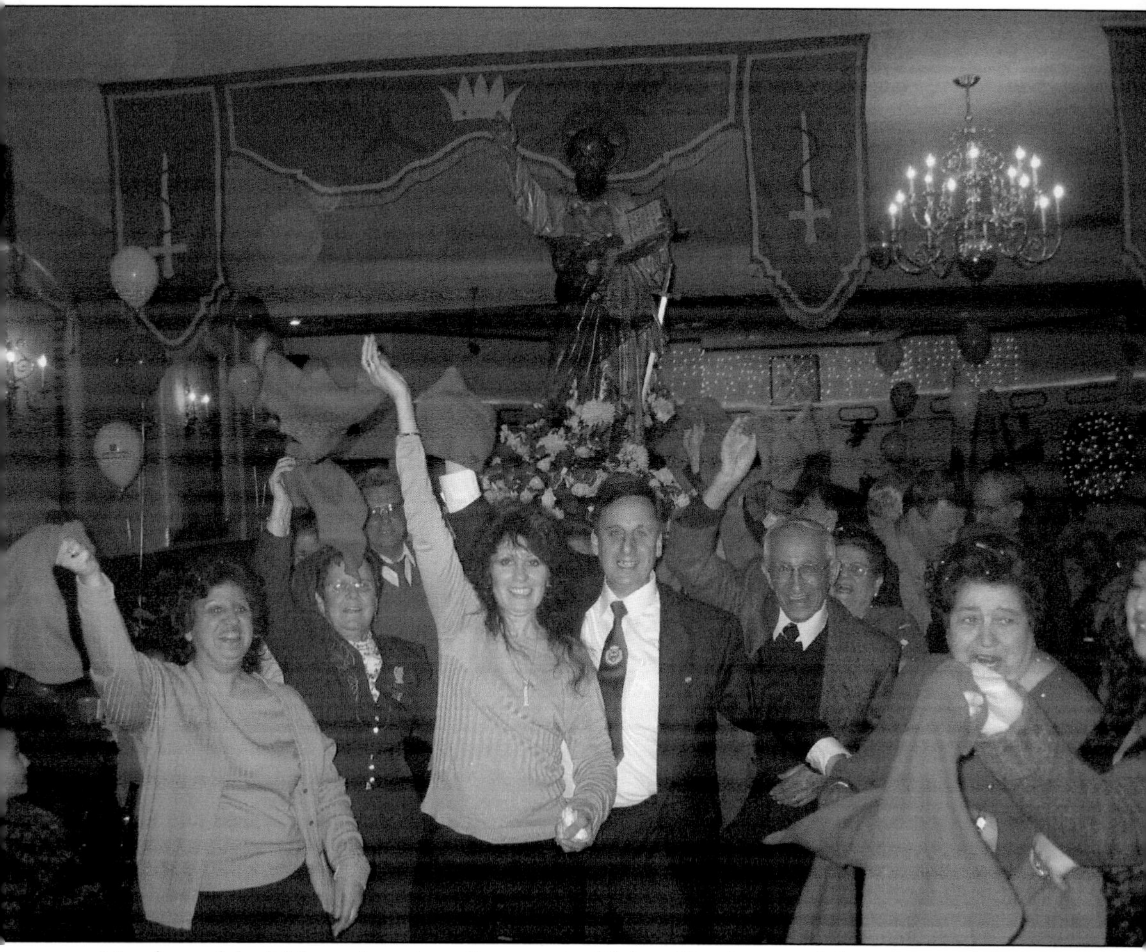

Members of the Maltese American Community Club in Dearborn and their guests celebrate at a party to commemorate the Feast of St. Paul at the club around 2005. (Courtesy of Paul Borg.)

From left to right, Robert, Mary Ann, and Francis Fenech are shown on Labrosse Street. (Courtesy of Frances Fenech.)

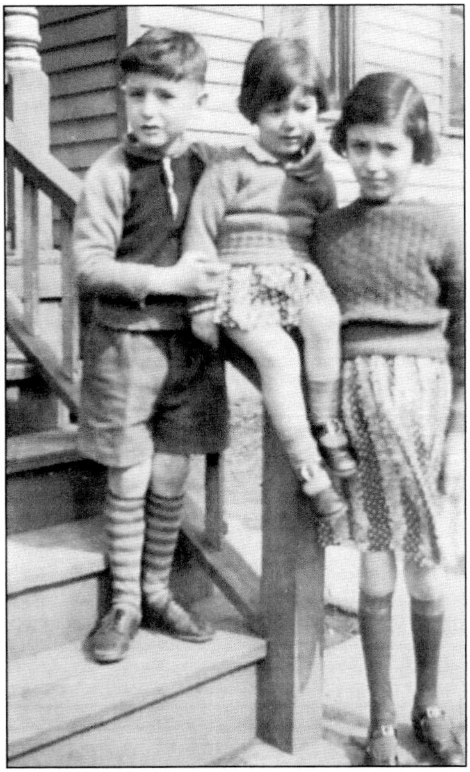

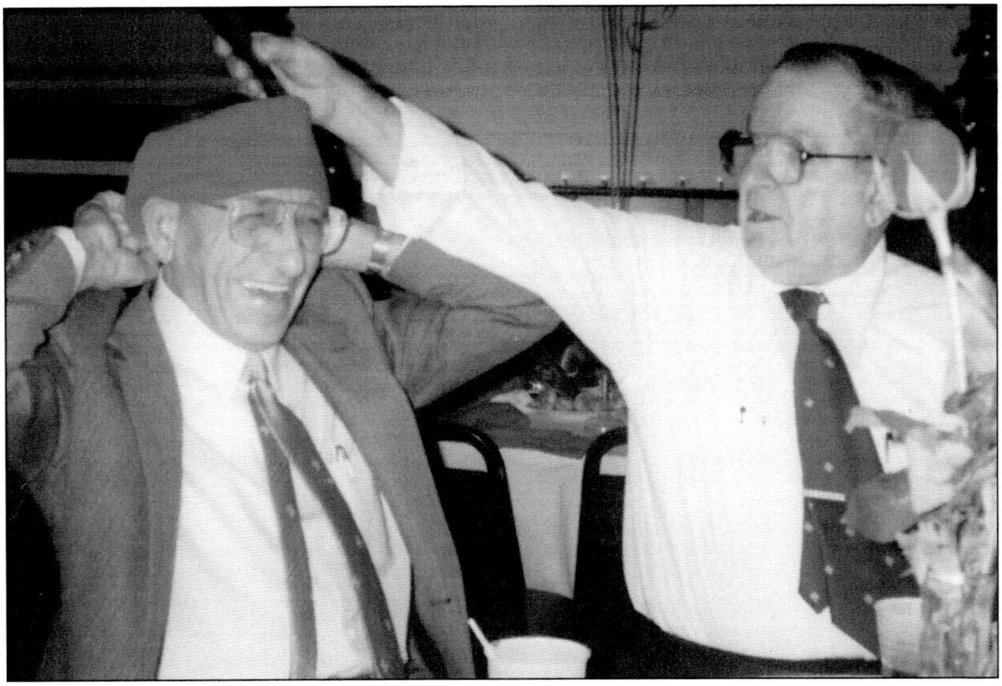

Andrew Pace and Louis Buhagiar are shown at the Dearborn Maltese club in 2002. Andrew worked for Parke Davis, and Louis worked for Ford Motor Company. Louis raised four children, and Andrew had six children. (Courtesy of Lisa Underwood.)

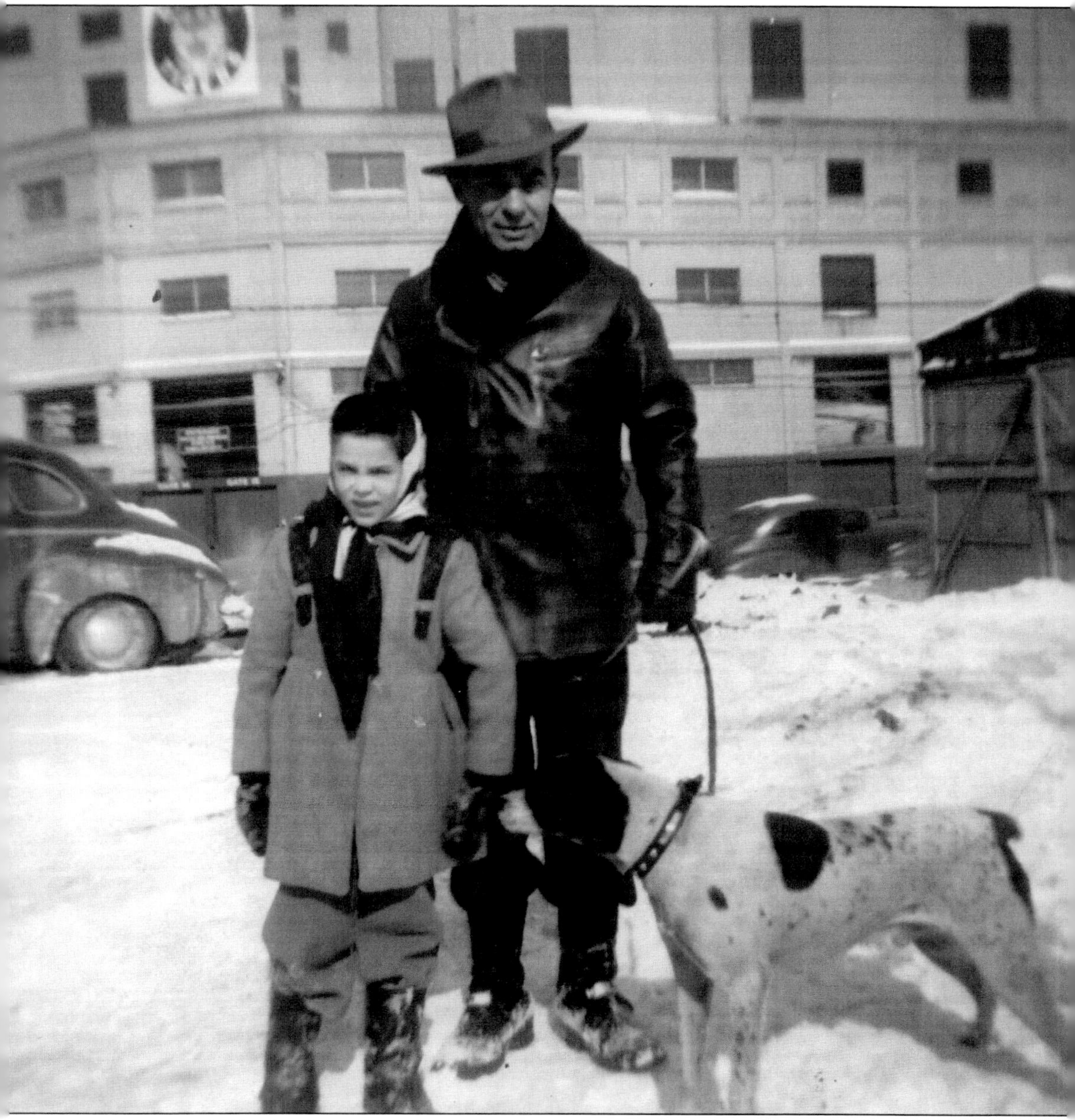

Carmen and Charles Attard are shown here just outside of Tiger Stadium, obviously during the offseason. (Courtesy of Theresa [Attard] Srock.)

Joe, Freddie, Paul, and Carmen Attard are pictured here. Carmen and Freddie are brother and sister, and Joe and Paul are their uncles. (Courtesy of Theresa [Attard] Srock.)

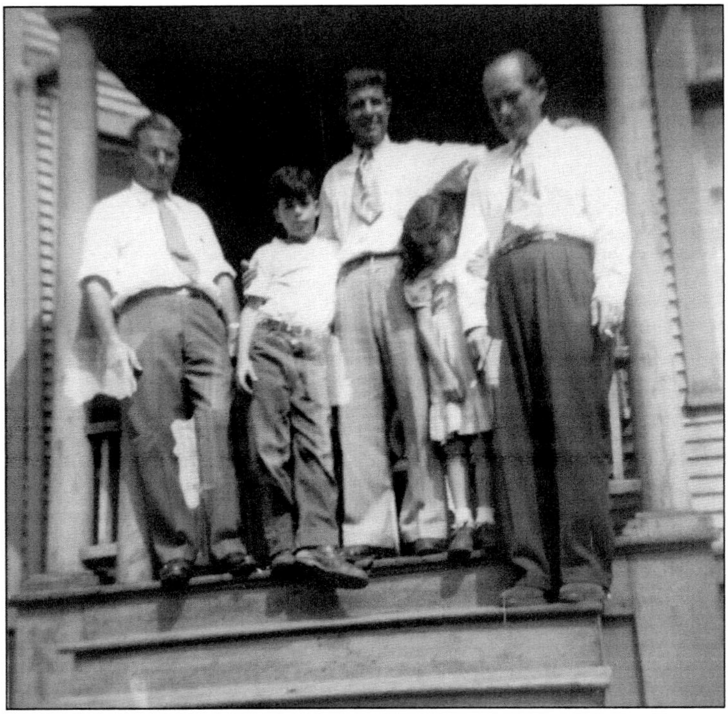

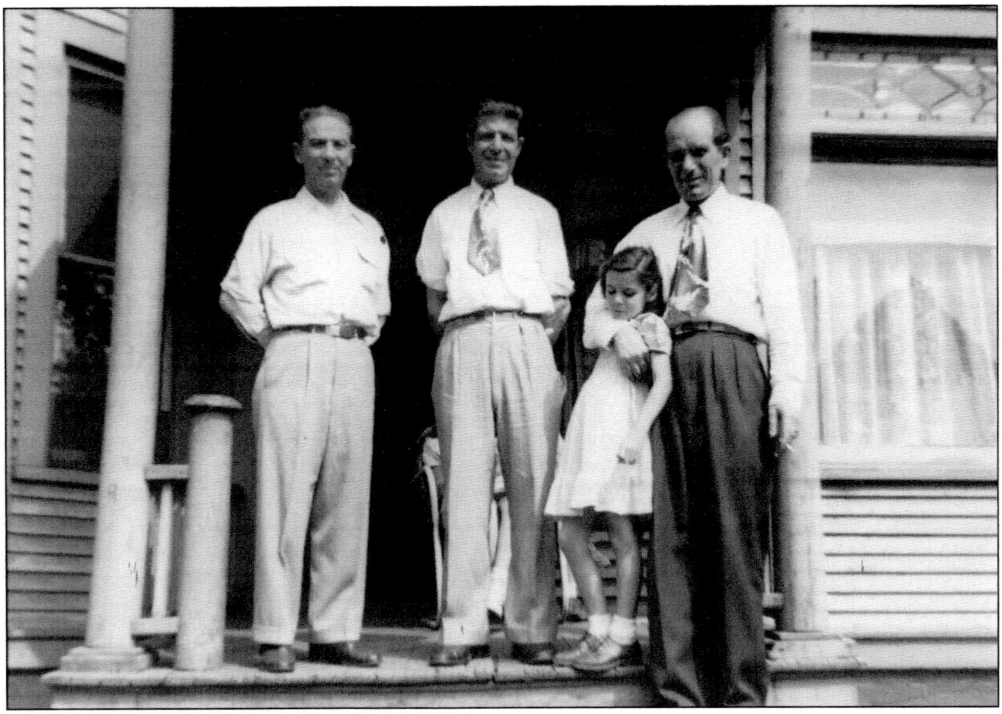

Here is Joe, Charles, Paul, and Carmen Attard; Carmen is with her father, Charles, and her uncle Paul. (Courtesy of Theresa [Attard] Srock.)

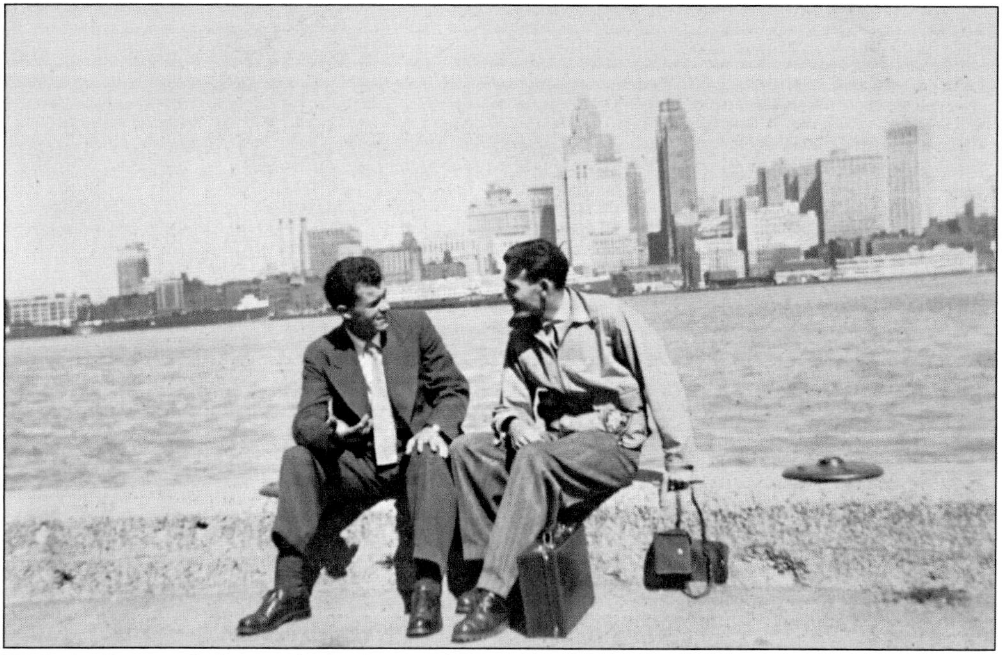

With the Detroit skyline in the background, Tony Pons and an unidentified person are shown in Windsor, Canada. (Courtesy of Tony Pons.)

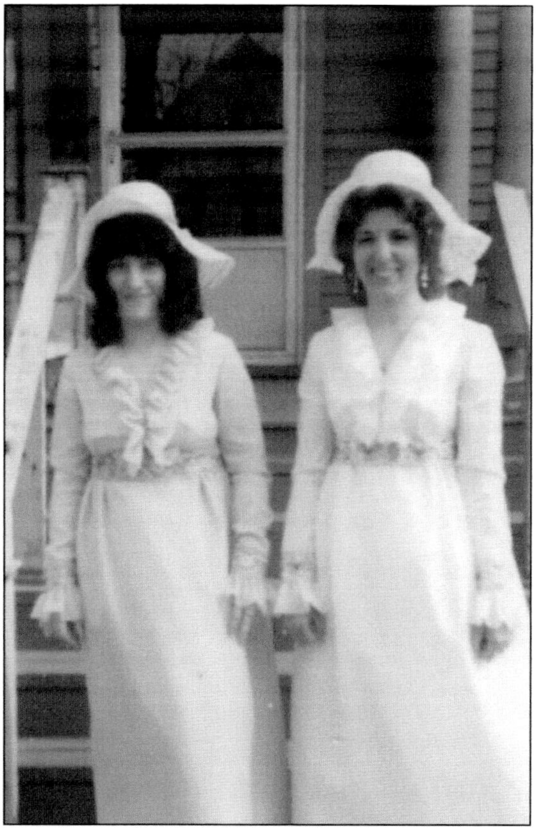

Cathy Czarnecki and Mary Ann Fenech were in the wedding party for John and Sylvia Fenech in 1982. Mary Ann was the maid-of-honor, and Cathy was a bridesmaid. (Courtesy of Norma Jean Philip.)

Seven

Clubs Serve the Community at Large

Apparently the first attempt to form a Maltese club in Detroit was made in 1920 by Tony Agius. Agius rented a small tenement on Michigan Avenue and created a meeting place for his friends. A club that followed was the Maltese Social Club, located on Trumbull and Porter Streets, which was headed by Joseph Fasi. A more formal Maltese club in Detroit began around 1922 and was called the Sons of Malta, with president John Spiteri. It was located on Howard and Third Streets. Other Maltese clubs followed.

The Independent Maltese Club of Detroit was established in 1940 and relocated to the current facility at 1832 Michigan Avenue in Detroit. The nonprofit club took on the new name of the Maltese American Benevolent Society, Inc. An eight-member executive board runs the organization, and membership had been limited to Maltese, their descendents, and their non-Maltese spouses. In 2007, the bylaws were changed to allow non-Maltese membership. The famous Maltese pastizzis are also sold at both clubs.

The Maltese American Community Club of Dearborn, Michigan, was organized by Maltese immigrants in 1958, and the first president was George Zammit. In 1972, the club joined other local Maltese clubs in organizing charter trips to Malta. Since the club did not have a building in the early days, members met to plan activities in basements, restaurants, and other locations. Annually the club organized a dance on New Year's Eve, which was the most popular event. In 1979, the Dearborn club bought a building, formerly owned by the Ukrainian American organization, on Oakman Boulevard in Dearborn. "The building needed extensive work both inside and out," commented Larry J. Zahra, past club president and the Detroit area's consul general of Malta. "Many club members volunteered to help, bringing skills from all walks of life, to renovate the facility. The hard work continued for a number of years and still takes place today as constant improvements are made to the facility. . . . Ed Carwan was the most memorable president, because he was able to pull together the community and all types of resources to make the purchase of the building happen," Zahra said. "Since his term as president, he has been followed by other leaders of the community who have volunteered their time and energy." Other club presidents include Horace Spiteri, Ninu Abela, Edward Camilleri, Anthony Camilleri, Robert Fenech, Sam Flask, Larry Zahra, and Paul Borg.

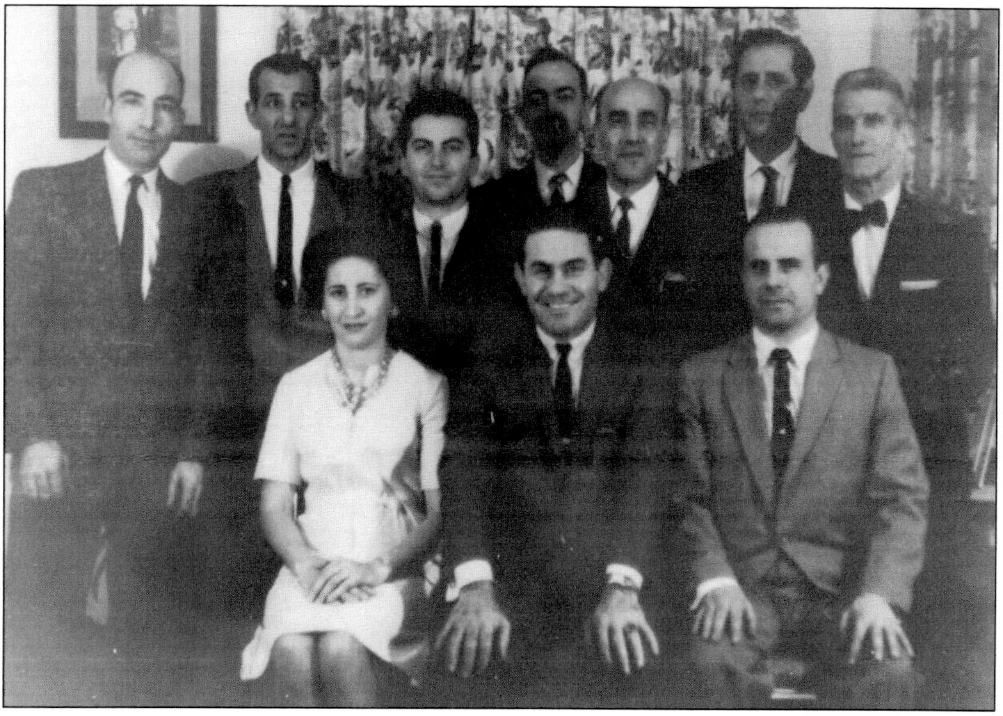

Here are the first organizers of the Maltese American Community Club in Dearborn in 1958. They are, from left to right, (first row) Carmen Borg, correspondent secretary; George Zammit, president; and Nino Abela, treasurer; (second row) Manuel Farrugia, entertainment chairman; Anthony Fenech, trustee; and Paul Scibberas, trustee; (third row) Larry Grech, secretary; William Parnis, vice president; and Frank Borg, trustee. (Courtesy of the Maltese American Community Club.)

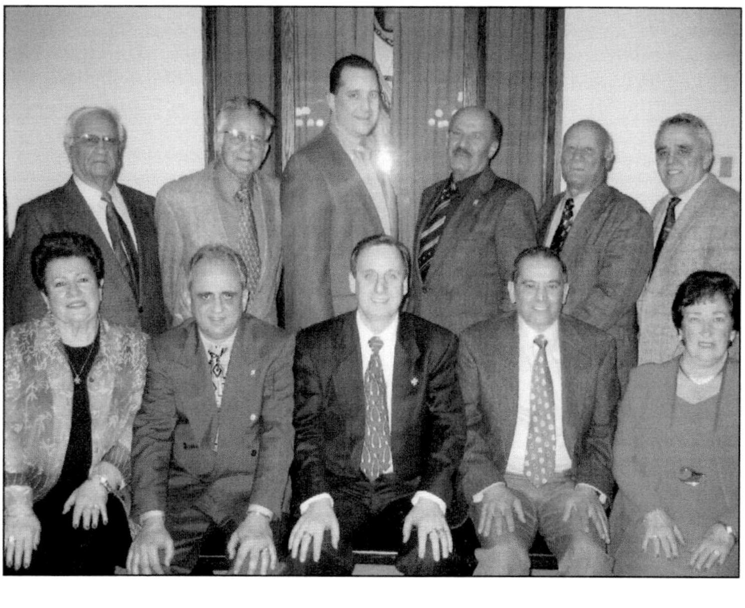

These 2010 Maltese American Community Club Committee members are, from left to right, (seated) Maria Coyle, Sam Flask, Paul Borg, Joseph Formosa, and Elsie Spiteri; (standing) Mike Camilleri, Manny Agius, John Micallef, Piju Muscat, Joseph Chetuti, and George Theuma.

Paul Borg has served as president of the Maltese American Community Club in Dearborn since 2000 and was named Maltese consul to Michigan in 2010. Born in Malta, Borg is married to Angela and has two sons, Shawn and Paul Christian. He launched Printwell Acquisitions, Inc. in Taylor with Angela in 1983. It grew to be one of the largest commercial printing companies in Michigan. While serving as club president, Borg sponsored many Maltese musicians, including world-famous tenor Joesph Calleja in November 2010. Borg also developed a website for the Maltese American Community club, www.MalteseAmericanClub.org. (Courtesy of Paul Borg.)

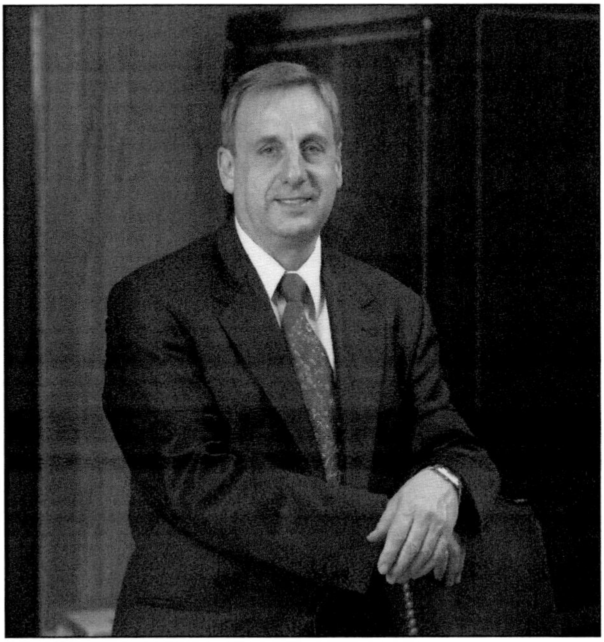

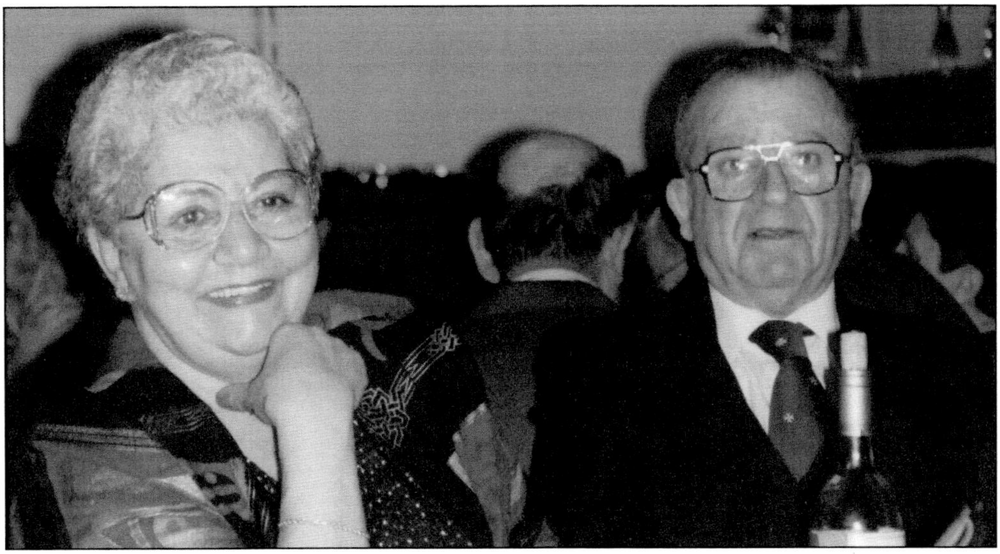

Mary and Louis Buhagiar are shown at the Maltese American Community Club in Dearborn. "At every club function, they made the desserts and donated them to the club," stated Joe Formosa, the club's vice president. (Courtesy of Lisa Norwood.)

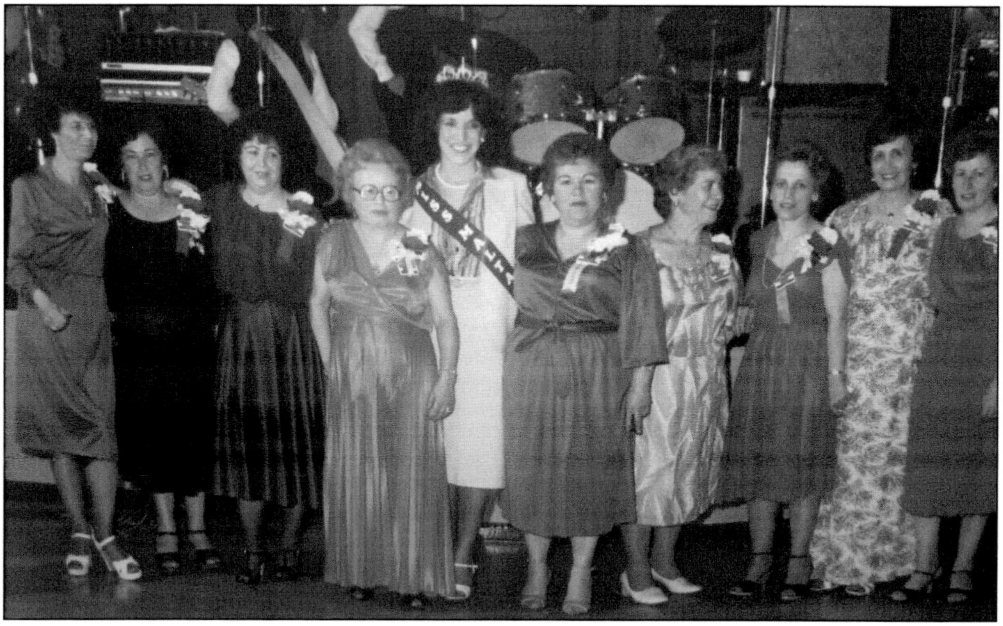

Pictured around 1980, members of the Maltese American Community Club Woman's Auxiliary included Mary Grech, Elsie Spiteri, Censina Caruan, Rose Cam, the Dearborn Maltese club's first Miss Malta Diane DeBono, Richie Muscat, Maria Grech, Mary Abela, Gracie Farrugia, and Lena Saracino. Muscat started the women's group and worked hard to make sure the Maltese club in Dearborn opened and remained viable. (Courtesy of Richie Muscat.)

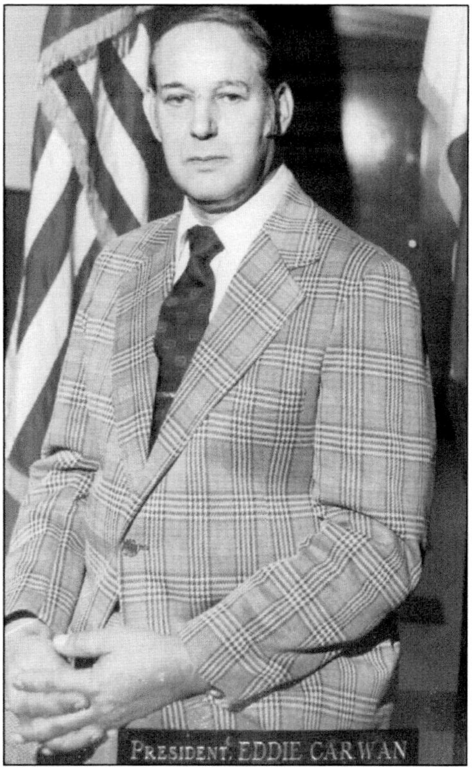

Eddie Carwan was one of the first presidents of the Maltese club in Dearborn. (Courtesy of Maltese American Community Club.)

This sign hangs on the building at the Maltese American Benevolent Society of Detroit. The building is maintained well on the inside and out in an area that has been deluged with urban blight. The Maltese club stands as one of the few buildings in the area that serve as beacons of hope for a long sought-after revitalization in the city.

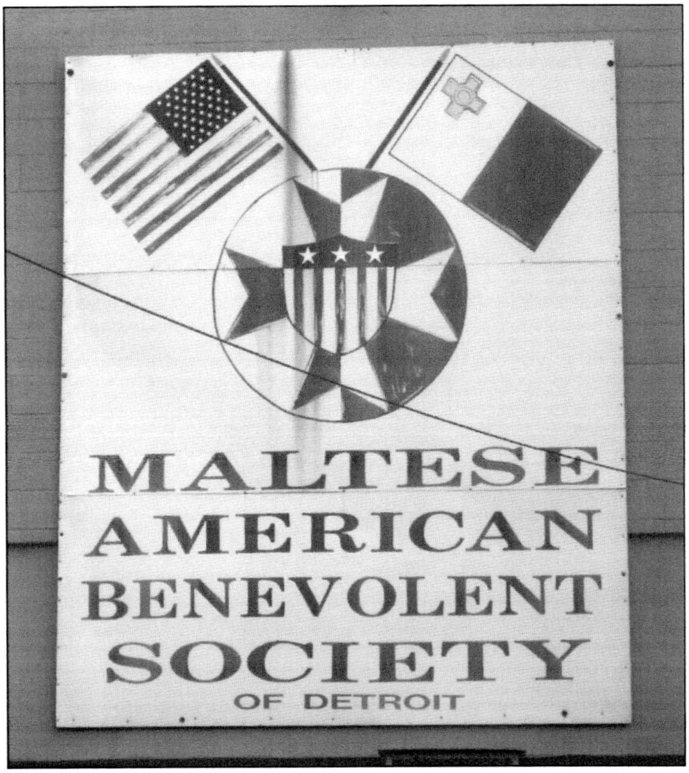

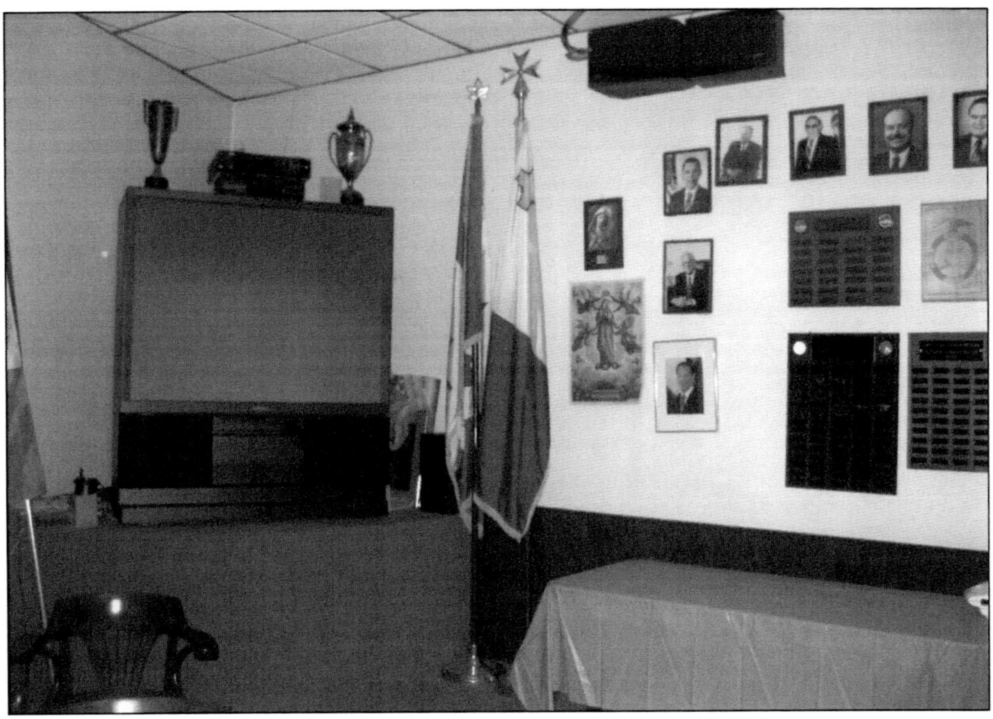

This photograph is from the inside the Maltese American Benevolent Society in Detroit and shows the trophies won by Maltese sports teams.

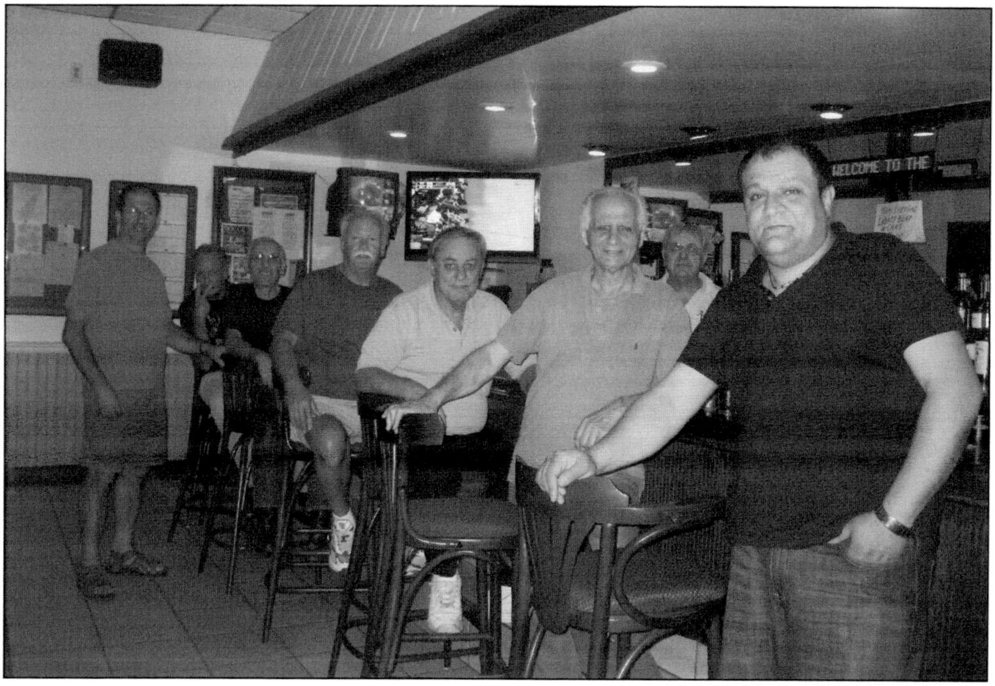

During the summer of 2010, men gather at the bar at the Maltese American Benevolent Society of Detroit. The Maltese club on Michigan Avenue remained well kept over the years while many businesses left in the area were in a decaying state.

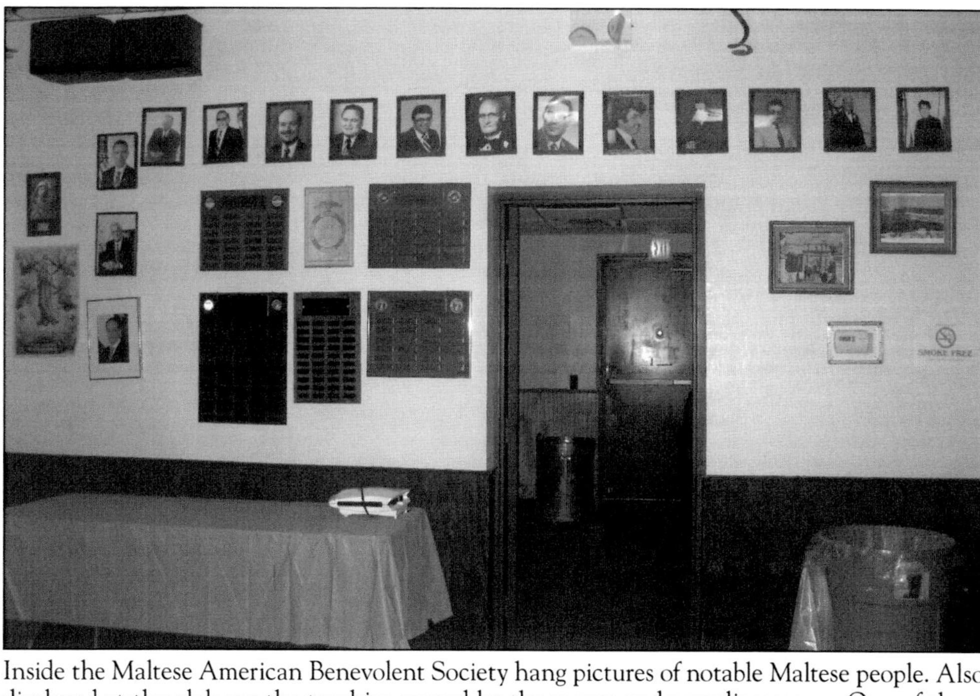

Inside the Maltese American Benevolent Society hang pictures of notable Maltese people. Also displayed at the club are the trophies earned by the soccer and wrestling teams. One of those pictures is of Mikel Scicluna, who was born in Malta and involved in the World Wide Wrestling Federation. He was also known as the "Baron" and "Mikel Valentino."

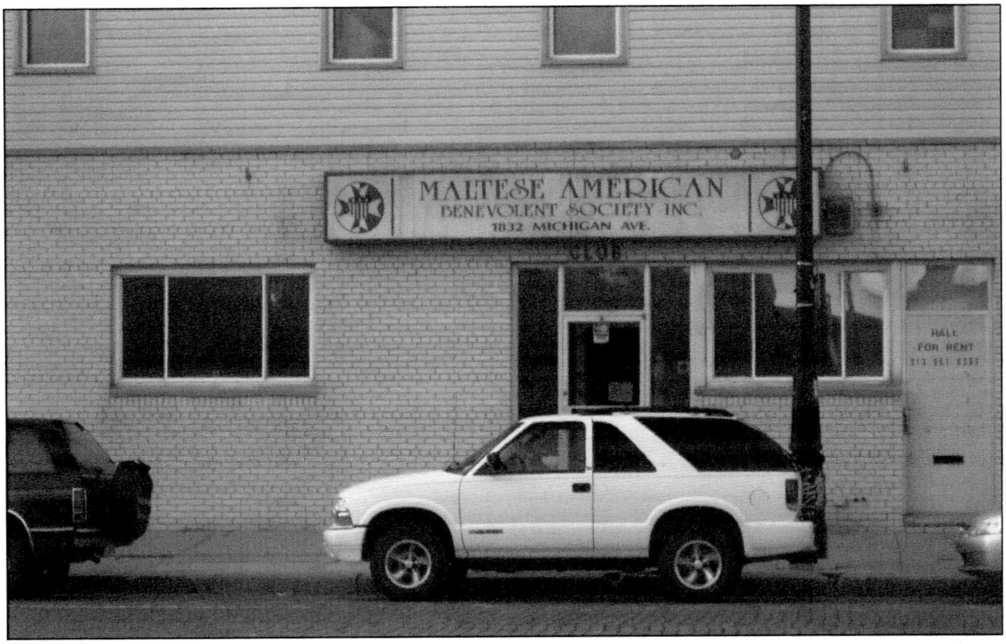

Maltese American Benevolent Society of Detroit is located at 1832 Michigan Avenue. There were various clubs that served the Maltese before the onset of this Michigan location. Each of the clubs served as a place for immigrants and their descendents to find other Maltese in an effort to socialize.

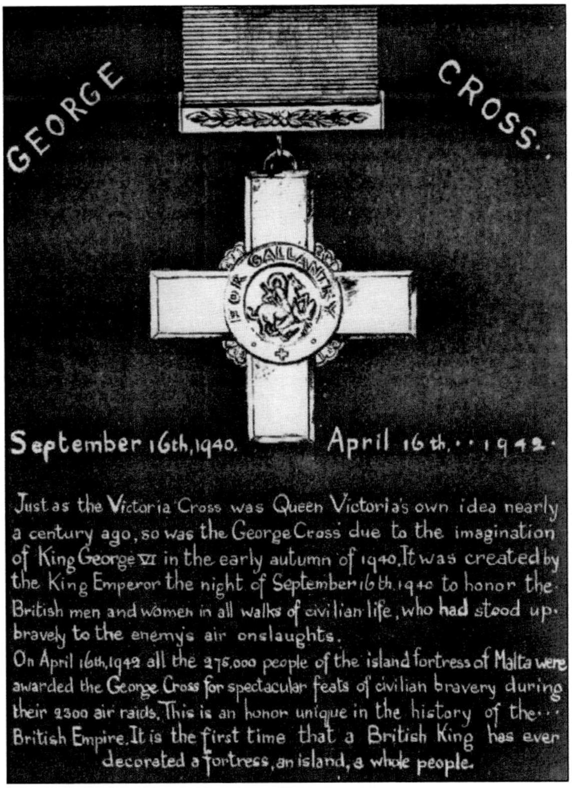

This is an explanation of the George Cross, which hangs in the Maltese American Community Club in Dearborn. Maltese immigrants and their descendants continue to take great pride in this honor. It says the following: "September 16, 1940. April 16, 1942, just as the Victoria Cross was Queen Victoria's own idea nearly a century ago, so was the George Cross due to the imagination of King George VI in the early autumn 1940. It was created by the King Emperor the night of September 16, 1940, to honor the British men and women in all walks of civilian life, who had stood up bravely to the enemy's air onslaughts. On April 16, 1942, all the 275,000 people of the island fortress of Malta were awarded the George Cross for spectacular feats of civilian bravery during their 2,300 air raids. This is an honor unique in the history of the . . . British Empire. It is the first time that a British King has ever decorated a fortress, an island, a whole people."

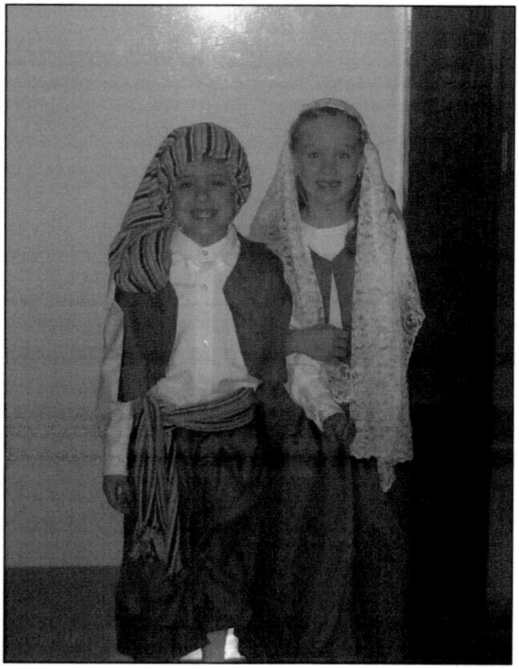

These children took part in the Miss Malta pageant at the Maltese American Community Club in Dearborn around 2005. They are wearing traditional clothes that children wore in Malta years ago. This photograph is part of archived pictures saved by the club. (Courtesy of Paul Borg.)

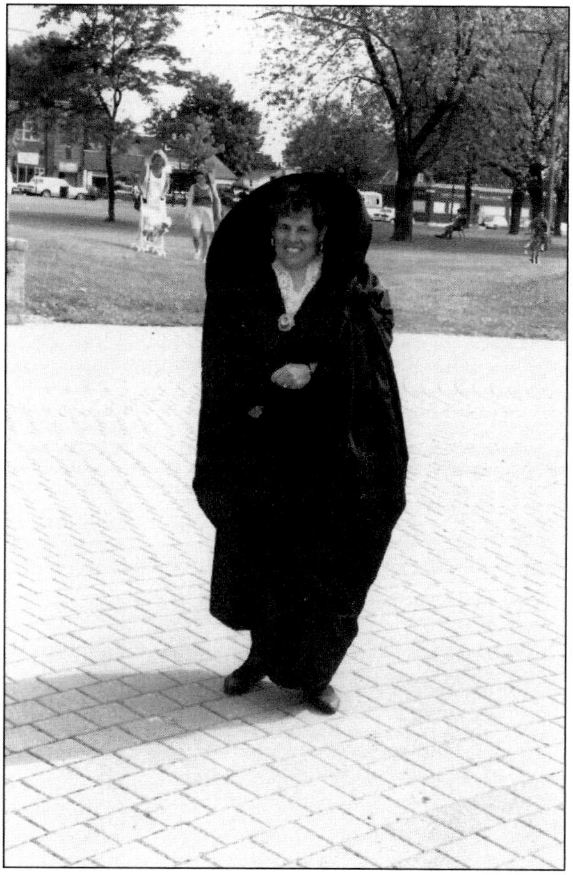

Pictured is traditional Maltese clothing. Some woman wore the ghonnella, or faldetta, until the beginning of the 20th century. Later it became a costume worn by older ladies. The ghonnella is made of black satin, using whalebones as stiffeners, while the wedding version is made of pure white satin. (Courtesy of Rose D'Amato.)

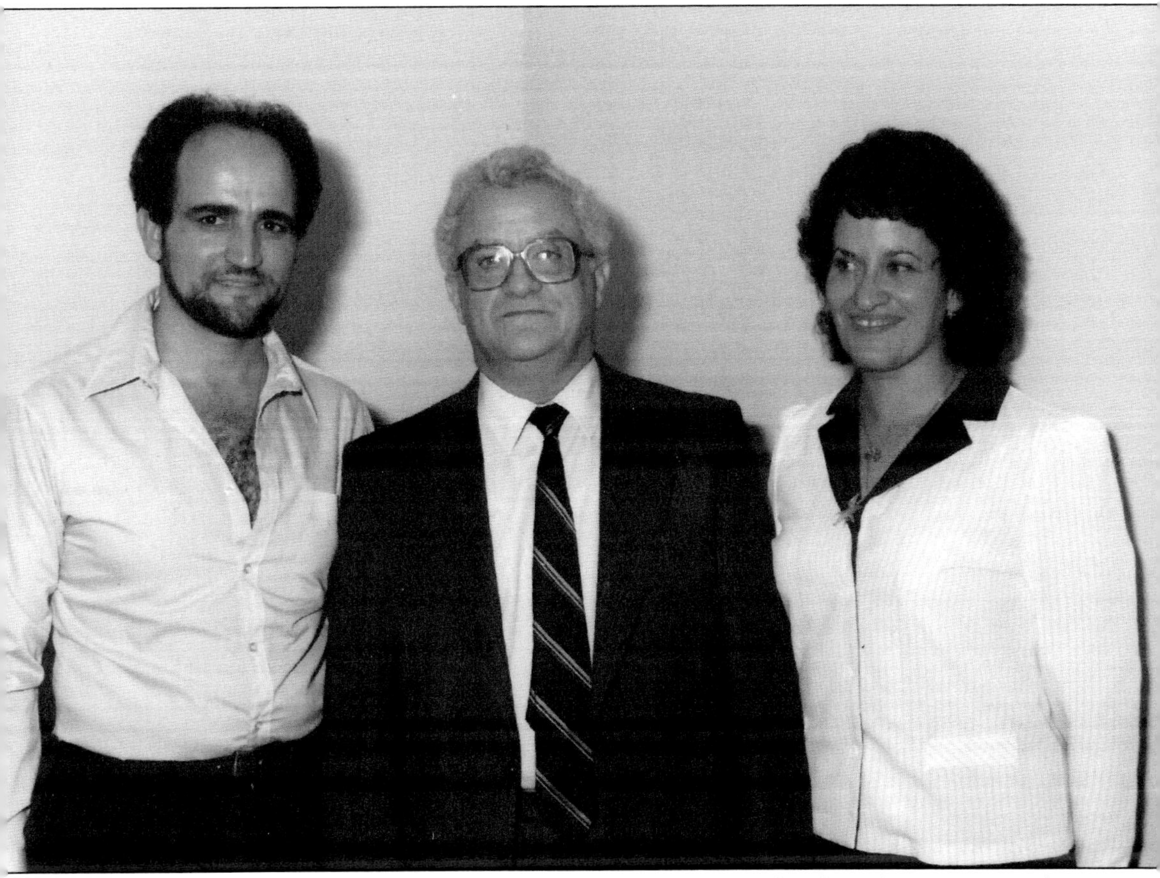

Rose and Mario D'Amato flank Maltese prime minister Eddie Fenech Adami during a visit to the Detroit area in 1986. The Canadian residents greeted him at the Maltese American Community Club in Dearborn. He was prime minister from 1987 to 1996 and from 1998 to 2004. He subsequently served as president of Malta from 2004 to 2009. (Courtesy of Rose D'Amato.)

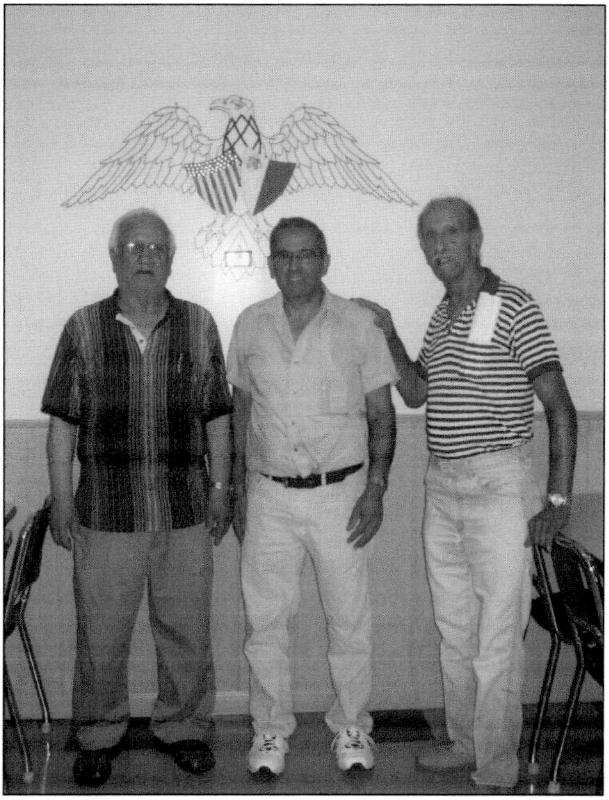

Mike Camilleri, Joe Formosa, and Joe Grech, all active members and volunteers at the Dearborn Maltese club, stand under a wall plaque in the shape of a falcon holding the Maltese and American flags.

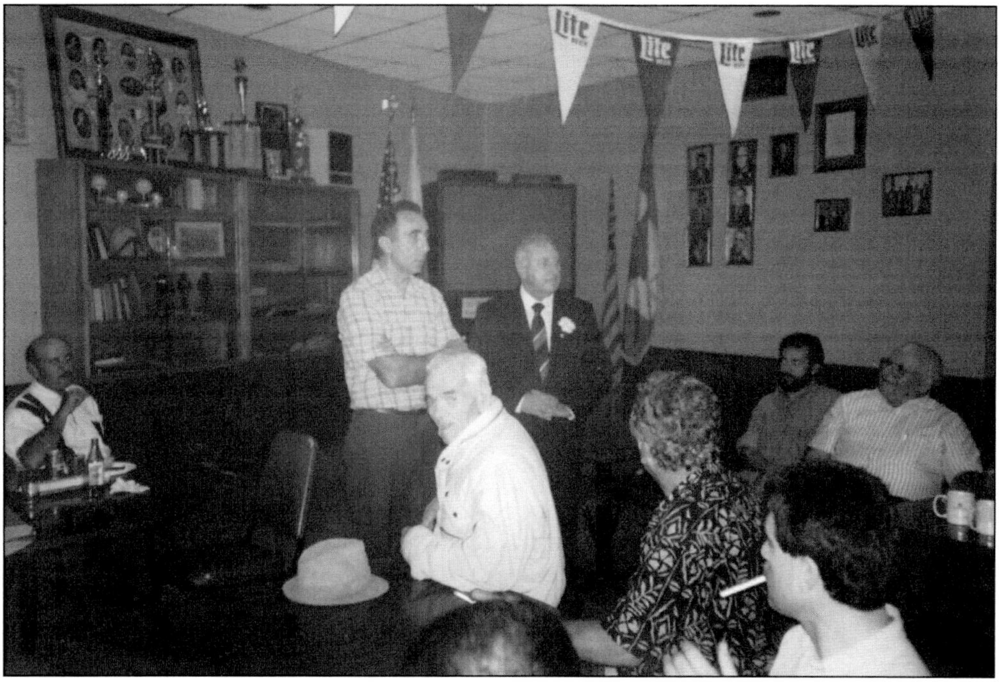

Tony Mifsud (standing, left) accompanies Maltese minister of education Vincent Tabone (standing, right) at the Maltese Benevolent Society in Detroit around 1996. (Courtesy of John Caruana.)

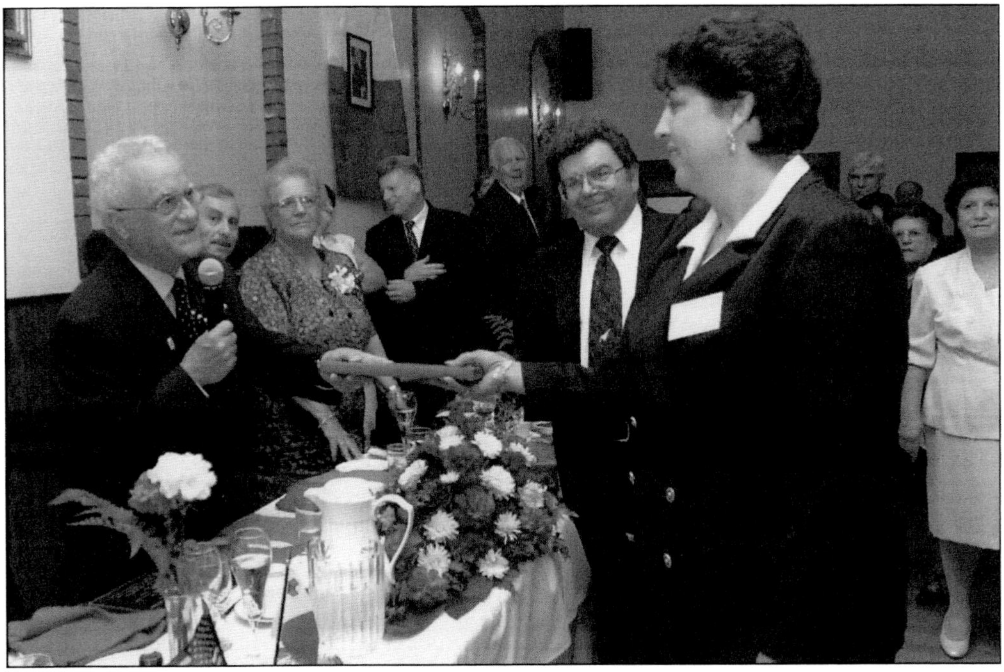

Maltese prime minister Eddie Fenech Adami greets Maltese American Benevolent Society of Detroit president Gina Nino and Maltese American Community Club president Larry Zahra. (Courtesy of Larry Zahra.)

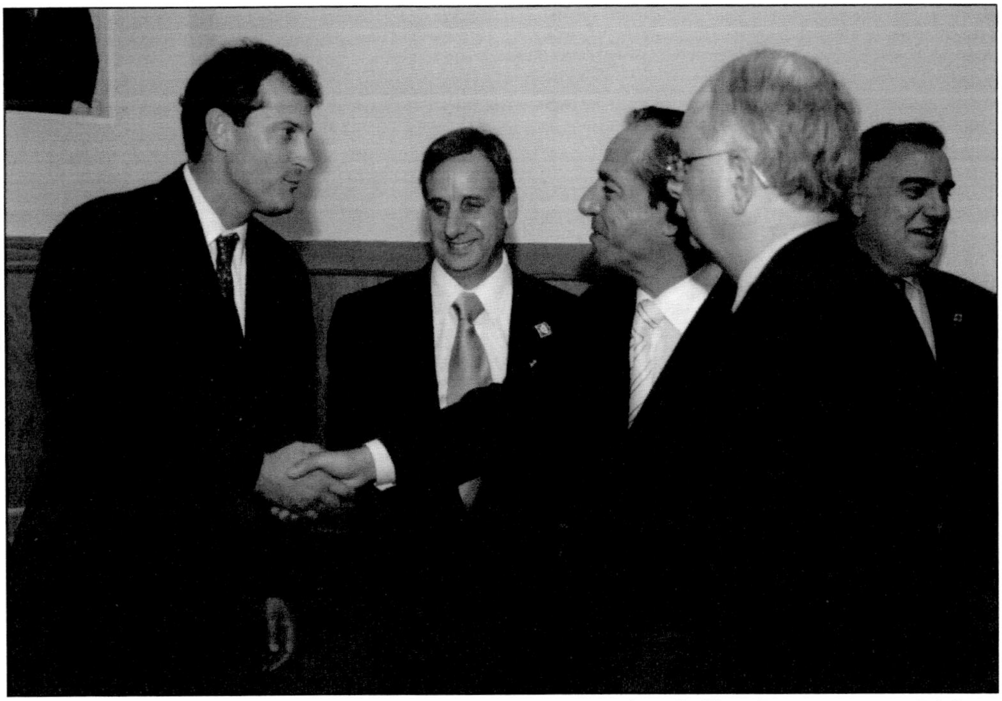

Michigan First District Court of Appeals judge Brian K. Zahra (left), a first-generation Maltese descendant, greets Maltese prime minister Lawrence Gonzi in the Dearborn Maltese club, with the club's president, Paul Borg (center), looking on. (Courtesy of Larry Zahra.)

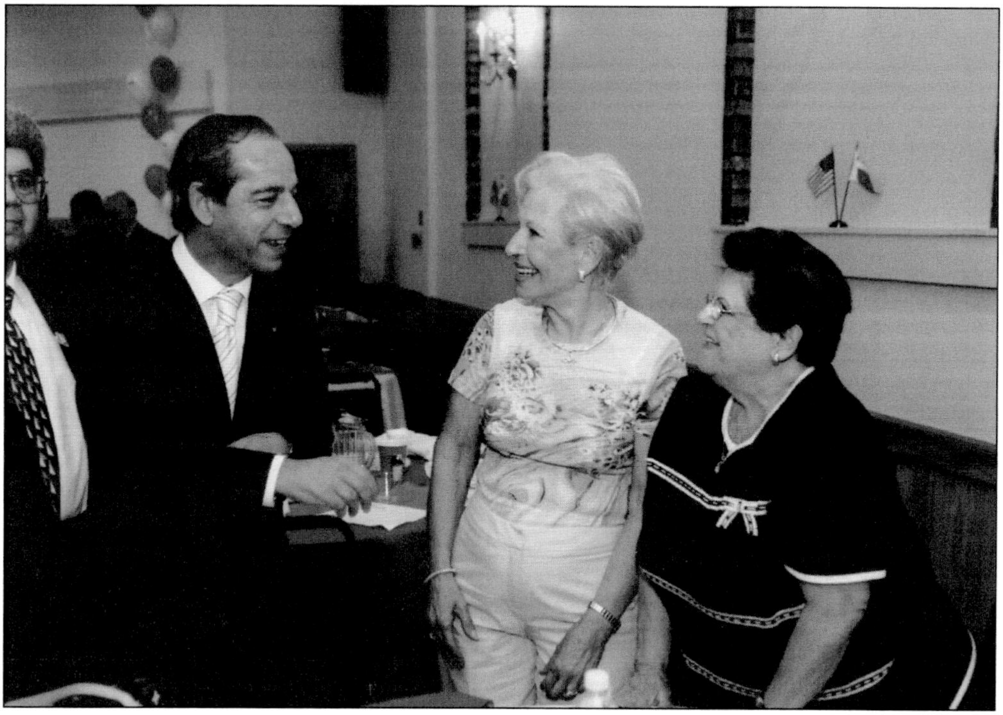

Prime minister Lawrence Gonzi talks to visitors at the Dearborn Maltese club in 2005. Visits from dignitaries like Gonzi were treated with special attention by the Maltese community, which often included Masses at local clubs, dinners, and other festivities. (Courtesy of Larry Zahra.)

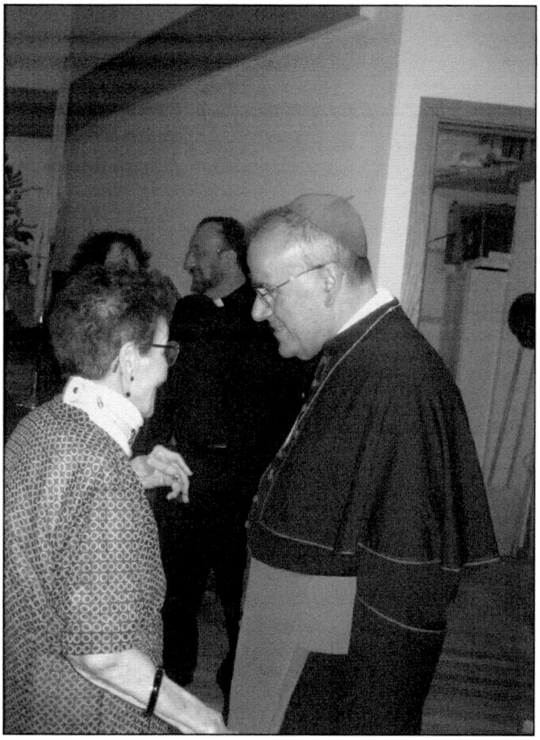

The Maltese community took part in a dinner celebration welcoming Maltese archbishop Paul Cremona during his visit to Detroit and Dearborn in 2010.

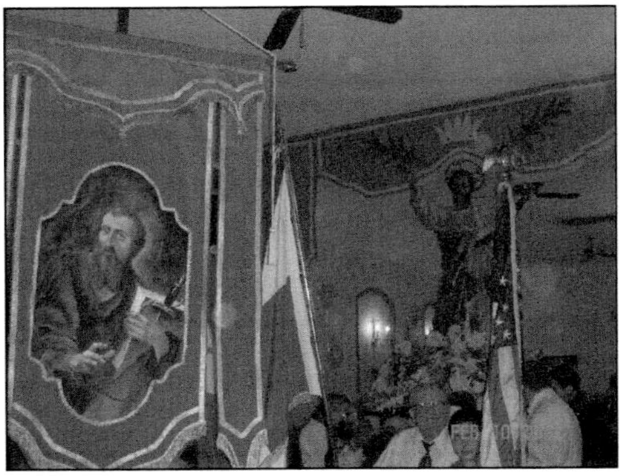

This statue of Mary (right), used during festivals at the Maltese American Community Club in Dearborn, was made in Malta by Mike Camilleri from Gozo, Malta. Decades earlier, his father, Wistin Camilleri, made this statue of St. Paul (above), which is also used during feast day processions at the Dearborn club. During these festivals, the statues are carried on the shoulders of members through the club for all to see. This has been a long-held tradition in Malta and continues today in the island nation as well as the Detroit area. (Above and right courtesy of Paul Borg.)

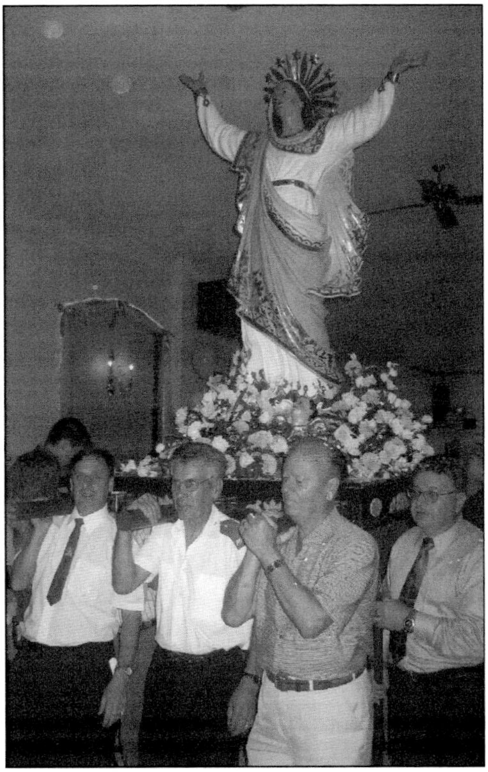

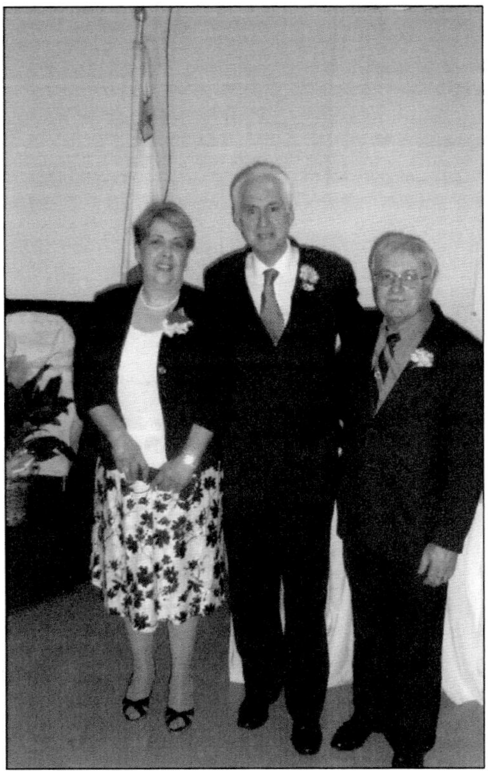

Maltese American Benevolent Society of Detroit president Carmen Nino (left) and vice president Leno Sammit (right) meet with a representative accompanying the archbishop. (Courtesy of Larry Sammit.)

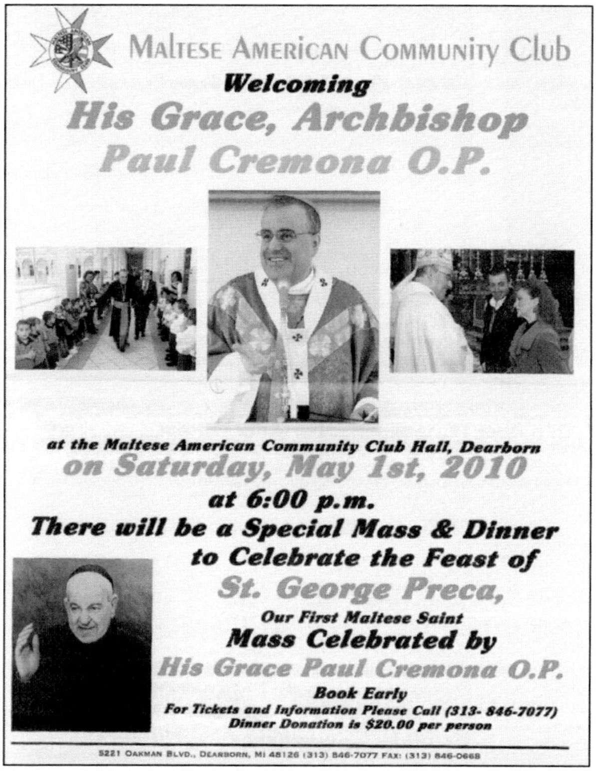

Maltese archbishop Paul Cremona visited the Maltese communities in Dearborn and Detroit. He studied at the Montessori School in Valetta, Malta, the Lyceum in Hamrun, Malta, and the Pontifical University of St. Thomas Aquinas in Rome.

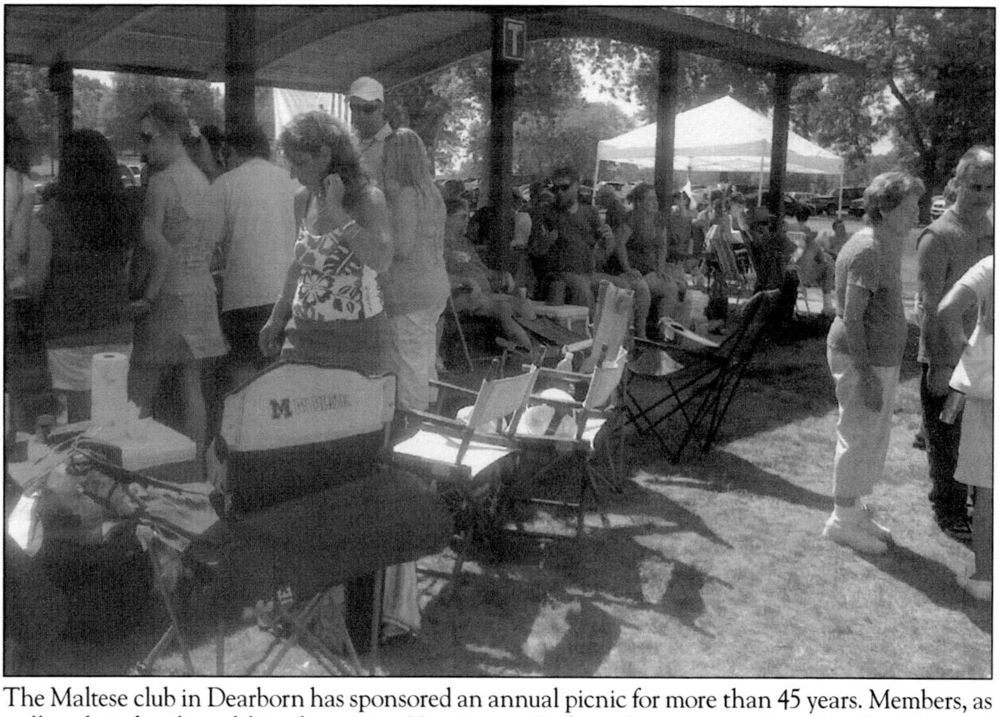

The Maltese club in Dearborn has sponsored an annual picnic for more than 45 years. Members, as well as their family and friends, meet at Kensington Park to play games and eat free food donated by Bob Farr. This image was taken at the 2008 event. (Courtesy of Paul Borg.)

Fr. Robert Cini celebrates Mass at the Maltese club in Dearborn around 2005. He retired and moved to Malta that year. (Courtesy of Paul Borg.)

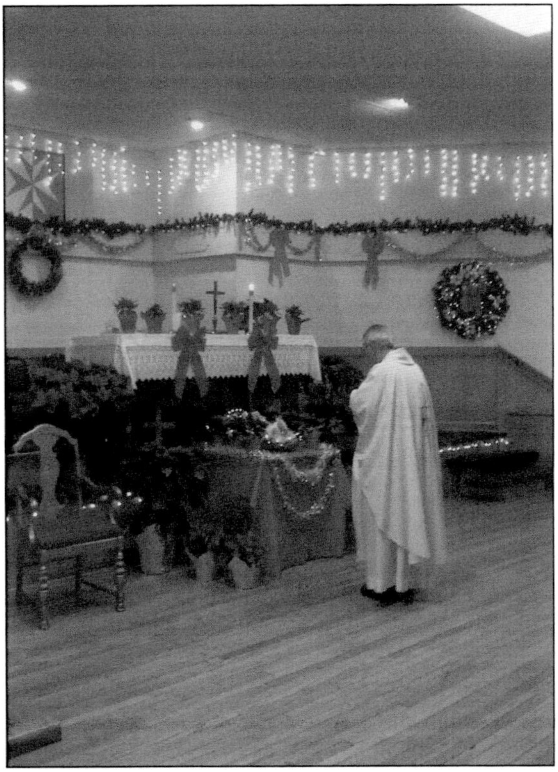

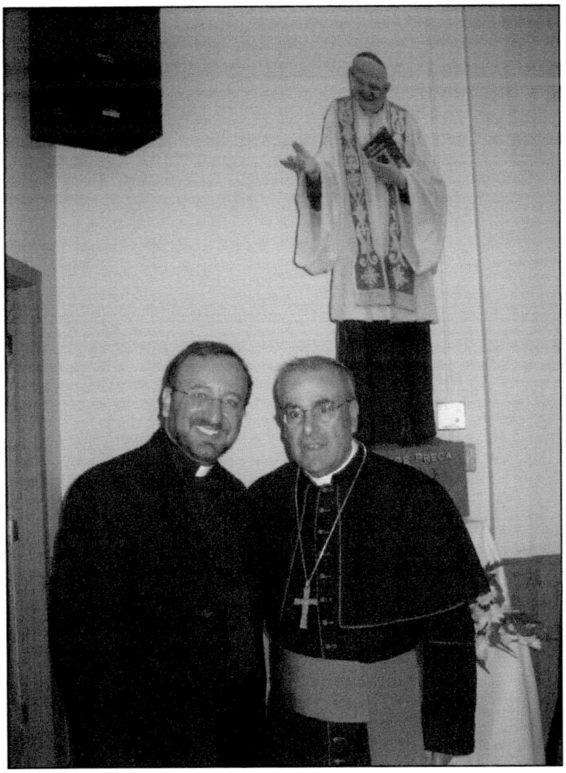

Father Mallia (left) and Maltese archbishop Paul Cremona are shown at the Maltese American Community Club in 2010. Cremona was announced as the 11th Archbishop of Malta on December 2, 2006. The ordination was in St. John the Baptist in Valetta, Malta, with the rites of ordination led by the outgoing archbishop of Malta, Joseph Merceica.

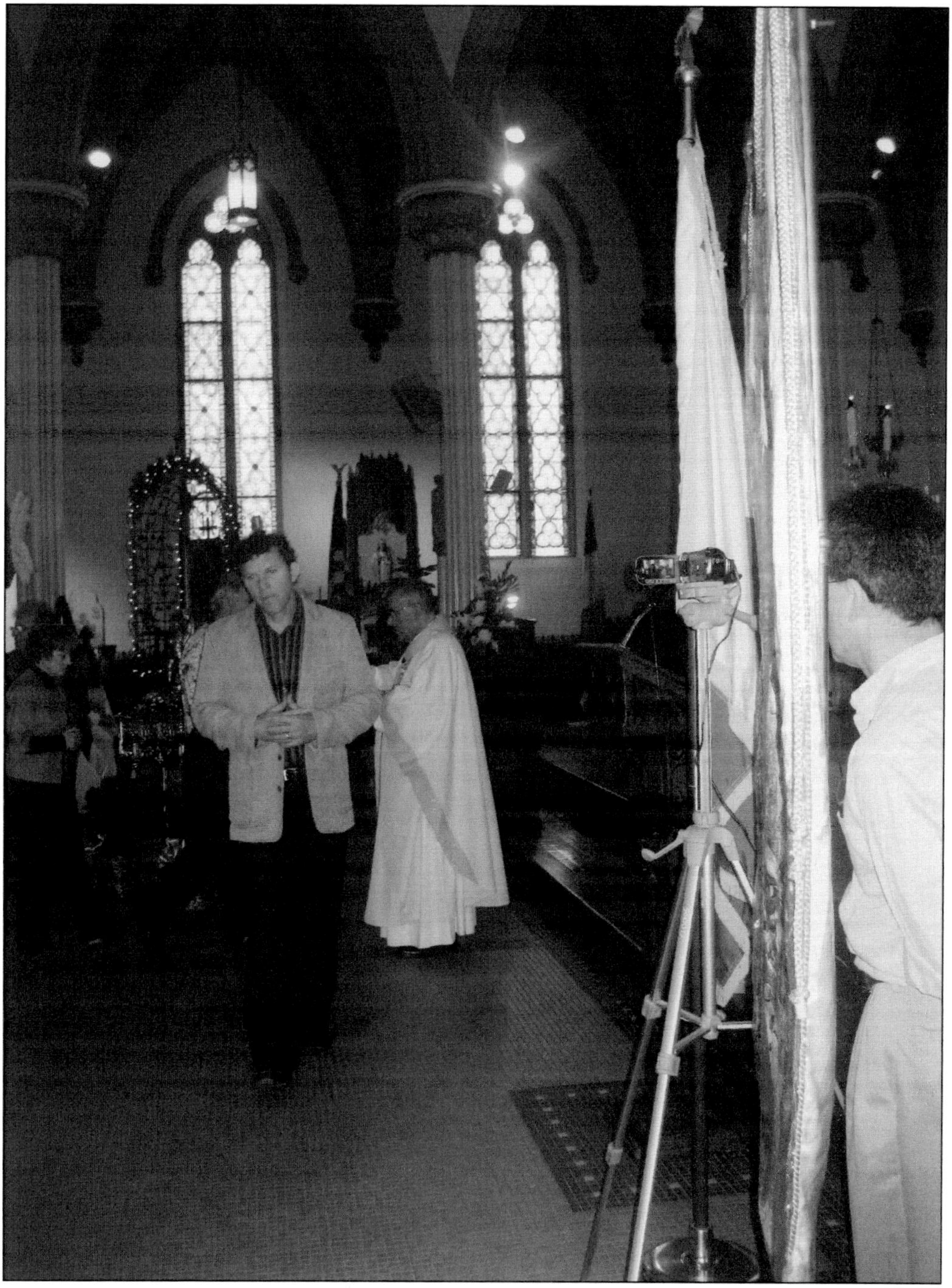

Archbishop Paul Cremona is shown giving Communion at Most Holy Trinity Church in Detroit during his visit in 2010.

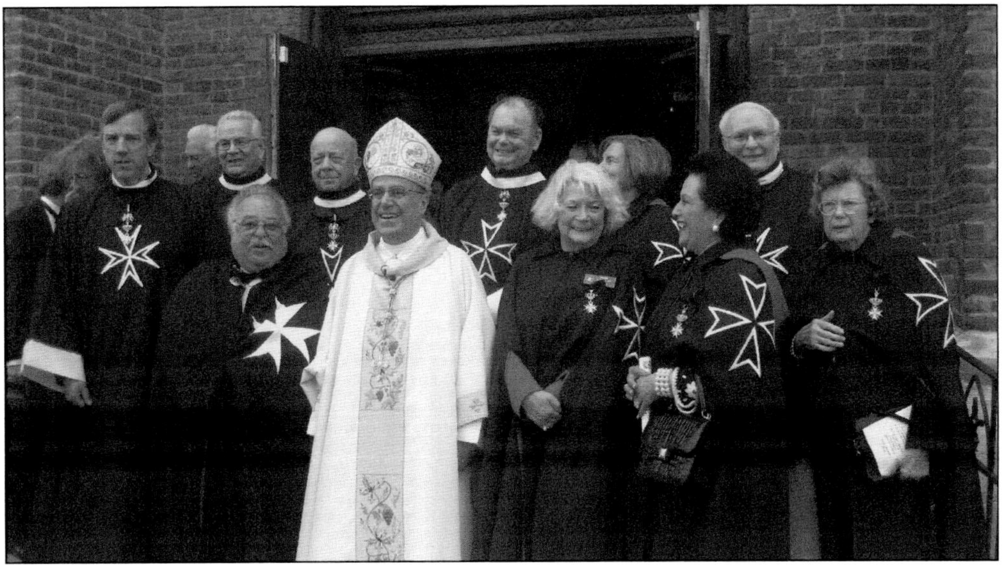

Knights and Dames of Malta attended a Mass at Most Holy Trinity Church in Corktown in 2010. The service was presided over by Maltese Archbishop Paul Cremona. The Knights of the Order of St. John of Jerusalem were formed in 1085, or possibly 1099, as a community of monks responsible for looking after the sick at the Hospital of St. John in Jerusalem. They later became a military order, defending crusader territory in the Holy Lands and safeguarding the routes taken by medieval pilgrims. The Knights and Dames support programs in 75 countries. In 2009, there were 99 men and women invested in the cross. They promised to bear witness to and defend the church, to live their lives accordingly, and care for the sick and poor. The Dames of Malta are female members of the Sovereign Military Hospitaller Order of St. John of Jerusalem, of Rhodes, and of Malta.

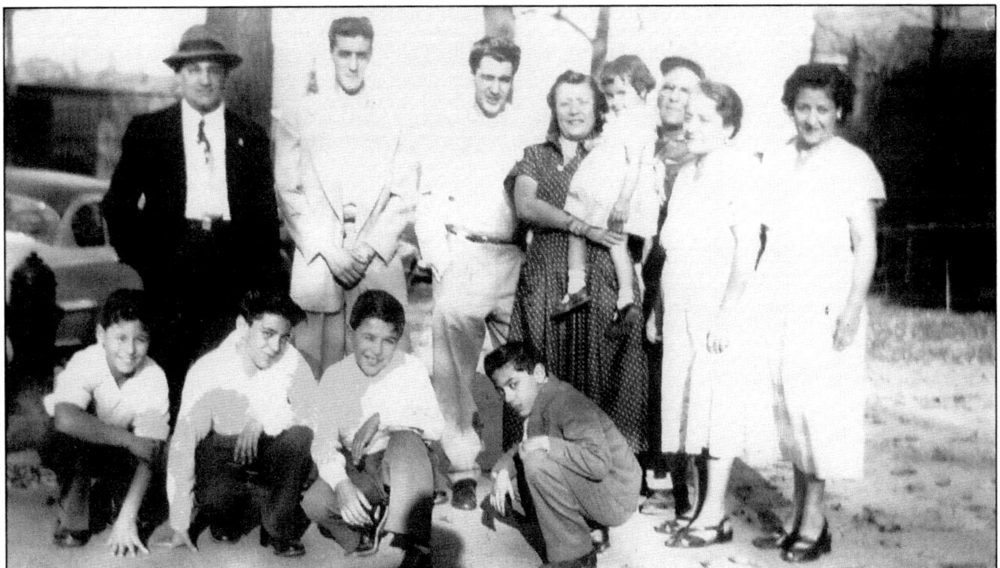

Family gatherings like this one were common. Emmanuel DeBono, Frank DeBono, Emmanuel DeBono, Delores DeBono, Linda Gale, John B. Haley, Nina Haley, and Rita Gale are shown standing; those kneeling are James Gale, Joe DeBono, Charles Gale, and Vic DeBono. (Courtesy of Linda Morasso.)

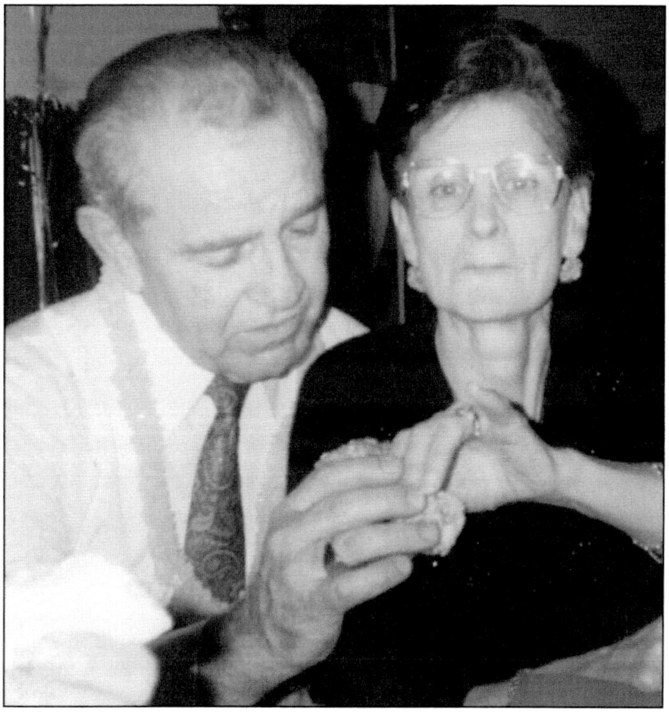

Joe and Pauline Vassallo are shown at a New Year's Eve party at the Maltese American Community Club in Dearborn in 2002. Joe worked at Parke Davis. They raised two daughters. (Courtesy of Lisa Norwood.)

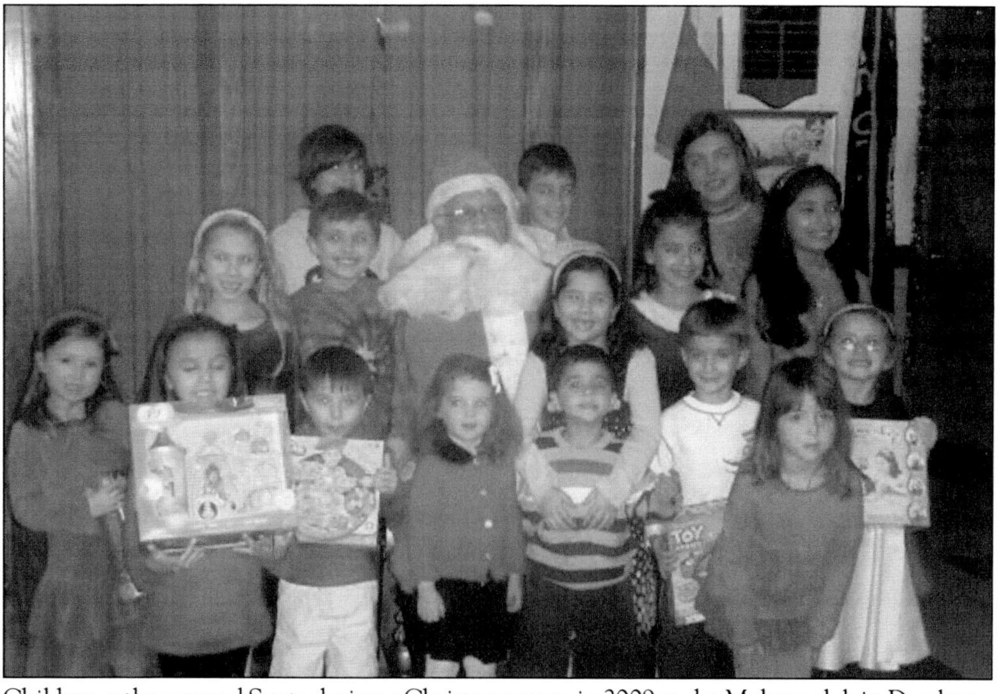

Children gather around Santa during a Christmas party in 2009 at the Maltese club in Dearborn. (Courtesy of Danielle Diacono.)

Eight

Maltese Today

Many Maltese who once lived in Corktown have moved to surrounding communities, like Dearborn Heights, Redford, Livonia, downriver cities, and even across the river to Canada. However, there are still many Maltese living in Corktown and other parts of Detroit, and they remain proud of the community that the first Maltese immigrants found when they left Malta. Images representing the community can be found at Most Holy Trinity Church, which displays a Maltese flag.

In the 2008 American Community Survey, there were an estimated 50,691 Maltese Americans, which was up from the 2000 United States Census that listed some 40,159 Americans who claimed Maltese ancestry. This includes Maltese-born immigrants to the United States, their American-born descendants, as well as numerous immigrants of Maltese origin from other nations.

The Maltese clubs in Detroit and Dearborn continue to thrive with events, including the Miss Malta pageants, visits from church hierarchy from Malta, and feast day dinners.

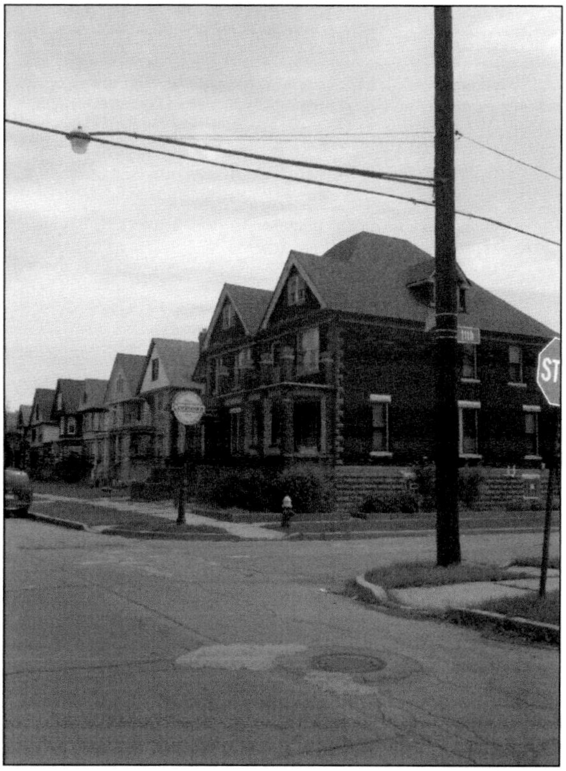

Here is Church and Eleventh Streets in Corktown in 2010. Detroit's Corktown is the oldest neighborhood in Detroit. In 2010, the boundaries were Interstate 75 to the north, the Lodge Freeway to the east, Bagley and Porter Streets to the south, and Rosa Parks and Twelfth Streets to the west. The neighborhood was listed on the National Register of Historic Places in 1978.

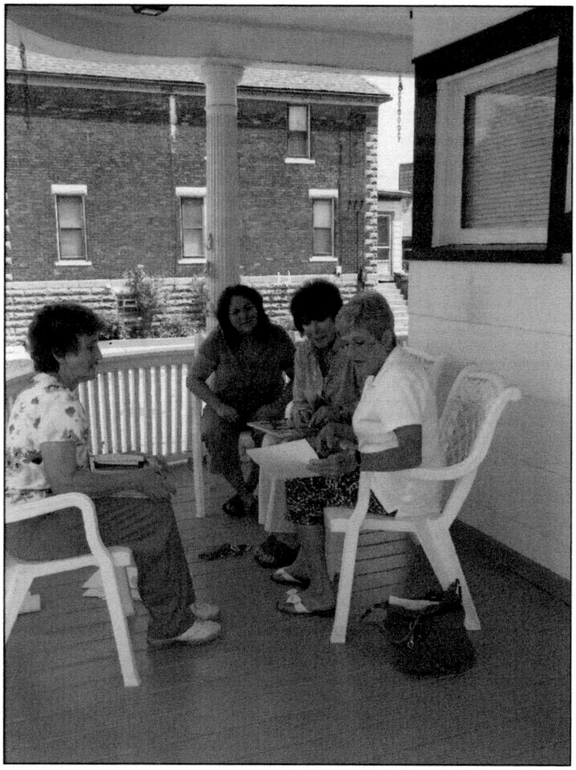

Josie Formosa, DeeDee DeBono, Terise Okasinski, and Norma Philp are shown sitting on DeeDee's front porch on Church Street in the summer of 2010. The DeBono home was always busy in the early days of Maltese in Corktown.

Danielle Diacono was crowned Miss Malta 2010–2011 at the Maltese American Community Club in Dearborn in November 2010. She works with the youth group at the club and recently received her teaching degree. With the honor of being crowned, Diacono also won jewelry and a trip to Malta. (Courtesy of Danielle Diacono.)

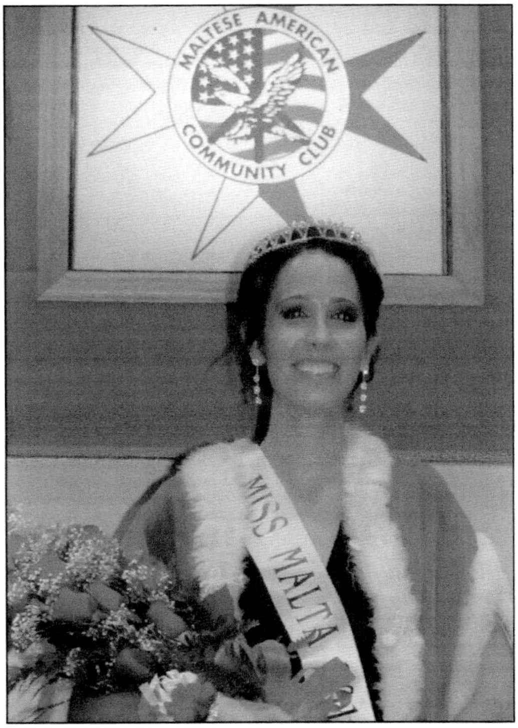

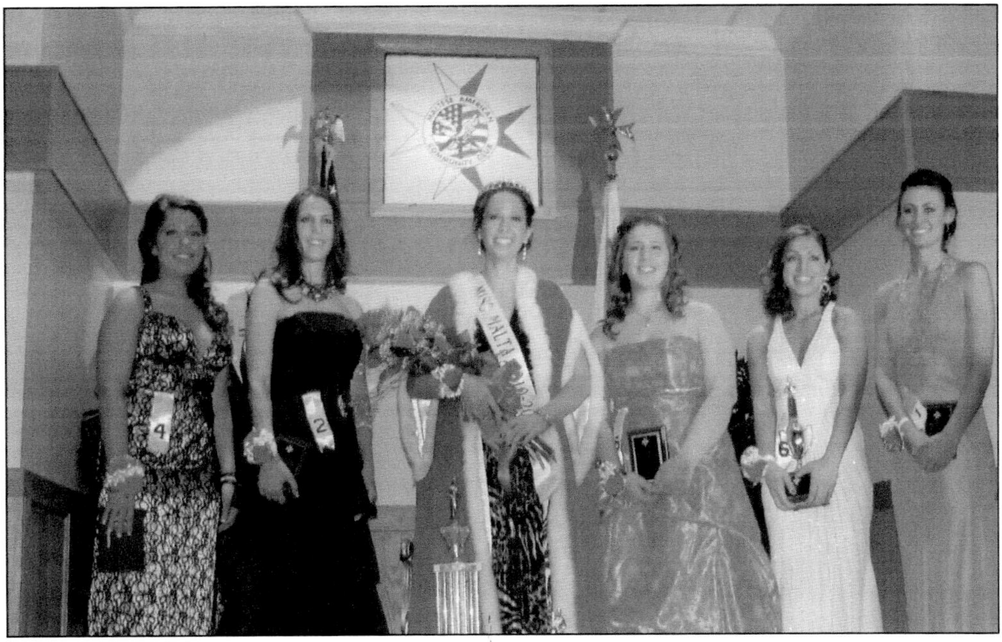

Miss Malta contestants from the 2010–2011 contest are, from left to right, Samantha Velazques, Melissa Shrimpton, Danielle Diacono, Elizabeth Grima, Bethany Hine, and Natalie Pizzimenti. Each of the girls was asked during the pageant how they would bring more awareness and shed light on the Maltese club in Dearborn. Diacono, who is active with the youth group at the Dearborn Maltese club, works hard to promote programs and emphasized that the future of the club is in the hands of these young people. (Courtesy of Danielle Diacono.)

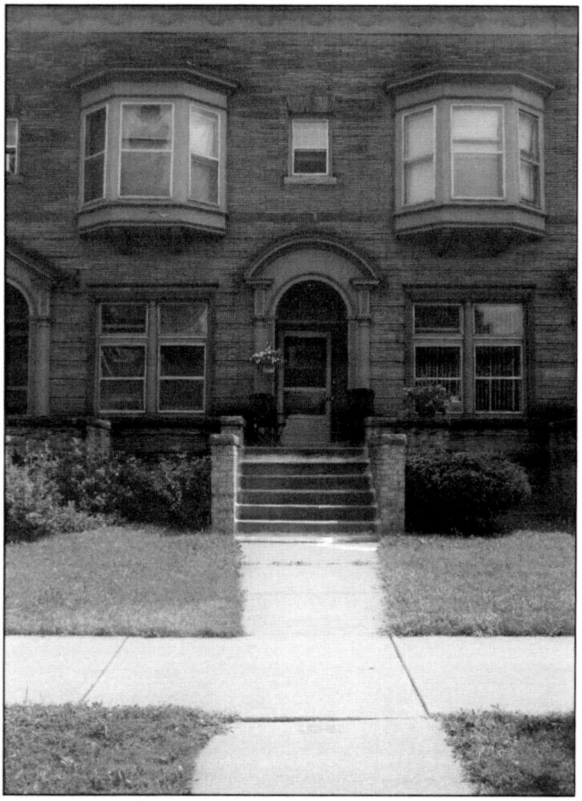

These rental units on Leverette Street were rented by Maltese families and were much bigger than the frontages would suggest.

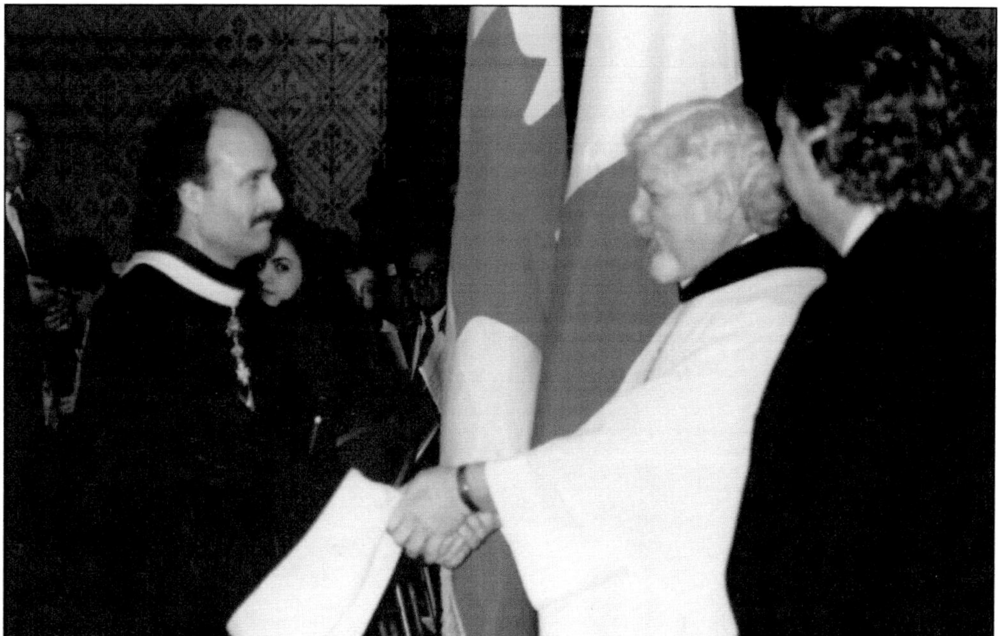

Around 1997, Fr. Russell Kohler (center), pastor of Most Holy Trinity Church in Detroit, greets Cavalier Louis Cumbo during the Festa of San George. The Toronto Band Club members are in the background. (Courtesy of Larry Zahra.)

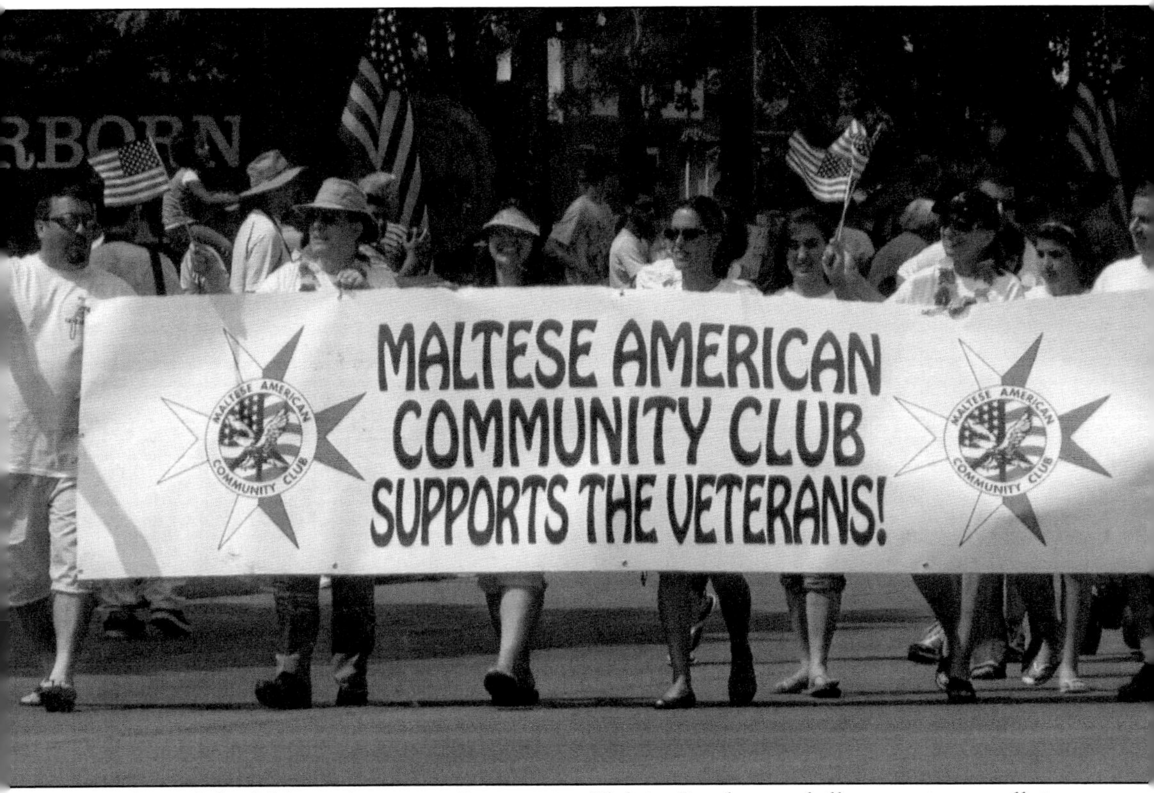

Members of the Maltese American Community Club in Dearborn, of all generations, walk in July 4th parade in Dearborn in 2010. In November of that year, Joseph Calleja performed at the Ford Performing Arts Center in Dearborn. Calleja has sung around the world in places like the Houston Grand Opera, the Metropolitan Opera, and many European venues. Calleja's recital in Dearborn was organized by Paul Borg, Maltese consulate to Michigan and president of the Maltese club in Dearborn, as well as Dino Valle, artistic director of the Bellini Opera Theater in Dearborn. The money raised from the performance went to the Malta Community Chest Fund for charitable concerns in Malta. (Courtesy of the Maltese American Community Club.)

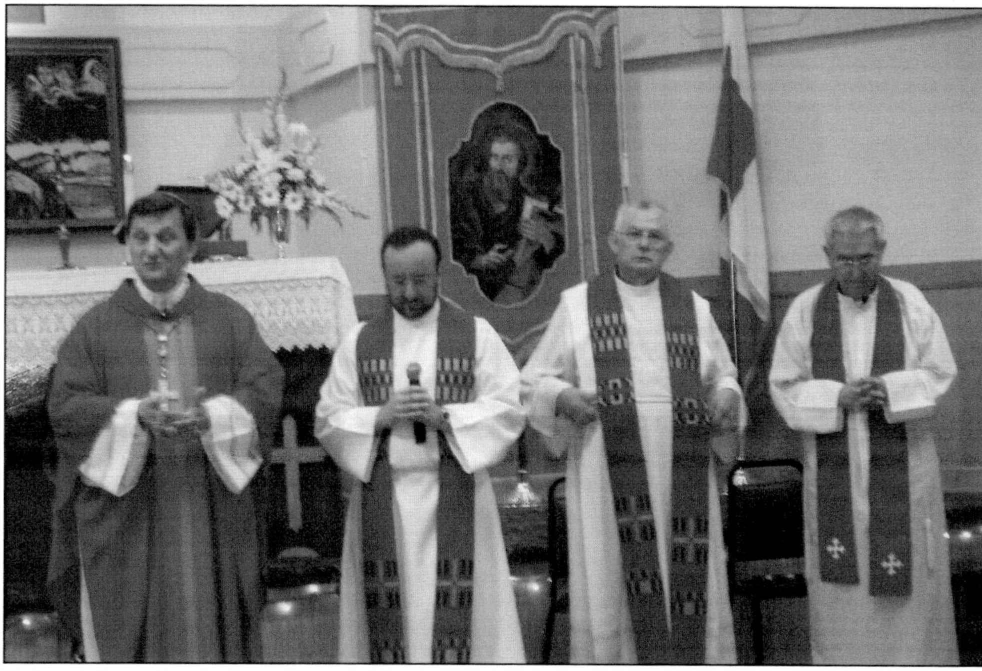

Bishop Mario Grech, from Gozo, Malta, performs a Mass at the Maltese American Community Club in Dearborn around 2007. (Courtesy of Paul Borg.)

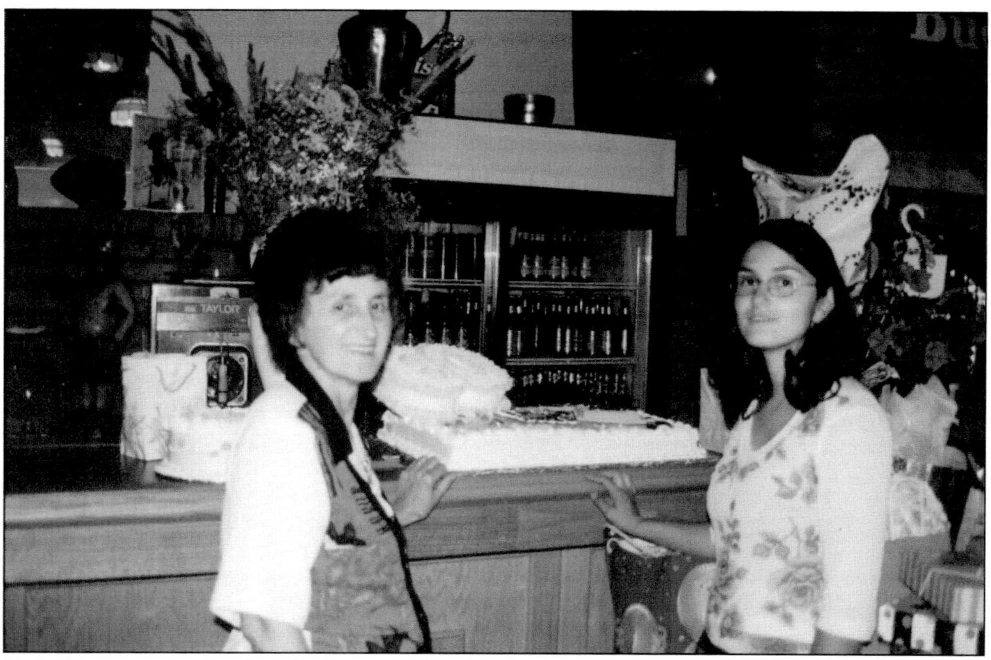

Josie Formosa, who lived in Corktown all her life, had her daughter Rose meet her at a Corktown restaurant to celebrate her 60th birthday in 2000. (Courtesy of Josephine Formosa.)

Shortly after he arrived from Malta around 1962, Charlie Schembri relaxes at his Detroit home. When he arrived, he rented a room with a Maltese family for $15 a week. His first job in the United States was as a stock boy at Hudson's. He then worked in the kitchen at Henry Ford Hospital. His third occupation was at Ford Motor Company in quality control, which was where he worked for 35 years. (Courtesy of Charlie Schembri.)

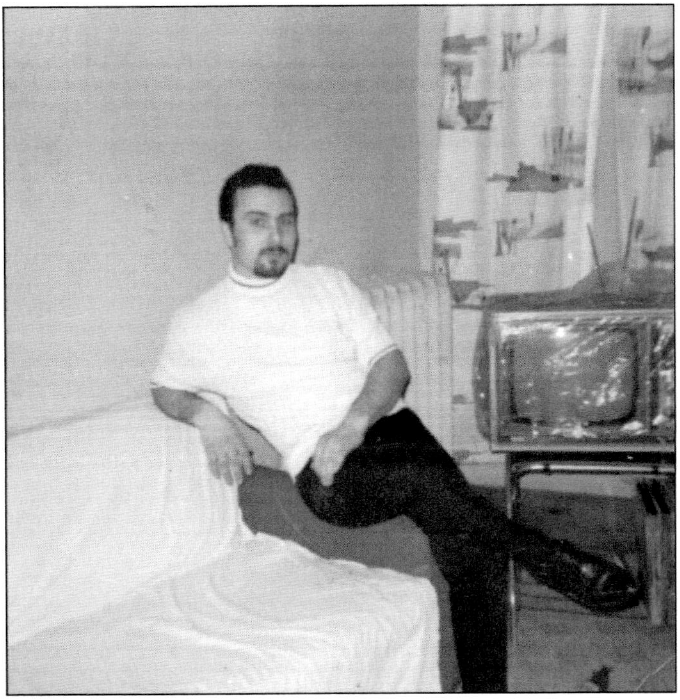

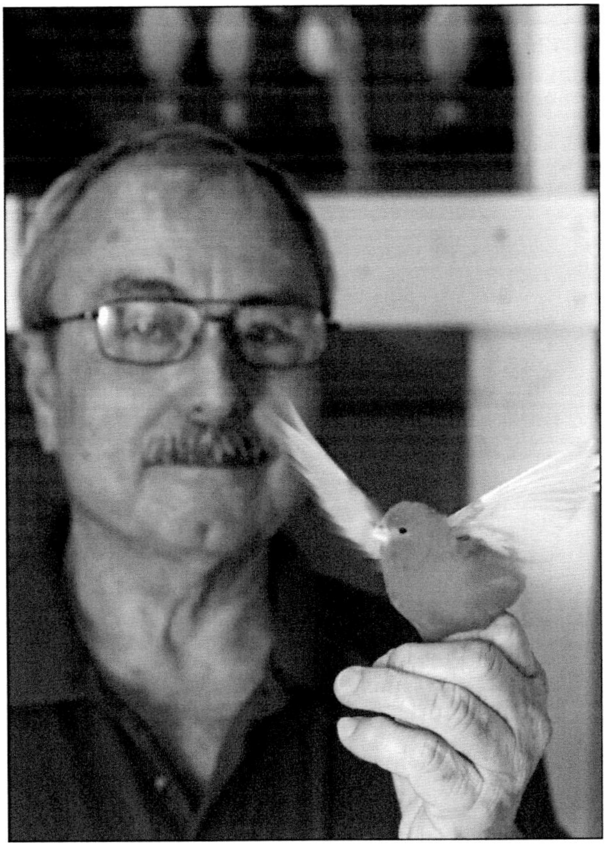

Charlie Schembri lived in Corktown until he moved to a Detroit suburb, where he continues a common Maltese tradition of raising birds. Schembri sells more than 150 canaries, finches, and other types of birds. (Courtesy of Charlie Schembri.)